THE GAZEBO LEARNING PROJECT

A Legacy of Experiential & Experimental Early Childhood Education at Esalen

THE GAZEBO LEARNING PROJECT

A Legacy of Experiential & Experimental Early Childhood Education at Esalen

Jasmine Star Horan, M.A.T.

The Gazebo Learning Project: *A Legacy of Experiential & Experimental Early Childhood Education at Esalen*

Copyright © 2020 by Jasmine Star Horan

Printed in the United States of America

ISBN 978-1-7346519-0-4

SILVER
PEAK
PRESS

PO box 366, Big Sur, CA 93920
www.silverpeakpress.com
email: Jasmine@silverpeakpress.com

This book is dedicated to my daughter,
N'Nady Elena Bangoura
and all of the children of the world.

My daughter is my true guru and children are
my wisest teachers who continue to humble me, bring
me joy, and the gift of presence.

CONTENTS

Contents, cont.

Acknowledgments

For my family who has been patient beyond measure with my writing process and the sacrifices we have made to see this through. I want to thank my mother, Peggy Horan, for being a rock in my life and supporting my dreams. To my dad, Richard Horan, for teaching me and my daughter the love of the land. To my sister, Lucia Horan Drummond, for cheering me on all the way through this process, and for all your unconditional and ongoing love and support. To my love, Jeya Chandran, thank you for your kindness and for nurturing me and my dreams as a writer and educator. To my daughter's father, Mory Moussa Bangoura, for giving me the gift of being a mother to our beautiful daughter. To my brother Jonathan, whom I always hold in my heart, and to his mama Gabrielle, who always believed in me as a writer.

I want to thank my teachers named and unnamed and all those who led me down this path. To all the Gazebo teachers and directors over the years for your service and contributions to this work. To all those who contributed to this book, thank you for your generosity and support of this project, and for sharing your words and experiences.

Thank you to Janet Lederman for your strength, brilliance and vision.

To my circle of trust. The wisdom keepers. To my Gazebo teachers, who became my aunties, uncles, mentors, and angels. To Lia Thompson-Clark for being my mentor and guiding light for my work as a teacher. To January Handl for being a guide, and friend, and supporting this work, especially in its early phases. To Joanna Classen for being an ongoing resource. To LaVerne McLeod for giving me strength to carry on when I was weary. To Penny Vieregge for the light she shines so brightly and her ongoing presence as Gazebo grandmother. To Bette Dingman for belief in me and in Janet's work. To Sydelle Foreman for your sweet caring ways through all the ups and downs as well as your faith in me. Thank you Martha

Clark and Zeet Peabody for your brilliance. To Martine Bitman for your dedication to children. To Glen Cheda for your ongoing love and support.

To all those who offered moral and emotional support during the course of this project—friends too numerous to name. Thanks especially to Chris, Dorothy, Jenny, Rudi, April, and the Tribal Ground Circle for your loving support for my daughter and me.

I especially want to thank Nancy Sanders and Alan Perlmutter for your encouragement and support of this project. A special thanks to my generous Zuncle Alan. Thank you, Ken Dychtwald, for your influence and input on this project and the love you give my family and our community. PJ Novotny, for your enthusiasm around Gazebo philosophy and its potential.

I want to thank each and every one who donated to this project—each of whom carried me in many ways to continue working. Alfred Tao, Ama Delevett, Amber Ryan, Anne and Alan Morrison, Anne Ribelow, Alan Perlmutter, Alicia Hahn Peterson, Andrea Juhan, Andre Couture, Arthur Munyer, Barbara Wilson, Ben Kalayjain, Blane Birchby, Brita Ostrom, Bob Doleman, Catherine Milner, David Hanson, David Molk, Douglas Drummond, Dorothy Charles, Erik Meuller, Eliot Goldward, Georgene Crow, Glen Cheda, Grace Macris, Gretchen Lee, Harry E. Breaux, Holly LevenKron, Jane Patmore, January Handl, Jennifer Price, Jenny Hernandez, Joanna Classen, Joe Write, John Hirsch, Joti Singh, Jules Henry, Julie Miller, Ken Dychtwald, Lia Thompson-Clark, Lucia Horan Drummond, Martha Toll, Michael Covey, Morgan Rae Burk, Molly Field, Nancy Sanders, Pamela Espinosa, Pauline Kirby, Peggy Goodale, Peggy Horan, Philip Ribolow, Rachel Morrison, Raven Lang, Robert Ansell, Sally Sumida, Sarah Faith Priddy, Seema Chistie, Shawna Garritson, Steven Turtle White, Sydelle Foreman, Susan Mohen and family, Theda Zawaiza, Tiffany Barry Bonbright, Tim Birchby, Rose Chapman, Sonya Pongsavas, Tzila Dunzel, and Vicki Topp.

Special thanks to Esalen for holding Gazebo in its living system for forty years and continuing to keep the children in their sphere with Big Sur Park School. Gratitude for Esalen Institute for your tolerance of the Gazebo Writing Project and giving the space for several writing gatherings to take place on the property. Thanks to Dawn Fielding and Jerlyn Hess in Esalen programs in supporting the Gazebo Writing Project. Thank you to Big Sur Park School teachers, board and staff for carrying on the legacy of Gazebo through your hard work and perseverance and in keeping Gazebo Park alive with the laughter of children.

Thank you to the sweet aunties and uncles who cared for my growing child during this project, Molly Field, Sarina Fernandez, Steven Turtle White, Kim Cory, and Elizabeth Appel.

Thank you Freya Peters for your legal counsel and your friendship. Thank you Karen Lemon for your ever beautiful photographs. Special thanks to Brian Hendrix for the beautiful art and design for the cover and emblem. My deep gratitude to Annie Elizabeth Porter at River Sanctuary Publishing for the book design and supporting my independent publishing process.

Special thanks to my readers Bob Dolman and Samantha Silverman for your valuable input on my writing and editing process. Thank you Nancy Knapp for inspiring me at a young age to write and fanning the fire of this project in the early stages. Thank you to my editors, Douglas Cruickshank and Magdalena Montagne.

In humble gratitude for the grace of an angel of the Gazebo, Olivia De-Sola Barnes, a wise and joyous being. May she rest in peace. And to her mothers, Libby Barnes and Daniela Desola.

I want to thank my ancestors—my grandparents and beyond. Thank you to the ancestors of the land at Esalen—the Native Esselen Indians—you are not forgotten.

There is a special magic on this land where I was born and I am so blessed to have been able to learn and grow up here. I offer the documentation of this history back to the earth—the sacred land—in hopes that future generations will learn to take care of Mother Earth, and all life, with kindness and respect.

The Gazebo Writing Project

The course of Gazebo Writing Project process occurred over the course of six years between 2013-2019. Creativity and life were gestating and growing in me as this project was concurrent with the conception, birth and early life of my child. My daughter has had the blessing of attending Gazebo and Big Sur Park School on the grounds of Esalen. She went from being a baby in my belly when I taught there, to being the baby crying at the gate when I left her for the first time, to being a big five-year-old girl guiding her baby cousin on her first day in the Park.

The research for this book took several years with ongoing additions in subsequent years. Many community members shared stories throughout the Gazebo Writing Project. The unpublished sources for this book are to numerous too be listed in the notes. My research focused on Gazebo alumni, Gazebo parents, and Gazebo teachers.

I hosted several writing gathering events on the Esalen grounds for parents, teachers and alumni—each with written and oral components. The attendees could choose to submit written submissions at the end of the event with their permission. Attendees could also chose if they wanted to give permission for the oral conversations to be shared in this book. Esalen graciously allowed these events and supported them as day-long conferences.

The previously unpublished submissions from community members were collected in three ways: 1) Written submissions based on a set of writing prompts or questions. These may have been sent to me directly via email or mail over the years or collected at one of these writing gathering. 2) Transcriptions from conversations at the writing gatherings. 3) Transcriptions from one-on-one interviews.

I was granted permission from unpublished sources. I have made every attempt to respect fair use laws. I have done my best due diligence to respect copyright laws. Published works are cited appropriately in the bibliography.

These are my memories from my experiences of Gazebo and the synthesis of other people's stories and ideas in relation to their Gazebo experiences. The events, locales, conversations, and teachings are from my memories of them, and I have changed the names of individuals to maintain anonymity in some instances.

I have made every effort to ensure that the information in this book is correct at press time, and as the author and publisher, I do not assume and hereby disclaim any liability to any party for any loss, damage, or disruption caused by errors or omissions, whether such errors or omissions result from negligence, accident, or any other cause.

This was a community project in the sharing of ideas and also it was partially funded by my early Indiegogo campaign. Ultimately, since I am working as an independent author, for the most part this project was completed through my personal perseverance without publisher advances or financial sponsorship.

This is not official Esalen material, nor is this book selling this pedagogy, curriculum, or method but rather honoring a legacy inspired by the culture of Esalen. I am not representing Esalen Institute or the beliefs of the institute, but rather am a catalyst for documenting a primarily oral history in the name of cultural and historical preservation.

I realize that the public may not know the community sources. So, I will include below a list of contributors and their role in relation to Gazebo and to the world. Keep in mind there are some crossovers; such as parents who were also teachers. Thank you to each one of you who contributed to this book. It has been my honor and privilege to weave these voices together.

Gazebo Teachers and Interns:

Arthur Munyer – Father, Founder of Neural Somatic Integration®

Catherine Wyatt – Mother, Grandmother, Educator, Director of the Michael Simonson Foundation

Glen S. Cheda – Land Steward, Vocalist

Dorothy Charles – Relational Gestalt Practitioner and Co-founder of Tribal Ground Circle

Eduardo Eizner – Father, Licensed Marriage and Family Therapist

Eliezer Sober – Author

Fatima Faria – Executive Director of Sunshine Valley Child Care Society in British Columbia

Iona Justyn Jones – Massage Therapist, Group Facilitator

January Handl – Mother, Grandmother, Parent Educator, Retired Teacher, Grandmother Extraordinaire

Joanna Classen – Mother, Early Childhood Educator and Founder of Early Ecology Forest School

Joyce Lyke – Mother, Grandmother, Workshop Leader and Founder of Awaking through Parenting

Josef London – Esalen Staff Member, Gestalt Practitioner

LaVerne McLeod – Mother, Grandmother, Author, Workshop Facilitator

Lia Thompson-Clark – Mother, Director of Children's School at Sonoma State University

Neil Baldwin – Early Childhood Teacher

Otis Kreigel – Educator, Author

Patrick Douce – Founder of Spinal Awareness, Student of Moshé Feldenkrais

Peter Myers – CEO of Stand and Deliver

Sharon Dvora – Educator, Artist

Sofia Snavely – Teacher and Director of Big Sur Park School

Steven Harper – Father, Outdoor Educator, Gestalt Practitioner, Workshop Leader

Sydelle Foreman – Godmother, Artist

Vivian Danzer – Interpersonal Communication Facilitator/Teacher

Gazebo Parents:

Christine Stewart Price – Mother, Grandmother, Gestalt Awareness Founder and Practitioner, co-founder of Tribal Ground Circle

David Nelson – Father, Land Steward

Hannah Reese – Mother

Joyce Lyke – Mother, Grandmother, Parent Educator, Group Leader

Kevin R. Harvey – Father, Land Steward

Libby Barnes – Mother, Architect

Peggy Horan – Mother, Grandmother, Esalen Massage® Teacher, Author

Perry Holloman – Father, Grandfather, Esalen Massage® and Deep Bodywork® Teacher, Gestaltist

Sarah Harvey – Mother, Midwifery Apprentice

Sharna Whitehand – Mother

Gazebo Students:

Abraham Wolfinger – Father, Teacher

Ama Delevett – Gestalt Therapist

Anne-Louise Marquis – Marketing for National Portfolio Brand Ambassador, Campari America

Chelsea Belle Davey – Mother, Artist, Server at Nepenthe Restaurant

Christopher Tarnas – CTO and cofounder of Biotique Systems

Lucia Horan Drummond – Mother, 5Rhythms® and Dharma Workshop Leader

Mac Murphy – Workshop Leader, Massage Therapist

Rose Chapman – Vocalist, Sales Associate

Rudi Price-Waldrip – Mother, Gestalt Practitioner

Samson Day – Husband

Zoë Beck – Mother, President of Big Sur Park School Board, Chair of Inequality Media Board

Gazebo Grandparents:

Bette Dingman – Mother, Grandmother, Retired Esalen Staff

Julie Miller – Mother, Grandmother, Retired Early Childhood Education Teacher

Penny Vieregge – Mother, Grandmother, Educator, Vocalist, Pianist, Poet

Seymour Carter – Father, Grandfather, Gestalt Practitioner, Workshop Leader, Poet

Bob Dolman – Father, Grandfather, Writer, Artist, Workshop Participant

Introduction

When I was a child, I didn't go to a school. I went to a magical fairy kingdom. I played in a wonderful park full of trees, gardens, animals, flowers, birds and friends. I could be free and be a child. My experience of the world was not limited to a classroom, a desk, or a set schedule of curriculum material written by some far off person at a far off desk. No, my life was dictated by my own interests, my exploration of the natural world, the rhythms of the day, the weather, and by my imagination and wonder.

My friends and I were given a lot of responsibility and respect for little people. We were given a set of tools to describe and process our emotions, a set of tools that were not set in stone but rather were a living, growing example of how to be in the moment with ourselves and other human beings. I learned about being in the natural world from my environment. I learned about being in my body from experiencing it with awareness. I learned my own boundaries and others' boundaries and limits from the people around me and from my own explorations with them.

I didn't realize until I was much older how unique my childhood was, and how my early education shaped me into an inhabitant of my body and heart. It was only later when I returned as a teacher to Gazebo Park School, the same preschool I went to as a child, that I was able to reconnect to and touch the innocence of being a child. I began unlearning some of what I had come to believe as an adult and what I had been taught at graduate school. During this time, I also gained a more conceptual understanding of what I had experienced as a child. As an educated intellectual who has traveled the world, I realized this was important work, documenting and preserving this body of knowledge, and I did not want it to be lost.

Childhood is so rarely honored in the way the Gazebo honored it. As a student and teacher, I feel inspired by the deeply held tradi-

1

tions of Janet Lederman and those who continue to carry her vision. Teachers such as Penny Vieregge, Lia Thompson-Clark and Joanna Classen brought to their work a very special kind of love and respect for children. The teaching was non traditional, allowing learning to unfold naturally by providing the appropriate circumstances and a safe framework.

I saw how different this school was from other methods I had studied. It was not Montessori, Waldorf or Reggio Emilia. This was something else, something that had been on the cutting edge for over thirty years. Now people like Richard Louv were writing about how important it was for kids to be in nature. Outdoor schools were popping up internationally and terms like eco-curriculum, sustainability, eco-literacy, emotional literacy, and emotional intelligence were on the table as part of the conversation in education and psychology.

The Esalen Institute and Big Sur community have such a strong connection to and a great love for Gazebo. Visitors to Esalen Institute who have brought their children there have seen a similar transformation in them as they have experienced in their Esalen workshops and in their own lives. Gazebo has enriched the lives of many children and families and positively influenced the lives of many teachers and interns.

Nevertheless, the Gazebo approach is not confined to the grounds of Esalen or the grandeur of Big Sur. It is possible to apply aspects of this learning to many educational settings. In spite of this, I have seen aspects of the Gazebo approach change faster than I felt comfortable with. I didn't want the essence of Gazebo diluted. I wanted to distill it so it would not be lost.

I have felt the threats of economic instability and the felt fear for the survival of the school, a fear many others have battled. I have felt the shifting of rapid turnover with the staff and wondered how this very unique philosophy could be saved if oral tradition were to fail. I also witnessed the closing of the school, and several incarnations thereafter. Nevertheless, it seemed important not to let time itself rob the future of the gift of this pedagogy for the children. I wanted both to preserve and share this philosophy, not just for me, but for the traditions of a tribe, a community, as a way to hold onto and honor something sacred. I wanted the world to benefit from this wisdom. I wanted to do this for the children so that they too could continue to experience such magic!

Thus, I began the Gazebo Writing Project, dedicated to recording and preserving the history and philosophy of Gazebo Park School. After I became pregnant with my daughter, I stepped out as teacher, but I kept alive my dream of writing about Gazebo. My goal was to gather stories from the community, parents, teachers and former students and to synthesize them into a book as a way to share the Gazebo practices with a wider audience—with educators, parents, administrators and anyone whose heart is open to it.

I have been a student and a teacher at Gazebo, and a parent of a Gazebo child as well. In this way, I feel I am in a unique position to do this work and I feel a great sense of honor to be trusted by the community to share their stories and experiences with me. I hope this book will become a vehicle for the Gazebo methods to be applied in education worldwide. We have so much to learn from the Gazebo environment and practices. It is truly a time to recognize that the Human Potential Movement begins in early childhood and that we need to honor this time in our children's lives.

I am blessed to have found the same magic and wonder that inspired my childhood from adult eyes, from the eyes of an educator and a mother. I realize now how different and unique my education was. I hope that you as readers give these words entry into your minds and hearts, so children may have the opportunity to experience being children—to learn and grow in the trust that they are truly whole beings—deserving of honor and respect.

VIVA GAZEBO!

Magic

Before I was a grown-up
I used to swing around in
this old tree
the flaming Eucalyptus
but then it was
no ordinary tree
but a place the fairies came to drink the dew
from the small acorns that hung from the tree
they only came early
just before dawn when the humans were still asleep
Before I was a grown-up
I used to play in the creek
with my friends
catch crawdads that seemed like lobsters
once I turned over a rock and found a bright orange lizard
with webbed paws and I ran to alert everyone of my discovery
when I was informed of the existence of salamanders

I used to sit up at the top of the hill at the Gazebo
on my a Hot Wheels bike with my curly pigtails poised
the hill that then seemed like a giant mountain and
I would yell "sketty rett go"
and let myself fly down the slope
pigtails following
like ribbons of gold in the wind
it was like I let go of more than just my footing
something changed as my feet left the ground
courage filling my ribs and head
something kept letting go
like slipping out of a world of magic
becoming more awake and less in a dream
or perhaps I just started to make the world around me
the dream of reality

I lost touch with leprechauns in the trees
stopped hearing fairy bells
stopped following their sounds into the forest
Perhaps I stopped remembering trees could talk
and be my friends
or maybe I just stopped having time
to love everything
butterflies were replaced with bills
sunshine with schedules
even my lost magic castle became an ordinary home
a place one could find me by an address

Sometimes I want it back
I want to believe my wishes will come true
when I blow on a dandelion
and watch it shimmy in the breeze
I want to search below the redwoods for four-leaf clovers
I want the passion vine to be my bedroom high up in the trees

Before I was a grown-up
my eyes were jade pools in the sun
followed moment-to-moment of joy like a hummingbird
let tears run free as wild horses
let everything exist
If I have a wish it will be to use those eyes again
sip from the fairy cups again
have tea parties with mermaids
and tell secrets that only the children still remember

Jasmine Star

circa 2006

History

My first experience of Gazebo was feeling the edge…the edge
of the land and sea, the edge of trust and fear, the edge of
organization and chaos, the edge of any knife of knowing, how
does one hone what is sometimes the most difficult thing in
the moment…I remember being awed by the soft boundaries
set by the hay bales, how do they get away with that? They
trust the kids won't leave? They (more importantly) trust that
other grown-ups won't invade? It marks the beginning of the
children's sacred space, and the warrior guides who guard that
space and all it encompasses. Then, I remember feeling the
pulse of the land, the fierce sense of protection that arose in me,
my Kali-spirit defending the individual's right to make their
own choices on the path of destiny set before them, the right to

veer off in unexpected directions, to flail about in mis-steps, to anguish over small things, and celebrate even smaller things. The honoring of our interior world, our right to create our own universe and the beginnings of understanding that others had that right as well. The power of feeling the co-creation of the edge surrounding and protecting space by grown-ups who are willing to walk in uncertainty and re-live some painful growing moments to keep their own woundings from adding layers of difficulty to the growth of the most vulnerable youth in their care. The beauty of being in the present moment, to be with oneself deeply, providing the anchor by which to be totally with someone else at times too. The freedom to explore the edge of being, the edge of becoming, to declare that edge a treasure.

– January Handl

*T*he history of Gazebo is steeped in the history of Esalen Institute, a center for human potential that is a place for seekers in many disciplines to learn and grow. Esalen Institute offers workshops in spiritual, psychological, somatic-based practices, art forms, massage therapy, and more. It is a place in which the land itself is incredibly healing, and the offerings there inspire self-inquiry and personal growth.

Nevertheless, the history is even deeper and older. The Esselen Indians lived on the land thousands of years ago and are said to have come to the site to use the hot spring to heal their bodies and spirits. Sadly, the Esselen tribe was persecuted during the attempt at first nations genocide. Under the Homestead Act, many native people were legally murdered. Also, native tribes, including the Esselen people, were moved to missions where attempts were made to eliminate their language and culture. It is a sad history, one that I was aware of since my childhood growing up on land that used to be inhabited by the Chumash and Esselen tribes. I have always felt a deep reverence for the Esselen people and the strong powerful presence of their energy on the land that I was born on. I grew up hearing stories of the burial sites at Esalen, seeing Daniel Bianchetta's photographs and listening to his stories of the Esselen tribe, and finding pieces of the past, stones, shells and even bones, as I walked through the Esalen garden and farm.

When I worked at Gazebo, I had a special altar set up for objects such as heating stones we found on the site of the school. The children and I often talked about the people who came before us and lived on the land, how they lived, and how important it was to honor them and care for the remnants of the past. These stories sometimes morphed into special ceremonies and always organically formed into alternative pathways of education in which we investigated and celebrated the history of the land and people. Yet, there is very little education on this history for the adults who visit the Institute, nor is there a native presence on the privatized land. While the ancient and the new age have converged, and Esalen Institute and spirituality created a new wave in modern spiritual insight, there is little acknowledgment of the rich native history of the land. However, I include this information because it is the origin of the place, and in my view, it cannot be removed from what else was born from this place.

Furthermore, when Highway 1 was being built, there were shacks built on the property that housed convicts who built the road. According to the lore, the farmhouse, that was part of Gazebo, was once a convict shack. What is more, people have been coming to the land to use the hot springs historically before the Esalen Institute came to be. Slate Hot Springs was a hotel and restaurant that existed on the site. In 1962, Esalen Institute was founded by Dick Price and Michael Murphy. This became a center offering workshops and teachings which grew from the 1960s era during a time when society was in great flux. People were breaking the rules and escaping the social norms. The hippie culture was about freedom and exploration. The early days at Esalen were full of sex, drugs, music, dancing, and many expressions of this social revolution. Singers and musicians such as Joan Baez, Joni Mitchell, and Ravi Shankar played at Esalen. Teachers such as

Abraham Maslow, Frederick Perls, Joseph Campbell, Aldous Huxley, Alan Watts, Gabrielle Roth, Ida Rolf, Gregory Bateson, Stanislav and Christina Grof, among many others visited, lived, taught and developed their work there in the early days. Michael and Dulce Murphy created the Center for Theory and Research and conducted conferences with great thinkers from all across the globe.

It was out of this social and cultural revolution that Gazebo was born. Gazebo Learning Project, later renamed Gazebo School Park, and then Gazebo Park School, was a progressive early childhood center that served both Esalen families and families from the Big Sur community. The Gazebo Park is now home to the Big Sur Park School, yet another incarnation of the Gazebo. The unique pedagogy of Gazebo stemmed from Janet Lederman's vision and the innovation that was happening at large at Esalen. The wild splendor of Big Sur contributed to the creation of this outdoor environment for children. Gazebo, with a unique orientation of the child and teacher, was inspired by the multidimensional modalities and practices such as Gestalt and somatic studies, that were emerging out of Esalen, which especially emphasized both nature connection and human connection.

Esalen has historically been a place of living in community and experiencing personal and group retreats. This center has been a home for healing, for people to come discover themselves, to work on the land in the farm or garden, to explore their inner world, to learn and grow. Budding geniuses such as Henry Miller and Jack Kerouac lived in Big Sur and visited Esalen. Hunter S. Thompson worked Esalen for a stint. Some people came to Big Sur to exit the mainstream, to live as artists, or hermits, or simply to live off the land. At Esalen there was an added social dynamic of people from of all walks of life who had been provided a *container* for self-inquiry, personal growth, and healing. Esalen is a place where the playing field is leveled—where physicists could come and wash dishes, where your lodge keeper might sit in group with you, where anyone from a therapist to a complete beginner could practice Gestalt therapy, and where healing and spirituality have been embedded in the work and the culture of the place.

Esalen was a place where Gestalt practice was germinated. Gestalt has developed from a psychological approach to group and one-on-one therapy to an awareness practice and way of life for many at Esalen. Frederick Perls, also called "Fritz," who many call the founder of Gestalt, lived and taught at Esalen. Later, Dick Price became a leader and an important cornerstone for the community. He and his wife, Christine Price, brought Eastern wisdom to Gestalt, calling it Gestalt Practice, which was offered to the community. So many stories refer to the kind of community which they created in which there was always presence and emotional support, and Christine and Dick had a daughter, Jennifer Price.

At Esalen people were meeting, falling in love, and making babies. How did people include children in this social revolution? In what ways were these teachers' bodies of work including children? Well, truthfully sometimes they were not, and there were times when children were not always given the nourishment and protection they needed. There were certain spiritual groups who encouraged parents to join, but did not allow children. In the early days, in my opinion, there was a gap in how adults were given the space to grow and learn, and how children were being supported and nurtured.

Some people began to pay attention and look for solutions on how to support children within this social context. Lia Thompson-Clark shared that,

> In 1967 a Ford Foundation grant led to the creation of the Ford/ Esalen Project in Confluent Education, joining affective and cognitive learning. Dr. George Brown of UC Santa Barbara spearheaded this program. His work was summarized in *Human Teaching for Human Learning*, which sold more than 50,000 copies in the education field and was republished in 1990 as a Penguin paperback. George Brown was a leading advocate for what he called Confluent Education, and whose work fascinated me.

She continues by saying,

> The Ford-Esalen project, however, never included a look at the very youngest as potential students, and I'm willing to bet that no one did in those days, and that it was not until Jenny Price was born, and a few other toddlers appeared (Dylan, Flash, a few others) that the idea of what to do with/for/them became the impetus for Janet's vision of creating the optimal environment for the youngest to grow into their (human) potential. The 'Throw them over the cliff' story Janet retold to us many times, was the only way that she, as an Esalen manager, could make her point with this macho male-dominated group of guys, and secure a place to let the little ones flourish. She had Chris Price on her side (she would be a bonanza of history/herstory) and therefore Dick, who of course did rule albeit with a gentle hand. Gazebo was born.

Thus, in response to the needs of the community, Janet Lederman birthed Gazebo in 1977. Penny Vierregge, Gazebo teacher, elder, and long-time Esalen community member remembers this time as,

> For the first time Esalen was forced to accept that children are here. They live/exist on property. Esalen was then a place of many drugs, much sex and much self-expression. Gazebo became a refuge for the children as well as a training ground for appropriate behavior in the larger world. Environment was part of curricula. Responsible self-dependence was encouraged. The budget was enormous. There were field trips and dance costumes. For the adults there was full focus on the children's development. Parents were excluded from the Park as it was designed as the children's kingdom. Children were encouraged to take risks in the physical world, always with an adult nearby watching. Conflict resolution was encouraged with an adult supporting the exploration. The children were supported while they learned to empower themselves in communication, movement, mutual assistance. The staff was to focus on the children.

Though the training ground was ripe and well-supported at this time, Janet's intention was that it was a human experiment. Janet didn't label it as a school at first. She called it The Gazebo Learning Project, which was intended to be both experiential and experimental. It became a place to evaluate mainstream beliefs about education and child development, and to nurture new ideas that were radical at the time. Lederman was coming from an education and Gestalt background, and she was a visionary, she could see outside of the box, and thus she created something completely new and revolutionary for the times.

It is hard to separate Gazebo from Esalen. The hippie era of the '60s and the '70s created a wave of new thinking. It was a culture of learning and growth and the work there was all interconnected through the cultural and social revolution. Patrick Douce, student of Dr. Moshé Feldenkrais and creator of Spinal Awareness, implored,

> The Gazebo reflected the experimental and unusual nature of Esalen as a whole. Part of what was going on was a reflection of the general setting. It isn't that we put up with kids at Esalen, kids ruled! When you were in Gazebo, and Janet Lederman was in control, the whole property stepped to it. You had an area in the lodge, the stage, where kids could hang out. Actually Esalen as a whole is better with kids. It softens it.

Though I was born in the late '70s, when Gazebo was more solidified, I felt that while growing up around Esalen and at Gazebo, we as children were held in a way that many others have not experienced. By then, it was a safe container, a place where many of these ground-breaking teachers developed their work, yet they were like our aunts and uncles. Gabrielle Roth used to come teach movement at Gazebo. Douce was helping children with movement and mobility issues as he watched them move around the Park. Perry Holloman, Maria Lucia Holloman-Sauer, and Dorothy Charles, among others taught at Gazebo and went on to teach at Esalen as their work developed. Gazebo was a starting point for teachers as they learned from their experiences with children, and used their growth at Gazebo as the grounds for the development of their life's work. It was a symbiotic relationship between adults and children as they learned from each other. Douce recalls,

> Thank God that Dick Price was always available to work with us, so I did an extensive amount with Dick and Chris personally. (I noticed I didn't feel as open when I worked in a group of people.) I mostly worked with Dick and Chris, and it evolved into my Spinal Awareness work. How to get the joy, how to get the silliness, how to get the play, how to exaggerate feelings and play? How to use the group dynamic in the Gazebo, which is Gestalt, and it used to be at Esalen?

Douce openly credits both Gazebo and the children as his teachers and as being great contributors to the evolution of his own work, which he taught at Esalen for decades.

I have heard it said that when a child has strong bonds with more adult figures, aside from just their parents, it provides a stronger emotional foundation for the child. I was blessed to have so many people, my parent's friends, my friends, who were inspirational teachers influencing my life. As a child, I didn't even know their work or what they did, but I knew they were there for me. Because my mother, Peggy Horan, worked at Esalen, I had the blessing to be there often and be exposed to many of the practices being employed at the time. Many children who went to Gazebo had parents who also worked there and many families lived there. This experience was perhaps different than those students who lived outside the Esalen community.

In this way, those of us whose parents worked at Esalen were applying similar practices in our homes, and children were experiencing them at school and at home. There was a larger cultural context outside of the school, at Esalen in particular, that supported the practices within the school.

For example, former Gazebo student, Anne-Louise Marquis acknowledges,

It is hard to separate Esalen and Gazebo. It is hard to separate Esalen and growing up here and having the lodge and having the safety to be. I wouldn't come home till sundown. There was a lot of freedom. There is something about drums and music and that wild side; and in Santa Cruz there is a drum circle, but it is very associated with homeless rebels hippie kids. I guess that our parents were too, but the thing is is that it was so alive with community building. Anytime, there could be a circle of people making music together and dancing together.

This was a time before computers, Internet, cell phones, when people like my parents made art, grew gardens, did healing work, and had parties where wild music and dancing were normal. Douce recalls,

> What is important to understand is that we didn't have the media barrage that we have now, we had a movie once a week, we would have to rent a film and they would have to show it in the main room. We didn't have TV, VCR, some people had cheap stories, but we didn't have technology. Wednesday night program was a movie. For anything you had to find people. In staff units, there was a point where they would always have something different when you walked by. In one room there was a group of women knitting, in the next room there was a group of guys and women playing board games, in the next room people were making music together, and in the next room people were listening to a stereo. But every room had a different activity and you could join any of them, so it was a community that was always engaged with each other, there was nothing else to do. The idea was the interest in people.

In this way, the human connection was the emphasis at that time.

Furthermore, those of us who grew up at Esalen had a relationship to each other as we were part of a unique counter-culture upbringing. Mac Murphy, former Gazebo student and son of Esalen founder Michael Murphy, describes growing up in the cohort of Esalen/ Gazebo children as,

> What really came through is the sisterhood and brotherhood that we are a part of. People that get to be mirrors for each other throughout our lives. Seeing each other grow up through different ways and size and character, and how they develop in this life. It comes from Gazebo and our childhood experience on this land. So it is like a family of mirrors.

In this way, we grew up together on the fringe of a social revolution. Abraham Wolfinger, former Gazebo student and current educator feels that, "Growing up in this environment is an anomaly different than 99.9 percent of childhood experiences in our society."

In this way, our experience in this environment was one of privilege, yet however privileged this experience was, it had its challenges.

Yet for many children, the experience of community was one which felt safe and supportive, and Gazebo was a contributing factor in this. Ama Delevett is a former Gazebo student, and later became a Gazebo intern. She now works as a Gestalt therapist mainly focusing on trauma work. She reflects that,

> Our experience of community is a good experience. Other people don't see community like this, other people were brought up on communes and were tortured and abused and we grew up in this! It was utopia really.

The children who grew up at Esalen had parents that worked or taught there, so the teachings of Gestalt, farming, bodywork were all woven into their experiences outside of school as well. Rudi Price-Waldrip, former Gazebo student and Christine Price's daughter, remembers,

> One of my mom's favorite stories to tell about me as a child took place in the Little House living room where my Mom would have her workshops when we were at Esalen. I was about one-and-a-half, was barely walking, and could only speak a few words. I had set up my stuffed animals in a circle and was sitting there gesturing. Dorothy came in and asked what I was doing. 'Group' was all I said. From the very beginning I have wanted to be in the group

room *witnessing* and participating in what my mom does. That always took precedent for me over Gazebo and sometimes I felt like I didn't fit in with the other kids because of it.

She acknowledges,

I have been in group with mom since I was six months old, she would do session while I was breastfeeding. As I got older I would be sitting there with a box of tissues and I would learn when it was time to put out a tissue. That for me became my focus here, and I think I wanted to be doing that here. I think it was happening at Gazebo, but I didn't know how to integrate the adult version and bring it to the kid version.

Therefore, the work at Esalen and the work at Gazebo were interwoven in many ways.

For instance, long-time community member, Gazebo teacher and Gazebo parent, David Nelson says, "Gestalt is so much part of the culture here, so I think it probably made a difference." In this way, the work that was developing outside of the park, outside of the soft boundaries of the hay bales, was influencing the development of the work with children, through the parents, teachers, and children via cultural integration. Similarly, there was an exchange between Esalen Institute and Gazebo. It was not just Esalen principles and practices that were being adopted in the school, but the children and the school were also influencing the community at Esalen. Bob Dolman, writer, artist and workshop participant describes how the school touched him.

One specific notion stood out for me, by the way: that children are our teachers. And it's true in many ways. I can remember walking by the Gazebo school one morning, in a grumpy mood about something, my head down and my book bag hanging from my neck, when I heard some children shrieking with joy. I looked up and they were playing, dancing, laughing. I don't really know what they were up to, but they reminded me that: 'Oh yeah, that's why I'm here, here at Esalen, here on earth!' Children teach us what we far too often lose sight of.

Arthur Munyer, founder of Neural Somatic Integration®, and one of the original Gazebo teachers, describes in his Arf Stories an exchange between a passerby and a child in Gazebo:

Why is that man crying?

Jenny: (appears concerned) Arfur, why is that man crying?

Arfur: Why don't you ask him?

Jenny: (walks over cautiously with a caring posture) Why are you crying?

The Man: (looks up) Because I am sad!

Jenny: (wanting to share) When I'm sad and don't feel good I sometimes cry too!

The Man: (looks relieved) I feel better now that I have shared my feelings with you. What's your name?

Jenny: Jenny! What's your name?

The Man: Johnny!

This simple and sweet exchange might not be possible in all educational settings, but it demonstrates how in this particular window in time, Esalen was as influenced by Gazebo as Gazebo was influenced by Esalen.

Yet, for us Esalen kids, life was not always flowers and butterflies. Some Gazebo children had challenges within their experience. There was an intense amount of *process* going on, and sometimes as children it was hard to understand the complexities of the adult activities. For example, Delevett describes her experience as,

Walking by this yurt here and people were screaming in there and group was always a little bit scary. It was a little like, 'You are not allowed to go in while it is happening. Something is happening in there and grown-ups get really loud and scary.' But because the doors were shut and we weren't allowed in I wanted to know.

On the other hand, Maya Sotto Mayor, daughter of Perry Holloman and spiritual massage teacher Maria Lucia Bittencourt-Sauer, had a different response. When she was a small child, she walked by a group of people in a loud Gestalt process and said, "Oh, they are just throwing up their brains." In this way, for some children the cultural phenomenon of Gestalt process and other modalities was normalized, while for others there were points of tension. Regardless, it was woven into the fabric of our lives in both subtle or overt ways.

A strong memory for me personally was just after Dick Price had died. I was walking by the creek at about seven or eight-years-old and I heard someone weeping. I looked and saw that a community member, the late Ma Prita, was inside the meditation house crying and very upset. I went inside, and without a word, sat behind her, allowed her body to rest on my own, and held her while she cried and cried. This memory stands out as very poignant and strong for me. I think I learned how to be a witness, how to be there for someone emotionally without trying to change or fix their experience, and I think I learned this from the way that people interacted with me and from what I witnessed in those around me. Later, Ma Prita told me an angel had come to her and that it was me.

There were many sides to growing up at Esalen. Some of us kids would laugh and joke about the practices with some level of irreverence. Marquis remembers,

Dorothy would say, 'Hate is a very strong word.' This had the effect on me that words have power. Even today, I get uncomfortable when people say the world 'hate.' There was something about the Gestalt language that became kind of a joke for some parts of my life. All the places you would say, *but, with, and* and we would do it in ways that don't really make sense and because it is kind of funny.

> And lots of eye contact and lots of talking about your feelings, but it was a way for me to continue to connect with other Gazebo kids as some of us went to elementary school and middle school and high school together. Like Jez was a couple of years above me so he was a senior and I was freshman or sophomore. So we didn't run in the same circles, but we would see each other in the halls of high school, and stop each other, and put our hands on each other's shoulders and do this momentary Esalen check-in. It was like I am feeling your energy right now, and that was a way for us to connect but making fun of it but using that language as a connection.

While not everyone found the humor in our upbringing, I also spent a lot of time joking about the follies of my youth. The new age movement was very familiar to me and I found amusement in its popularity and even some of the falsities within it. In some ways, I feel I could identify what my Mom would refer to as charlatans, and I think my nose for authenticity came from the fact that I was encouraged to be authentic during my youth at Esalen.

Gazebo was framed within the context of Esalen, but it became its own organism. Funded by Esalen and inspired by the work that were happening at Esalen, the Gazebo Learning Project later was renamed Gazebo School Park. It still portrayed a fluidity in thought by which it was designed. Thus, drawing from the modalities that were blooming in the Esalen community, Gazebo established new pathways in education. Gazebo, and the first small cohort of Esalen children, were the beginning of a forty-year-long learning project that continued to cultivate new thinking in the field of education from this beginning. Munyer recalls the formation of Gazebo as,

> There was no Gazebo and the property was there. Nothing there, just the sage brush. We built it with the kids. Selig Morganrath, Dick Price and Andy Gagarin, and Janet Lederman, and Delevett [Ama's father] came out too. Art gazebo was one of the first structures and before there was the sandbox I built. Then I started to build out from the sand box.

Munyer talks about creating the Gazebo and getting their first pony, Peyote Karina.

> I planted more things that will be safe, built a corral with the kids. We had a great connection. She [Peyote] would do what I say. Riding was a big piece for me, everyone wanted to ride. We were all a family, and took care of her, cleaned her. It was different then. I would take the kids out into the canyon, and we would go frequently. Some kids would ride on my back, or whatever and everyone was connected, like a fabric, like the web, no one could let go of each other.

The Gazebo was expanded by the arrival of the notorious boat. Delevett remembers,

> Lederman asked my Dad to get a cable car to teach the kids about California history, but instead he came with a boat—which became a great place for hide and seek.

Douce describes how things worked.

> Janet bought a boat. We were all at the back gate excited about it when it came. Finally, this truck came with the most beat up piece of junk you have ever seen, and we were horrified when the boat showed up. But Janet was a master of getting people to help her, and she got notably, Bob O'Black, who had children there, to work on the boat. He was a boat man and he rebuilt it.

The boat and the original Gazebo structure, the old wine barrel, had both deteriorated greatly by the time I was a teacher at Gazebo, so much so that the staff and director decided they needed to be removed and replaced. The emotional response from the community to the departure of these old structures was quite amazing. Many people were saddened by the news that these structures were leaving and had many memories and much affection for them. I myself felt it was truly a renewal energetically, and with the level of decay, that they were no longer going to be safe for children. We did a special

ceremony and invited the community to say goodbye to these structures. We asked the people connected to Gazebo to send writings
or poems we could read at the event. Former Gazebo student, Rose
Chapman, sent this poem:

Gazebo Boat Poem

Rosy comes down from the magic castle
Or pottyville
She Crosses the little bridge
Onto the Boat
Jenny and Dillon are there
"What do you want to play?"
"I'll be the captain"
Steer the big wheel
"I'll be the carved lady my hair blowing back in the wind"
Eucalyptus feathers are like seaweed
"I'll wear a cape"
(And nothing else)
Feel the rope and the net
Feel the deck under bare feet
Voyage on our magic boat

A little older
Rosy crosses the bridge again
Imaginary games turned to classroom time
Down below deck her first time using computers
Turtle on the screen
Dank smell
It's moldy but we don't care
Lucia is there
Emily is the teacher
Or Perry
Math class, yuck!

As a big person
After she moved away
Visiting
Rose comes in the back gate
Stopping to let gazebo remind her of who she is
Crossing that little bridge again
She knows
She is all grown
But once she was one of the small people on a big magic boat

by Rose Chapman

These places in the Gazebo Park deeply marked our lives as children. Years later, Bob O'Blacks family came to visit his memorial stone where some of his ashes had been placed by the boat. There is a little garden dedicated to Lederman with her name painted on a stone. LaVerne and Kenneth McLeod held their wedding in the Gazebo. One of my first memories and my first birthday party was held in the Gazebo. I remember a big white cake and blowing out the candles in the beautiful light of the indoor-outdoor space. It had a winding staircase and a loft, and the staircase was missing the bottom step. The missing first step was an ingenious way to allow only children who were capable of maneuvering the stairs to go up them, and children were not allowed to bring a stool to help them reach. Up in the loft, there was a privacy in which make-believe games could come alive, and many of us became incredibly imaginative in this area. There was a little theater later added with costumes and a stage. There were always swings around the park, balancing beams between logs, and some props like balls and bats, and of course the Hot Wheel bikes.

In creating the environment of the Gazebo Park, the creation was a task that was completely child-centered. Moreover, many of the former Gazebo teachers and directors I spoke to identified that the process was about seeing through the eyes of a child rather than the eyes of an adult. Eduardo Eizner, former Gazebo teacher and director, identifies,

> When I was there, it was different because the kids where the ones who were doing the paintings. The kids were designing the environment with us, or they were telling us what they wanted and we worked together with them, and they would build whatever they wanted to build. We had a few structures, the Gazebo, the boat, the tipi for a while.

This was an organic process that had the components of a small farm including a farmhouse in which teachers could cook; there was also a school office, and a place for rest, and a shelter on rainy days.

Glen Cheda, former Gazebo teacher recalls,

> I believe it was was the summer of 1979 when I started at the Gazebo Park. Lia Thompson, LaVerne McLeod, Steve Beck, Sydelle Foreman, Perry Holloman were the core staff when I arrived. Janet Lederman was filming at the Gazebo. I didn't meet her for a few months. Only saw her about the Park with her camera, and she didn't interact. Jigsaw Blade was our mascot dog. Peyote Karina, our pony. We soon added chickens and goats.

The early Gazebo community essentially became a family. There was a lot of closeness within the staff and among the children which is why today I am still in touch with many of my Gazebo teachers. They were family friends, some even became my godparents, who kept in touch and followed me and my sister through our lives offering support long after childhood. I received birthday cards from my former teacher Glen Cheda and his partner Oscar into my thirties.

Sydelle Foreman, former Gazebo teacher and my godmother, writes,

> I began my Gazebo days in 1979 and spent a lifetime in a relatively short span. I suppose I gave and got what I needed before my tenure was abruptly ended as a result of my personal relationship with

Janet. A short stint here at the computer cannot do justice to the depth deserved. Each day with the kids was filled with magic as was the connection between the teachers who lived and worked together. We were a lucky group, Lia, LaVerne, Vivian, Glen, Perry, Oscar and Martine, a circle of mutual respect and caring. Gazebo was a family and community unto itself. The natural environment and the circle of adult support provided a safe lab for the children to explore, discover, grow and flourish. In our own spheres as teachers, the same was happening. You can see in my photos that the children had the space to work things out together, to learn to solve conflicts, to learn that they could take care of many of their needs, and that there was a subtle yet very present circle surrounding them and there for them. I had been a teacher in Los Angeles public schools after college. Never did I enjoy being with children more or in any similar way as my time at Gazebo. As I said, Gazebo was a family, a community, supported and nourished by the community of Esalen. We celebrated together, played, cried, laughed and loved.

Granted, there were of course changes and many different eras in Gazebo over the years. Gazebo was renamed Gazebo Park School making the "school" more the focus. There were different directors after Janet who had their own leadership styles and focal points for the school. Neil Baldwin, long-time Gazebo teacher, talks about the changes of the school—transitioning from the first cohort of Esalen children to serving the larger Big Sur community,

> I saw a lot of changes. When I first came it was still a lot of Esalen children with a few local Big Sur families. We had a few Big Sur community kids for a while and that went on for quite some time, and then the local community grew. Then, in the last couple of years numbers started going down. The fire kind of really quieted things down. There were lots of reasons. Esalen changed. It didn't have so many children, there wasn't that sense of this is a place that I can just come freely. Culturally it went through a phase of

lots of people having children, and really using the Gazebo. Part of the reason people wanted to stay at Esalen was to have their children here. I have seen Gazebo go through having lots of kids and only a few kids.

Eizner was a director after Lederman. He describes Gazebo when he worked there as,

> Kids exploring on their own, learning at their pace, and developing from physical emotional to social skills as they are ready to; rather than being taken to places by adults. That would be the main concept that Gazebo was always about—following the children's lead and following their interest.

Nelson describes that time by calling it the 'Eduardo era' and by remarking,

> He was really good and he was not Janet Lederman. But he reached out to the Spanish-speaking community and the local communities and because they could communicate I think that was a big golden era because there were more kids, more income, and diversity. He had them play soccer every day out on the lawn. Tyler still loves soccer. That was a great time. There was a lot of kids. Esalen supported it.

Nelson's son, Tyler, was influenced by his time at Gazebo and returned to teach at Gazebo after college. There were many directors and staff, too numerous to mention here, many of whom I couldn't track down or gather stories from whose lives were woven into this history. Lia Thompson-Clark was one of the early directors at Gazebo. She had a huge impact and subsequently took aspects of the pedagogy out in the world. Catherine Wyatt was also a former director and shared the philosophy in her work abroad.

Baldwin says,

> There were times there were lots of staff. On a busy day someone
> might be in the boat, someone might be in Gazebo, someone might
> be in the middle, and someone would be by the pony shed, and
> someone might be down by the animals and the kids would just go
> up and down. They often didn't need much care because the more
> children they had, the more they would look after themselves.
> You look at sometimes when you haven't got many kids and all
> they can do is talk to adults because they have never learned how
> to hang in a group of children. That is true of anywhere you have
> children coming in when they have never been to school. When
> you get a big group of kids and they are like, 'teachers are nice

people but...' —which is what Janet wanted—that we the staff are not very important, I mean we are important, but we are not really important at all. It is the park. You know it is called a park and that is the point of this piece of land. It a park and school comes second. The name got changed. It is semantics, but it used to be called Gazebo School Park and it is now Gazebo Park School. Well, actually it is park that is the key word. I learned that long before I ever became a teacher, and that is why Janet wanted me in this school, because I've got something that if you've not been a park keeper you might not see as easy. That is me, not Gazebo. In the big picture the park is very much me and the school not so much.

Joanna Classen, Gazebo teacher and director from 2008 to 2012, describes this later era at Gazebo:

I was trained by Neil and Marcus. Neil held a lot of the piece of the grounds in terms of being a park. Slated to be closed in six months, and I was hired for six months. That was when there was a big push to figure out if we could get more funding through grants. We got nature explorer (Arbor Day Foundation) program grant. What was happening in social context: *Last Child Left in the Woods,* so there was funding for outdoor education which was creating a context for this. After six months was up, we were doing pretty well and enrollment was up. Everything was going pretty well, and then I began as director. Summer program was packed, and the next fall they decided to close the school. That came out at Staff Week [a week of the year that the property was closed to public and held staff recreational events and business meetings]. The community rallied and the board put together the new agreement that required a minimal enrollment number, support from community, financial fundraising demands, limitations on our budget. It was also when there was a community meditation and proposal for board for funding ideas, one percent came in then. [Esalen staff donated one percent of their pay check to Gazebo]. One of the things that was part of this agreement was proof of outreach each year. It was so amazing, to watch a community take a hold of an issue and organize itself. It was good to be at the center of a grassroots, heartfelt, strategic movement that was successful; felt amazing. Really, really beautiful, stressful too. Penny was there through all of it. What came to the center was that we felt however long we do this, we do it with our hearts, and when it is all over we put all our love into it and so be it. It didn't feel like a fight, but it felt like an act of love and that was what kept it renewed. Since then it carried on the same. I did a lot of outreach, hundreds of teachers a year, visiting the school or attending my workshops.

This was a trying time for the school to remain open as it was required to meet certain criteria such as raising funds and keeping enrollment up. During this time a lot of focus was taken out of the park and teachers were required to do more administrative tasks and fundraising in order to keep the school in operation. At the same time, the community really showed great support for the program.

Further down the road, January Handl became head teacher and director. She recalls the climate at the time she was there,

I came to Gazebo at the end of May, 2012. I came because four years before, the director who was leaving, Joanna Classen, had almost offered me the position. Now, as she was leaving she asked me to again apply for the position. As I came aboard, Joanna had just finished 'saving' Gazebo from the budget cuts of the Esalen Board. There was a huge community outpouring of support, and the board had given Gazebo a mandate of three possibilities and criteria by which Gazebo could continue. In addition there was major upheaval at Esalen due to three dismissals and a perceived shift toward 'corporatism' by the administration at Esalen. And the Big Sur area's (demographics shift) population had shifted away from supporting family life. Two more preschools now existed, and the national/world economy had taken a nosedive. Gazebo felt mired in uncertainty with low enrollment and a planet in crisis funneling us toward making other models by which the precious gem called Gazebo could continue. Joanna was gone about six weeks when I finally got through the hiring process, and Gazebo had a new teacher (past alumni of Gazebo) [myself] of three months, and a veteran teacher of almost two years who were trying to teach, recruit children and split the duties of directorship. They were stretched thin. Within two months of starting, Esalen did another 'reorganization' and my supervisor went from the resident education director position to the director of human resources. Also, personally I was finalizing a divorce, and selling a beloved home, while helping to care for my mother on hospice. When one accepts a position at Gazebo, it is not just a new job in a new paradigm, it is a life-shift. Learning all the sub-cultures in Big Sur, Esalen, interdepartmental discourse, and the Gestalt basis, appears to be trying to know a moving target, yet strong feelings of identity and ownership abound. I could not go anywhere, do anything without people feeling compelled to tell me, with tears in their eyes, the preciousness of Gazebo and the Gazebo experience.

Handl describes a particularly conflicted time in Esalen's history. It had gone from a program that had a large budget and was supported very much by its umbrella organization to having to be more independent and sustainable – which was very challenging for the program and its staff.

Esalen had its own financial hardships with the wild fires and mudslides of 2017 that led to prolonged road closures, evacuation and closure of Esalen, and as a result many staff layoffs. Esalen faced numerous financial challenges (including a pricey remodel). Thus, it also became more and more of a strain for the Gazebo staff to meet the requirements for program to remain open. So, late in 2017, after a year full of natural disasters, the program became at-risk once again, and a new administration chose to close Gazebo after forty years in operation.

Instead of the forty year anniversary celebration that was planned, the school closed the farmhouse doors. It was a hard blow to many of us who depended on the childcare for our livelihood, and it also difficult to digest in terms of how cherished this program was to the community. On a wider level, the decisions made by the non-profit umbrella were simply a reflection of how education is viewed by society. It felt like cultural changes had been happening within Esalen—some people felt there was a shift from personal growth and human potential to more of a business mentality in which the organization was focused on finances and operations.

Capitalism has such a strong pull and although fiscal responsibility is important in any organization, even a non-profit, education, the future of our youth, and investing in human capital should be equally important. During this time, my three-year-old daughter had been asking to go back to Gazebo often. I asked her why it was so important to her. She first mentioned her friends, who by the way she seems more bonded to than children she has made friends with from other programs. Then, when I asked more, she tellingly said, "Gazebo is home." This touched my heart deeply, and touched the center of how it felt in her experience.

Again the Big Sur community, deeply affected by the closure of the school, mobilized and organized to create a community movement and a way to revive the Gazebo school or create a new version of it. Many of the parents, teachers and families within Esalen and without came together to help create a net to catch those without childcare and continue the tradition of Gazebo. The Big Sur Park School, a new non-profit dedicated to serving the children of Big Sur, was formed. After searching for a new location, and the dust settling, Esalen allowed the Big Sur Park School to use Gazebo Park as its operating location and the park was once again alive with children.

Gazebo Park is now a space for The Big Sur Park School forest school. Other programs like Gazebo have popped up all over the world, some of them lasting and some not sustaining for long periods. Nevertheless, Gazebo has been a seed that has been picked up by the wind, and perhaps this book will inspire other families, schools and business, to consider the pedagogy that lived at Esalen in an experiential and experimental way for forty years and greatly enriched the community.

When Lederman was alive, she stressed that "The Gazebo is always in the process of organization and development." The constant state of evolution is one of the things that makes Gazebo so unique and so hard to write about in a static form. Furthermore, the ideas presented in this book would ideally have a current model, though these principles and stories shared still have historical and educational value. I have worked tirelessly towards the record-keeping and preservation aspect of this work. My intention has been for other educators to benefit from this sharing and find ways to transplant the ideas of the school in the way the Big Sur community is doing now. My hope is that this book can be a torch, documenting of a set of theories and principles which other programs may find useful in alternative education. In the subsequent chapters, specific principles of the philosophy will be outlined— principles that can be applied differently depending on the environment, community, etc. Though this chapter is focused on the history, the material presented in the subsequent chapters is an offering in hopes that not only will Gazebo be remembered for its history, but will be an inspiration and an influence in the growth, development and education of future youth.

Though my heart has been heavy and there have been many discouraging moments, I am encouraged by other paradigms out there such as the model Patagonia presented in their book entitled *Family Business*. Patagonia as a company saw the value in investing in the future of their children and they break down the financial payoff in the first chapter of *Family Business*. Consequently, this is the model that Janet wanted to see, one in which business subsidized early education. She hoped to use Gazebo as a blueprint for other companies and organizations to provide on-site childcare. She had drawings and descriptions of the environment that could be created within business sites to make childcare accessible, and furthermore children accessible to their parents for nursing and visits during their work day. The comfort of the proximity and knowing there is quality care available for parents is invaluable.

In my own experience, it was very hard to leave my child at first, yet knowing she was just a walk away while I worked on the same property was reassuring to me. I also knew that she was in good care, was being challenged and that even the difficulties were making her grow as a person and discover who she was as her own person. There is a real benefit to parents being able to visit their children on their lunch break and mothers being able to nurse their babies on their breaks. More organizations would benefit from adopting on-site childcare as a way for families to stay connected and employees to stay happy.

Whether models are independent or subsidized by businesses, children matter, and investing in children is investing in our future. The saying "We cannot know where we are going if we don't know where we come from" applies to this chapter. As we step off into unknown territory, we must remember our roots.

Janet-isms

When a revolution can be Fun THAT WILL BE A
REVOLUTION and no doubt a REVELATION.

– JL

Janet Lederman, JL, the founder of Gazebo, was a true visionary. She was a character. Lederman was elusive. She was brilliant. She was loved and feared. She was direct and laser clear. Lederman was Jewish. She was openly gay. Lederman broke all the rules and created something truly magical.

I was afraid of her as a child, but there was also a great love and trust present because I knew she was our guardian and protector. She was part of my family and community. Now, I consider her one of my great teachers. Today, I see how truly brilliant Janet Lederman was. She created an educational philosophy that was not only unique, but it could stand on its own without her—which is a truly miraculous feat. Lederman was one of four managers that ran Esalen. Lederman, Dick Price, Michael Murphy, and Julian Silverman had shared leadership. She became deeply loved by the Esalen community for creating a space for the children. She was also deeply respected, not because she listened, but because she rebelled.

Perhaps the most famous story of Lederman was before Gazebo came to be. During an Esalen staff meeting, the problem of what to do with the children came up. According to the story, Lederman said, deadpan, cynical and of course in jest, "Throw them off the cliff." This shocked everyone into facing to the reality that the children were here to stay and that they must be responsive to their presence. She saw children and their education and development in a completely different light than anyone else. She wanted children to be free to express themselves, to have an outdoor environment that would support their exploration and growth, and she wanted them to experience life fully, including their challenging emotions.

The story goes that Lederman had visited a farm on a trip to England and was amazed at how the children were involved in every aspect of life. She was inspired to create a similar environment for children because she saw how children had been part of the fabric of the farm, participating in the responsibilities of the work and play. The Gazebo was created in this way as a place in which learning and living were not separate, generations shared in the experience, and real-life became the learning. Lederman said, "The philosophy involves the integration of generations, the inviting of children back into society, and the re-introduction of living into the content of learning."

She created the Gazebo Learning Project, an experimental school in which she could apply concepts of Gestalt as well as the agrarian lifestyle she had witnessed on the farm in England. She said, "We're supposed to know all the answers, rather than being encouraged to find out. We've left out something very important—we haven't given the kids any choices." Therefore, she created a space where children were given choices, responsibilities, and a right to be children.

Lederman came from a background of being a public school teacher in inner-city Los Angeles. Her long-time partner, Bette Dingman said,

> I could say that when Janet got her credentials to be a teacher, they sent her to regular school in Los Angeles, and she went to whoever you go to and told them that she wanted to go to the worst school known for children's behavior that they have. She did go to that school and one day the principal walked into the classroom and she had a saw horse and this kid was sawing wood and another kid was sitting on those tall bookshelves they have in schools doing something, and the principal just freaked out because there were no books or chalkboard. Then, she came to Esalen and became one of Fritz Perls' favorite students and became a teacher of Gestalt. So, she put the two together, Gestalt and children. And she wrote *Anger in the Rocking Chair*.

Her book, *Anger in the Rocking Chair*, was controversial. It is a poetic reflection of her work in the public schools. It does not follow a structured organization but is rather like script of dialogue and exchanges from her time teaching in the Watts district in Los Angeles. Eizner, a close collaborator with Lederman says,

> She got in trouble for her writings. She got in trouble because she wrote a line there that was *reflecting* on what was going on with the kids. People started to talk about her being abusive to the kids. That is when she said, 'I am not writing any more,' because people will do that—they misinterpret. That line was a line about sitting in awareness with a child and reflecting the child's experience. In Gestalt sessions people reflect and do empty chair [a Gestalt excercise which uses an empty chair] with the facilitator. It was a reflection of the child's experience that was taken differently.

This experience must have deterred Lederman from publishing her work; though she did write several books after this, they were never published.

Lederman didn't want her writings about Gazebo to be misunderstood. Eizner also said about Lederman that, "She was very concerned about writing about Gazebo as a curriculum. Everything depends on the environment, the time and place and what is going on." In this way it is important that the reader stays open to the fact that although Lederman had pure and distinct educational tenets, she also never wanted any of them to be fixed. One of her mantras was, "Nothing lasts forever." Lia Thompson-Clark, another close collaborator with Lederman, says, "Catch the evolving moment, make furrows in the earth, pause to savor." Lederman did fear being misinterpreted and having her work represented as concrete rather than evolving.

The issue of attempting to document a static body of work has been a challenging aspect of the Gazebo Writing Project—not wanting to stratify the work yet striving to document Lederman's vision and the philosophy of the Gazebo. I acknowledge that Lederman didn't want Gazebo to be a one-size-fits-all approach. Yet for me, I have felt the importance of cultural preservation and historical value while honoring Lederman's wishes. Gazebo is an experimental study of humanity that is rooted in growth and possibility.

Similarly, an important issue for me has been that I was seeing the core values were not being translated and some of the original wisdom from the founders was being diluted or even lost. The staff's training at the school depended on mostly oral tradition, and over the years elders and wisdom keepers moved or passed away, and there were gaps in directorship which left a staff with less than ample training and resources. What were they/we to rely on for learning and training in this specific philosophy where other approaches might have accessible written materials?

Eizner says that,

> Janet was always concerned about labeling things. The 'eco' this, and the 'environment' that is, because her concern, and I think she was right about that, is that once you label something that is what it is, and it can't be something different and that doesn't allow for change.

However, in researching this book, I have found that Lederman's interactions and her ideas have been etched in the memories of many community members as she deeply influenced people in their personal growth and learning. She was memorable both in her theories on education and also in her personality, which was both honest and fierce.

Lederman was in many ways a social underdog being that she was openly gay and Jewish in a time when the biases and prejudices towards Jews and homosexuals were very prevalent. She was an openly gay woman in the '70s, a time when it was not socially accepted to be openly gay in the same way it is today. She was also on a male-dominated management team in a time when sexism was even more common in the workplace. She had the ability to be herself in a radical way despite the social judgments. Perhaps being identified with marginalized groups contributed to her tenacity and in a way made her an activist of her time. I imagine that her fierce attitude towards the rights of children stemmed from both her personality and the fact that she herself was so authentic to who she was that she fought to allow others to be so too. Though her cultural identity or sexual orientation were a part of her personal life, they may have fed into her work in that she modeled to others a level of authenticity and bravery that was in itself a teaching. In this way, Delevett says,

> That she was Jewish—this became important later when I moved to Germany and learned in school that the Nazis killed everyone who was different: Jews, blacks, gay people—wait a minute! That seems everyone I loved would have been killed, Janet, Sydelle, LaVerne, Glen and Oscar. That's stupid!

Delevett's contact with diversity made her truly question history when she transitioned from Gazebo to Germany at a young age. Similarly, one of the original Gazebo students, Wolfinger reflects on the diversity among the Gazebo staff by saying,

> Janet was openly gay and that was a big deal for me. I was seven or eight, and I remember going over to her house one time and realizing, 'Wow those are girls and they are in love.' That made me open to that side of things too.

Peggy Horan, my mother, a massage therapist and long-time Esalen Massage® teacher, stated, "She was really the first openly gay woman I knew. She was a good teacher to us all."

Each of the people I talked to had their own takes on Janet, some feared her, some loved her and some were loved by her. Dingman described their twenty-year relationship by saying,

> I had no fear of Janet. Most people did on some level. There was no one at Esalen Institute that I felt intimidated by. She came to the table I was sitting at in the lodge, and it was definitely something I had not experienced. She fascinated me and I fascinated her.

The Gazebo recruitment stories carry a theme. Lederman would pick someone based on their talent and would ask/tell them to come into Gazebo for a specific purpose. She could see individuals for their gifts and wanted to put those gifts to good use. Munyer describes how he was recruited,

> Lauri, my partner, came home and said, 'Go see Janet. She wants you to build a school.' What reason would she want me there? Because I let children cry. I guess she sees me. I felt seen. She was very good at seeing.

In this way, Lederman could tune into people's gifts and she hand-picked her staff very purposefully based on the individuals and the needs of the Gazebo and each individual's skills.

Similarly, Baldwin, who worked closely with Lederman describes how he was hired, "When I worked in the office Janet would come up and say, 'I want you in Gazebo.'" It was this simple, she hand-picked the staff from people that mostly already worked at Esalen. She could see either Gazebo needed them or they needed Gazebo. Peter Meyers remembers,

> I was working in the kitchen as a lodge keeper, and during one of my breaks, I found myself on the lawn with a bunch of children and I was telling stories to them (which I love to do), and this woman came over with a long Moore cigarette with the ashes so long you wonder how could the ashes still stay on that thing. And she crept over while I was telling the story and she said, 'Who are you?' I said, 'I am Peter Myers,' and I said, 'Who are you?' She said, 'I'm Janet Lederman.' She said, 'What are you doing here?' I said, 'I just got here, I work in the kitchen as a lodge keeper.' She said, 'No you don't—you're a tree. I want you tomorrow at Gazebo.' And she walked away as if it was already done. And I turned to the kids and I said, 'What is Gazebo,' and they said, 'It is a school, this little preschool we have on the other side, and I said, 'Dumb question, but what's a tree?' They knew what a tree was, and I am not talking about the kind with bark, but they said it's like a new teacher that comes over. And low and behold I had been drafted to the Gazebo where I had the honor and the privilege of working for one year and I saw an amazing educational process.

Meyers' story describes his recruitment by Lederman and her Mafia godfather like persona as she spoke with perfect assurance in her raspy voice, often smoking a long thin cigarette.

Conversely, Thompson-Clark found Lederman and sought Lederman out to work with her. She remembers that,

> One day in my favorite Camden town bookstore that carried books on Humanistic Education including George Brown's work, I found a little volume called *Anger and the Rocking Chair.* I read it over and over and said to myself, 'That was what I want to do.' That

was before knowing that Lederman was at Esalen. As an educator she used Gestalt with a classroom of the most 'difficult' children.

Thompson-Clark became a protégé of Janet's and later Acting Director of Gazebo, and she also went on to direct two Gazebo-inspired schools including the Children's School at Sonoma State University. Nelson says,

> I was one of the lucky ones because Janet liked me. Probably because she could tell that I liked children a lot and that I was afraid of them, but that I could talk to them, and I had something to give them, so she picked me. She knew I was building stuff around her. I helped build the solarium when it was new, so she had a job to do in the kitchen and she said, 'Can you do this?' The people she brought in were not cut from the same mold, they were all individuals with different skill sets.

Thus, Gazebo was designed and built with the oversight of Lederman. Baldwin talks about her need for balance in this way,

> Janet wasn't about, 'You have to learn this so you are good at this particular skill.' It is more about between us all together, with our own skills, we could balance each other out.

She formed a staff in which teachers had different personalities and skill sets and could complement each other and create a more diverse and supportive group. This was reflective of her understanding that different children gravitate to different adult caregivers and teachers and it benefited the learning community to have a diverse staff.

Aside from creating a team at Gazebo of diverse and talented individuals, Lederman used Gestalt to work with staff members on their issues and sometimes during staff meetings naming these issues with unbridled clarity. Many of the teachers who had contact with Lederman relayed stories in which they felt she saw them beneath the surface and beyond ego trips. For example, Munyer says,

The paradox was that she gave me the loving open heart side, and she knew that I had been abused mentally. Once you read body language, the truth is in your body, it's not in your head. That's what Gabrielle [Roth] taught, it's not about words, it is about body language, everyone had their own dance.

Nelson remembers, "She had a great bullshit detector." Baldwin illustrates with this story,

> For instance, a woman loans her car to some guy. The guy drives it off the highway, and trashes it completely. Three days later, at the lodge, Janet's in the middle, she sees the guy walk in, she sees the girl walk in, so they are coming towards each other at the top of her voice she goes to the girl, 'Has he paid for your car yet?' She goes, 'No.' Janet turns around to the guy and says, 'You pay every penny for the car you crashed.' Because the guy was just going to kind of slide by. She is taking care of business right up front in front of everybody's faces—you have to take care of business here. There is an element of there is no hiding place. There is an element for us where we had to be up front, we had to be careful. Janet was watching. She was watching, even if you didn't see her for a couple of weeks it didn't mean she wasn't there. She always had a way of looking at stuff at a different angle.

In the same way, Munyer says, "Those people that had bullshit going on couldn't look her in the eyes. She had good intuition."

Another common theme in stories about Janet is that she was both loved and feared. Eizner says that, "Janet was a special character. She was either loved or hated or both. I happened to get along with her wonderfully. She loved me." I believe one of the reasons people feared her is because she had that ability to see people and essentially call them out without holding back. Sometimes this was done in inquiry and questions and other times statements. Perhaps due to her Gestalt background, Lederman was clear and direct in her reflections of people and their behavior.

Catherine Wyatt, former Gazebo teacher and director and educator says,

> Janet was an interesting teacher. My big learning with her was that I don't think she really liked me as I was in a much more fearful place, kind of wimpy and fearful, and that *triggered* her. She said 'I don't need to like you and we just need to get along and work.'

She had close working relationships with people regardless of whether she liked them or was feared by them and each person seemed to have their own experiences with her in that way. Lederman may have been direct in some ways, but was very illusive in others.

In the way she ran the school, Lederman was like a phantom. Her presence in and out of the Park was transitory. Wolfinger states, "I always felt like she was behind the scenes. I did see her but she always was talking to a teacher and then she would wisp away." Baldwin states,

> You wouldn't see Janet in the Park hardly ever. She always seemed to know what was going on like she had that psychic hold on the place—it was her Gazebo. She frightened the woolies out of lots of people, she certainly didn't bother me much. Her role at Esalen was so much bigger than anyone we have here now. She was a real leader and really looking out for every angle.

He also speaks to her view on things,

> She had some really interesting takes on things, she was always looking at the bigger picture. She set it up so well that when she died it wasn't like, 'How are we going to operate without Janet.' She set it up. She had a very very interesting way of looking at things. Very much the broad picture. Not doing things the way you expect.

Nelson echoes,

> She was a pretty amazing person for me. There were so many times she would say something to me and it was this mystical Piscean

presence, because she was a Pisces she would say something when I was there with her and I would say, 'She is so right on,' and she would zero in on the point of the whole incident and summed it up with great insight and later the next day I couldn't repeat what she said.

Similarly, Peggy Horan says,

You never knew what she was going to do, it was always a surprise. She always surprised us, her response to things, and her answers to questions always surprised me. I would never ask her something and expect that I was going to know what she was going to say, because she was such an original person, and so smart.

Lederman thought outside the box. She didn't follow the rules and according to the Esalen management structure, she didn't adhere to the hierarchy that most others acquiesced to. Her partner tells the stories of her rebellion with Dick Price, the founder and director of Esalen. Dingman says, "I think for me what stands out is how clever Janet Lederman was. Because she didn't ask Dick Price, no one knew what Janet was going to do." She continues,

One day, I'm in my office and Dick Price comes in and says, 'What's that woman doing now?' 'What woman? I said.' 'You know what woman, Janet!' 'I don't know what she is doing,' I said. 'Just look up there on the highway, there's cars hundreds of cars behind her and this huge wine barrel. What is she doing?' I said, 'I don't know what she is doing.' He said, 'Alright.' The wine barrel came down and the maintenance men loved her and they hauled it to the place where we have Gazebo and thus became the home of Gazebo—the huge wine barrel. Then, I'm in my office and Dick Price walks in and says, 'What is that woman doing now?' I said, 'What woman?' He said, 'You know what woman, Janet!' I said, 'I don't know Dick.' He said, 'Look, look up there on the road. It is a boat! That woman is bringing a boat!' 'So,' I said, and I go out on the oval and out comes the boat.

Janet didn't wait for permission, answers, or recognition from authority. She did want she wanted and felt was the best thing for the children, even if it meant bringing a boat to Esalen. Peggy Horan says,

> Janet Lederman, the founder of the Gazebo, had infinite wisdom regarding child rearing, although she never had any children of her own. She supported families at Esalen and the Big Sur community in a way that had not existed previously, and gave endless counsel to new families, single mothers, and uncommitted fathers regarding the need for focus, love and attention to the precious being they were bringing into the world. She was not only an advocate for children, but for women, especially those of us who were practicing midwifery and delivering babies at Esalen for families that did not choose the hospital way. Her passing left a hole in many hearts. I am forever grateful to Esalen for hosting and supporting Gazebo for many years, to the teachers who gave themselves to the children, to Janet and to the children, who continue to be our teachers in life.

My mom didn't always agree with Janet for some of the same reasons Dingman disagreed, such as the instinct to help a crying child by picking them up. This was a very difficult point for a lot of people within Janet's approach. Peggy Horan says,

> We had our differences too over the crying baby thing because it was very hard for me to leave Lucia [her daughter] at Gazebo and hear her cry and know that the teachers weren't gonna pick her up. That didn't work for me at all. I didn't understand it and I had a lot of trouble with it.

Similarly, Dingman describes her experience having her own granddaughter visit Gazebo.

> The main rule Janet had with Gazebo is that you [the adult] do not come and jump over the hay bales, which was the protected area. I had my granddaughter. She was at Gazebo and she was two or three and I was walking through the Garden. It was lunch time,

and I think every mom knows the voice of their child of their cry, and I heard her crying from the garden. I walked down the hill, of course over the hay bales, and she said to me, 'You are never to cross the hay bales.' I said, 'That is my granddaughter.' She said, 'I know it's your granddaughter.' 'What you don't know is I am not gonna have her struggle because I know your going to tell me Janet that it is good for children to struggle and my children and I have struggled our whole life so this isn't gonna work for me.' She said, 'We will talk about it later.' I left, and my granddaughter had her sandal or bare foot stuck in mud.

Lederman, however controversial, created Gazebo and the philosophy stemmed from her approach to being with children, and from her beliefs about early childhood. The philosophy of Gazebo is grounded in her early ideas and experiments with children, beliefs that broke free from social norms and societal influences. Her personality and identity were as unique as were her approaches to working with children. Over the course of the years, based on Lederman's quotes and principles, the tenants that follow were and handed down through conversations and oral tradition, and were adopted as teaching tools at the Gazebo.

Gazebo Tenets

"A child who is able to 'pay attention,' to attend to what he or she is doing with awareness, will be a successful learner. We teach paying attention by paying attention."

"As the child attends to his or her learning, we are careful not to intrude."

"The environment is there to maximize the body experiences.... it has slopes grades, terraces, and many textures to give a varied body experience from moment to moment. It is an environment that Rewards the child for every movement."

"The Gazebo is designed with the educational goal of maximizing the FULL use of the child's growing body and unfolding intelligence."

"Some children learn by exploring everything, some by staying in one area; some learn by touching all objects, others by building around them familiar items; some are more interested in pouring water and others in slopping it. All of these proclivities balance and change in time."

"Gazebo is a place where children explore who they are, what they can do, and how they feel – apart from parents....and in doing so discover who they are, what they can do, and how they feel ...with parents."

"The philosophy involves the integration of generations, the inviting of children back into society, and the re-introduction of *living* into the content of learning."

"The Gazebo is always in the process of organization and development."

"The tools for gardening and developing the land are critical learning materials. The landscaping and surprise developments become the overall learning project for the children, the staff, and the neighbors."

"When experience and learning are partners, resourcefulness follows."

"Take the focus off the focus."

"Teach respect by being respectful."

"What the parents resist the children persist."

"Experience precedes knowledge."

The View of the Child

After all a person is a person no matter how small.

-Dr. Seuss from *Horton Hears a Who*

The two toddlers, Tayden and Dodge, best of friends, but lots of push and pull. They were on the kangaroo toy and Tayden fell off and he was crying. He immediately asked for his daddy, then mommy and then ran to me and hugged. I looked and there was a little bruise on his knee; within a minute he was back on the kangaroo and said, 'I'm happy now.' Both he and Dodge yelled out, 'Rock and roll. Oh yeah!'

*T*he Gazebo view of the child invites the perspective that children are whole humans worthy of respect. Children are held in the light of being capable of independence and responsibility. The view of the child is one of mutual respect, respect for the child's process, respect for the child's abilities to lead in the learning, and respect for the child's potential to master their own body with a freedom as well as self-responsibility. Delevett recollects, "I remember being treated with respect, that our feelings matter, that we matter."

As a teacher, I don't do for the child what they can do for themselves—turning on the sink, turning off the sink, washing hands, throwing away diapers, and walking. The children maintain their connection to the earth without being held constantly and they learn to walk, move, balance. They navigate the terrain of earth which offers challenges for fine and gross motor skills all around the child. Children frequently fall, and then look to an adult to dictate whether they should be upset about the fall. If they don't see a concerned adult immediately reacting or running to comfort them, they often get up, brush themselves off and continue to play. As a teacher, I attempt to leave the space for the child to determine how any given situation is going to affect them rather than applying my own judgment about it first.

The exception is for health and safety, which has been a firm Gazebo guideline. If there is the possibility of injury or a safety issue then it is important for the adult to step in and be more directive and firm. Otherwise, children are given more opportunities to learn about their own resilience, to fall, to recover and see how the experience informs their movements in the future. Kids fall down as a fun game. There is a way in which they fall, notice their fall and say, "Wow, big fall," and get up and move on. If there is crying and the need for comfort, the teacher goes to the child's level, offers comfort or first aid, if necessary, in a form in which the students participate.

Children can participate in administering first aid and learn compassion, care and empathy. If a child is hurt in the Park, it is amazing to see the children gather round, support, help and learn how to check in and see if the injured child is alright. They develop skills to comfort a hurt friend. They are cultivating a system of care through the way one person's problem becomes a group problem. Or not. The child that is hurt might turn away and want their space.

They may want to be alone and they are honored for that if they don't want to talk or have their owie attended to right away by the group. Penny Vieregge, who taught first aid at Gazebo for thirty-nine years, notes that,

> The kids are able to do so much more than we think. And particularly at that age, if they see the relevance, and can use imaginary play. You might remember the manikins and the owies, 'First you wash it then you cover it.' And washing and practicing with the Band-Aids to put them on. I mean that is relevant and for years, the children would handle their own owies at the Park.

There is a lot of intentionality around the Gazebo philosophy that many of us children were not aware of until we grew into adults. Marquis reflects on this by saying,

> When you're a kid you're just in it and you don't know the difference. You don't know that there's a philosophy at work or an intentionality in the way people are with you, that they are aware, that they are making specific decisions in how they interact with you to help you become the person, well, the person this philosophy believes you can be. Childhood is very special. It's a tiny moment in a long life and yet the most formative time. Then there was a moment when I grew up and was at Gazebo. For one reason or another and a little girl crawled into my lap and when I picked her up, I was asked to put her down, and she started crying. The teacher said, 'I really wish you hadn't done that.' I realized that there was so much at play here than I'd ever realized—so much intention and careful interaction.

Marquis goes on to express,

> You let kids be kids. You let them express and play and wear what they want, and cry and when there's conflict you help them with communication tools, but never do the talking for them. You teach them to respect you, like they respect their other friends, but that

you're just there if they need you, or want you, but it's not about you. You encourage creativity and deny the existence of boredom, while explaining how we are all a part of the system and that we are all responsible for the earth. You teach them to care for themselves and for one another. You explain the idea of consequences, not of any man-made law, but the consequences of nature. If you climb a tree, you should be able to get back down. You don't offer crutches, you don't soothe, you teach them to self-soothe and leave the protectiveness to parents.

Handl noticed,

The view of the child is what struck me the most deeply when I first came to Gazebo. The environment did not look like any licensed facility I knew—hay bales for boundaries, trees allowed climbing, loose parts, unkempt wild areas, a crumbling foundation as a Magic Castle, and children given freedom—freedom from time, from artificial transitions and allowing the biological clock back in to reign our days together. This trust extends to the experiences that children choose, or ones that the land or community imposes. Children can be free to experiment and discover their own strengths and frailties, their own boundaries on any given day, with any given place, situation or other being. Though the teachers may look for what the next step might be in offering curriculum, from finding the field guide to setting up a mud pit, it is the child's own inner teacher that dictates what they may want to explore. The teachers model cooperation and speak about their own feelings, 'I don't like the shovel in my face, stop,' or ' When people scream in my ear, it makes me want to move away,' or 'I feel crowded, please move back and give me space.'

In this way, a deep trust of the children was a unique quality in the culture at Gazebo.

Children as Capable, Equal, Responsible

Teach respect by being respectful.

-JL

A Growing Capacity

Two years old. Messy hands with paint.

Adult conditioned response—"Wait! Wash your hands over here! Let me help you. There you go."

Pathway towards self-reliance {new adult response}—"I see your hands are full of paint. What's next for you?" Wait for response {verbal or non-verbal} "Do you want to wash them off?" Wait again. "There's a water fountain over there. Here's a rag for you."

Then a step back to take in the growing capacity of the young child.

In this case, the practice was so rewarding and sensory-rich {new experiences can be intoxicatingly refreshing}, the process was repeated a few times—plunge hand into cup of paint, rotate fist back and forth, rub hands together, feel the smooth sensation, take in the colorful visual of smooth green on fingers, sense what's next, back to the newly discovered water fountain, pull down on slippery faucet, delight in the downpour of water, wet the rag, squish, one hand cleans the other, repeat entire process at will.

-Sharon Dvora, Gazebo intern

"Children are just as intelligent as adults, they are just learning."

– Patrick Douce

In my involvement with Gazebo, I saw that the program approached early childhood in a way that children are given trust and respect. These are given based on the belief that they are capable and that each child has their own interests, timing and experiences. The environment was designed for them to explore rather than be directed. The materials were available and the opportunities for social interaction were provided through the environment. If they wanted to paint, they were given tools to paint. They were given the conditions so that they could then explore the possibilities. If they choose to paint, and then they don't want to paint anymore, they are given the responsibility to clean up and wash their brushes and pallets. They are taught responsibility for clean-up of materials and this is as important as the right to choose their own activities. Price-Waldrip says,

> Giving power and choice to the child, the child as decision-maker, because they are able to know what they want and allowing them to try to go after it. Adult as a shadow, leaving the child to have their own experience. Child as a capable being, adult as support to intervene only when necessary, allowing child to make mistakes, get hurt, have conflicts, express anger. Adults are always there for safety and protection, but are not getting in the way of the child being able to embody their experience fully. Each child as part of a community, but not forcing them to participate, giving space and time for them to choose to be a part of the community or not.

At Gazebo, there was an honoring of potential and self-mastery. Children were not given a strict schedule with structured lessons. This alone demonstrated a deep trust of the child's process. Teachers were not constantly engaged in leading, teaching, or even playing with children. They were often modeling land stewardship, and offering invitations for children to get involved or explore their creativity with an attentive adult nearby. The teachers shared their passions and the students took part in this as they chose. While teachers were still engaged, they were not always interacting in direct ways with students, but rather *holding space* and awareness for the child's process. Sometimes, especially with students who were not used to having this kind of leadership, they expressed boredom. Yet, as teachers, we trusted that they would break through their boredom and find creative play on the other end of that challenge. The play and creativity are like the pot of gold at the end of the rainbow. Wyatt remarks,

> Getting down to the essence of what Gazebo is, I really think it's an outlook, a perspective. How I see the child primarily, and the world around me with myself. The world around me starting with the child, as capable, as I want to say equal, were are not equal—but being to being. A certain kind of coming without an agenda, but with a curiosity to meet this other being who is as full and rich as I am and has something to teach me.

She continues by saying,

> I want to reiterate wherever I go, this piece that I found in Gazebo that children are capable, about coming in as an equal teacher. I am not sure that people see this. A lot of people, even teachers, see kids as deficit in some way and I need to fill them, or impart something to them. That's not what I learned from Gazebo and that has not been my richest experiences. It is this exchange, this dance, it's a co-creation that happens together in the present moment and there is definitely a respect that comes in there that I don't see out in the world. I see a lot of agendas in the world of education. There are people that get it, that get down on the kids'

levels and listen and are respectful, but not tons of that. Definitely in terms of education there is this view of needing to put something on the children. It is such a missed opportunity, because for me as an adult, I am missing such opportunity for growth for myself. There is so much that that child has to teach me, and when I have an agenda, I am not really open to the present moment, right?

There is a undercurrent when I walk into an early childhood center about the orientation being towards the adults or the teacher. Are the children are all gathered around a teacher who is "teaching." Are they asking questions? Are they exploring on their own? The environmental design also very much supports children's self-directed play and whether they are as reliant on adults. For example, having sinks and water fountains at the children's level sends a subliminal message of "you can do this" and also gives them opportunities for practice. Does the environment make the children reliant on adults or does it send the message that they can do this with practice?

Then, there is the way the adults interact with the children and the exchanges between them that further signal this orientation. Wolfinger describes his perception as,

Seeing kids as humans. The child is full of potential. The child is self-developed through choice-rich environment. The child is self-directed through choice theory. The child is best left to feel freedom to discover and explore and have the freedom of self-expression and discovery.

In this way, adults can accept the natural state of childhood, without having to control, but rather openly learning from that special state of curiosity and wonder that children live in. Eizner expounds,

The whole concept of living environment and changing with the environment and listening to kids differently, paying attention to kids differently, appreciating kids for who they are without having to change them. Meeting kids at their level. Learning about kids' development by watching them. There is so much knowledge when it comes to the basics of where kids are, and that is the beginning. There is so much that people can learn from watching this. It is to perceive another human being with their own experience, their own knowledge, their own interest, their own self as they develop. Gazebo provides a sense of safety and understanding and support and love and care. Seeing the kids as another human being for who they are.

Julie Miller, retired early childhood education teacher and Gazebo mentor, says,

> What I see is honoring the children's humanity, and letting them take the lead in figuring out what they want to do and how to do it. Honoring where they are rather than making assumptions. This is very different from elementary and Early Head Start, where there is lots of talk about deficiencies. Gazebo doesn't worry about what children should be learning and rather looks at what they know and prompts their knowing and growing in the world. It is far less directive of the children's behavior. That is the philosophy, and Gestalt—honoring and believing that children know what's best for them. It still means they need guidance, but it gives them an opportunity to do that before we start pulling them in.

Nelson adds,

> I kind of saw ways, before I had kids, that I could treat my kids on an equal level not like a possession or a pet. I think it can still happen in the early childhood, in Gazebo. Teaching self-responsibility at an early age is the only time it can happen. I tried to talk to them as equals, when they were babies I did some baby talk but once they were communicating vocally I talked to them as equals, as peers, well not quite as peers but on many levels peers, people with feelings, thoughts and ideas.

The social trend in education and parenting is to help children by picking them up or doing a lot for them that they might otherwise do if given the time, space and opportunity. It is commonplace to talk to children as children by solving their problems for them, providing assistance before we give them a chance to try. Are we really helping them or are we taking away their experiences because we may have more practice or ability?

The implication here is that if children are given the space, and if adults approach them with more faith in what they can do, a whole different and more dynamic experience is possible for both adult and child. Former Gazebo intern, Iona Jones, depicts the scene at Gazebo by saying,

> Children are respected as individuals with wisdom and empowered to understand themselves and communicate their needs without assumptions being imposed upon them. Children are considered whole and capable human beings. We encourage and empower them to excel in life as individuals with the skills and permission to speak their mind, stand up for themselves, experience the consequences of their actions, and know that they have accomplished something on their own. Teachers do not interfere by speaking for a child, defending or rescuing them, or assisting them to climb, paint, build etc.

Though teachers may at times assist, the distinction here is that they generally do not do what the child can do for themselves. The adult might talk them through a challenge rather than providing physical assistance. So often parents and teachers approach children as if they cannot handle certain tasks because they are adult tasks, though they have never tried to give them the chance. For example, a mother I know recently complained that the father of their child was allowing her four-year-old to use scissors. I remarked that I thought cutting while supervised was actually a great fine-motor skill and would help build confidence for the child. Similarly, at Gazebo one might historically have seen a child hammering nails into a log or boards, cutting papers, or slicing bananas with a butter knife on a cutting board, with a teacher nearby supporting the process.

At the time the original Gazebo team designed the park, the descriptions above were not at all common practice. Therefore, the world of early childhood education has, in a sense, caught up to some of the principles that Gazebo began as one of the first outdoor schools in the state. Some of these Gazebo approaches are now seen as best practices in education such as kneeling down to talk to children and speaking to them physically on their level. Also, having child-sized toilets, sinks, and water fountains are environmental designs that support this kind of independence and self-mastery. The environmental design is in itself a metaphor for seeing what children can do and are capable of, given the opportunities for risk and responsibility. Classen says,

> Another thing that blew my mind, watching a one-and-a-half-year-old child crawl up to the sink to turn on the water, and her arms were quivering. She was so far beyond what I had seen a child of her age do. We can do so much more than we can expect them to do because we are so dumbed down. At Gazebo I was watching her turn on the water and no one around me was trying to help her or stop her, and because she was used to it, she wasn't looking to anybody for help or trying to get away from something she wasn't allowed to do. There was nothing to stop her, or keeping her apart from her purpose. Witnessing that changed the way I work with people forever.

Several Gazebo principles were controversial; even though they were adjusted over time as a response to social and cultural changes. First, the idea of not picking up children and babies was a radical practice. Two, allowing crying and emotional release. Third, allowing a certain level of physical conflict. Lastly, permitting calculated risk. On the outside, these practices may have been perceived as inhumane, but there is intentionality behind each process that is based on the belief that the child is capable. Working through challenge, through experience, being supported, the learning is much more meaningful.

In the end, the relevance and meaning in working through challenges, seemed to be so much more profound than being told by an adult that they "should" or "shouldn't" behave a certain way or do something because of the risk involved.

Climbing and Calculated Risk

Calculated risk was built into the environment and the teachers at Gazebo allowed exploration within these edges. For example, historically it was a Gazebo practice to allow children to climb trees as long as they could get themselves down. For example, a child might climb up a tree or onto a structure, and they were responsible to get themselves down. This meant they were provided the verbal support of a teacher or friend if needed, but they would have to physically find their way back. This was a hard point for children and adults alike and sometimes it took a lot longer to get through these processes, yet in the end the learning was so much more meaningful. Cheda remembers,

> I liked the idea of protecting from a safe distance. Not putting a child in a place where they wouldn't be able to get to under their own power. Giving them the space to challenge themselves and each other.

Douce also states,

> That was Janet's point, don't help them do what they can't do. Like climbing if a child wants to climb and they are not able to do it, don't help them. You make them dependent on the adult. The thing is to encourage them to learn how to learn which is the same as [Moshé] Feldenkrais. How do you learn? Not, 'We are going to program you with this information.' It's more about teaching and encouraging a way of learning where the child makes their own decisions. 'You're tired now? Go take a rest. You want to run now? Let's do some running.' How to support them rather than just have a preconceived script? I don't think we had a preconceived script. It was very much in the now.

Douce refers to his teacher, Dr. Moshé Feldenkrais, the Ukrainian-Israeli engineer and physicist, who founded the Feldenkrais Method®.

Many times children would climb trees, as it is much easier to climb up, then they would find themselves up high, calling for a teacher to help them down. As a Gazebo rule of thumb, teachers would 'talk' a child through getting down rather than physically helping them. Sometimes this meant that a child had to stay up there for a good long time while crying, calculating how to get down, being angry at a teacher for not helping, and in time, getting the courage up to take the risk of coming back down. This was a challenging point for many parents and bystanders, and often a strong and empowering memory for former Gazebo children. On the other hand, I do remember feeling really upset at being allowed to stay in a situation where I remained upset. Looking back, I see why it was done though it was upsetting to me at the time and I felt it was not fair. In fact, it was more fair than if I had been helped because that would have sent the message that the adult is more capable and stronger than me. Baldwin recalls,

> I remember and I don't know if they still climb Pottyville, but if they did get stuck, the teachers job is just to hang with them until they got down on their own. The other children help them. We would have children sitting on top of Pottyville for forty minutes. It's not like you abandoned them, you are right there, and the other children are like, 'You put your foot here and you put your foot there.' After a while these kids will sort of lose their nervousness, and if they are really still there after forty minutes, I will come and sit down and really support them in getting down. They will learn, or they will fall off, but before you whisk them off, the way they can learn is with experience. That is how the first time can be very, very difficult, and the second time isn't, and the third time, and after a while you're climbing that tree. I will support them in that, but they can do more on their own. Remember that great big tower with the telegraph pole with the netting? It broke the law because it should have only been four feet tall, so we had to

pull it down, but all the years we had it, no child ever got stuck. By the time you got up there, you knew what you were doing. It's dangerous, and the kids learned that. You did not idly try and climb it. It was always available for them to climb, it wasn't fenced off, there wasn't certain times they could do it. At any time one of those two-or three-year-olds could try and climb it, but they never did. What would happen was the four-and five-year-olds would go up—the ones who just had enough skill. There was something about it that was so 'whoa!' that children are learning from that and they would follow them. Because once you're up, you're up, and we will support you in getting down. That is not necessarily help, that's support. There is a difference.

These benchmark challenges became events and big memories for Gazebo kids.

I remember what Baldwin described above as a deck with a giant rope netting along the side and you had to climb up the rope to get to the platform. As a child, I was often floundering at the bottom, frustrated watching my sister and our friends having fun at the top. I remember not making it to the top or going only halfway many times while my friends all played above. It seemed so huge at the time. I also remember how I felt when I finally did climb to the top and the triumph and confidence I felt after so long trying. No one helped me up or down. The teachers waited patiently, even for months, until my body was capable of this feat. Marquis recollects,

> I have a very formative memory of being stuck on top of the shed. It felt like all day, but it was probably like fifteen minutes. My memory is I climbed up there.... cut to—I realize the entire class was sitting down there staring up at me, and I was sobbing. The teachers had to have a very serious conversation. They were all gathered over there talking and really thinking about it and then Yalitza came over and said, 'I am going to help you help yourself.' She said you can hold onto the branch, and just in case you fall, I will catch you; but that is as far as I will go, Anne-Louise.

This level of independence is a pretty foreign approach to early childhood education. This has been an area of discomfort for parents and interns, yet children have breakthroughs in these ways. Adults underestimated them or they themselves may have fears, yet there were huge triumphs involved in these situations. This is one of the growing edges, sticking points, and more controversial aspects of what went on at Gazebo and an area where so much growth took place.

Wyatt speaks to these practices by saying,

> Why don't you help kids up trees? Why don't you break up fights? Why don't you pick kids up and down? To give them the opportunity to experience their capability. When I help a kid out of the tree, I am saying that you can't do it; that you need my help. That is the message they get whether I say it or not. 'You need my help, you are not capable.' It is hard for parents because we have that very real time where they are dependent and they are learning and growing and expanding and we are always catching up. That was my experience with my daughter. 'Oh, you can do this now and you are capable of this now.'

Wyatt also reflects that without a rigorous time schedule, Gazebo allowed situations to play out fully and thus the child to progress at their own rate without the pressure.

> Why don't we pick them up? I think it is very empowering to children to stand on their own two feet. As soon as you pick them up they are completely dependent on you. They are not independent, they have no power.

Picking Up and Carrying Children? How Much Do You *Do* for the Child?

Parents and outside witnesses have found specific Gazebo practices are not easy to digest. In particular, there was a guiding principle from the start of Gazebo where teachers did not pick up or carry babies and children. It is not that teachers couldn't get close to children or have them in their laps, but they didn't lift them off the ground. The connection to the earth and to their own power was the basis for this premise. Handl notes,

> The idea of competency is a constant mirror the adults offer the children as well. The child is seen as competent within their own progression, that they can do lots more than they think they can. What choices lie within the boundaries of physical safety are theirs to make and harvest the consequences of. In the end, our power as human beings truly does not lie in what happens to us, who happens to be interacting with us, what is being said or done with/to us, it is in our response to those things, and to the meaning we give it. How empowering, how integral to building our own construction of life and the world to find out that whatever we choose to do will have outcomes, and we can only control our own choices, not the choices of others.

It seems like human nature to pick up a crying child, to calm them by bringing them up into your arms, to want to soothe and comfort them by rescuing them from discomfort. There is nothing wrong with this, and in many contexts, this is the appropriate response. It is also a very instinctual response—as if humans are hardwired to not be able to tolerate a crying baby without wanting to do something about it. Why did Lederman implement this protocol of not picking up babies? Through the lens of viewing the child as capable, equal, responsible, and even resilient, there is much more possibility. Jones describes, "Not picking up a child enables them to develop their own feet, sense of groundedness, and capacity for supporting and directing themselves in the world."

McLeod's response to why don't we pick up a child within this philosophy:

> Because it deprives exploration and initiation and learning to feel the pain of a rough surface and actually knowing one's one abilities and inabilities to do something. Without being grabbed by an adult, they will get the motivation to leap forward and take a risk with an inability—transforming to ability. It may sound a bit abrasive or unnatural. It is one of the pieces that makes Gazebo an experimental learning center, the cutting edge, a human growth and potential seed. You see Gazebo is the space for the learning to take place (safely) otherwise kids might as well be at home where most mommies can pick them up and do everything for them. In Gazebo philosophy, as I learned it, picking up a child at Gazebo was overstepping boundaries. Why? Because it keeps a child dependent on the adult (not allowed to be an independent thinker and problem solver).

Nelson feels,

> When a kid falls down they don't hurt themselves at all, it's a little shock. So, if someone comes up and slobbers all over them then they can kind of train parents and other adults that they just have to fall down to get lots of attention. Some awareness of that potential dynamic is good for parents and teachers. I think that

you can teach a kid to be helpless or be needy by giving them too much reinforcement for being needy. I really noticed how, it was easy for me to do those unintuitive things that we were supposed to do like not pick the kids up, and slobber all over them, and play first aid. If they fell down, just go up and be present for them. If they were injured then take care of them.

Chelsea Belle Davey, former Gazebo student and Vieregge's granddaughter, feels the reason children were not picked up is to encourage "independence and responsibility":

> Don't climb up if you can't climb down. Don't say something hurtful, or act out against your peers because there are consequences. Consequences. Action and reaction. If you are helped as a child over every step, through every argument, etc., how are you supposed to know what the consequences are once you are alone? There is also the gift of independence and sense of self when you are able to manage on your own. I remember knowing that someone could get hurt—if someone was climbing very high in the tree or hammering a nail—owies would inevitably happen. Looking back on this, I admire the trust the teachers gave the kids, and the parents gave the teachers.

Vieregge worked at Gazebo longer than anyone else in its history. Though she worked outside of the park, her frame of reference for the philosophy is such:

> Picking up and running to help: Only in matters of health and safety. Babies (before crawling) are securely chest carried while facing outward when possible. Contact with the earth (bare feet is essential for grounding and balancing. Child encouraged to take the first steps toward comfort. This gains control over environment. Crawling/toddling bare feet on uneven ground. Contact and balance. Trust in Allah and tether your camel. Again, mutual respect. Encourage the child's strengths. Adults' protection is always quietly nearby, encouraging the child to discover its own

strengths. When rushing in to comfort WHO RECEIVES THE MOST BENEFIT/PLEASURE. ALWAYS ASK YOUSELF.

Vieregge mentions carrying babies, and as time went on, Gazebo did shift to a time some teachers began to hold the very young babies more frequently in baby carriers for napping etc. Yet, traditionally it was really focused on them being close to the earth and grounded in their own movements. In fact, there was a special garden and open tipi area with different herbs on the ground Lederman designed to stimulate the touch and smell senses for the babies.

During Baldwin's many years of experience at Gazebo, he saw so much growth and progress around these practices and the issues connected to them. He says,

Why not pick up a child? Why, because the child is capable of moving on their own. There are three stages of crawling, and the more you let a child crawl without picking them up the better. Allowing those three stages to go fully through is important, and when a child is ready to walk, they do it using their own body. It's like when you get into your car and start it, you don't then get out and push it do you? That is the point of your car, it goes. A child goes. They have legs, they have arms, unless obviously they have a problem there, they operate. And they need to operate at their own speed, learning to crawl, learning to walk. The worst possible thing you can do for a child is give them one of those stupid 'dingly dangly' things where they learn to stand early. They are not building up their muscles. If you want to go to the moon then that's great, teach your kids that. But they are not going to the moon, they are going to be on a planet with some really serious gravity. The more their bodies learn that gravity, the better. That is the physical development of the physical side. You also have the emotional side.

Baldwin expounds,

A lot of time the picking up of the child has nothing to do with the kid, it is all about the adult. Little Emilio, he was the golden boy. He was so cute. When he was six months old, there were queues of people in the lodge to carry him. Literally people had kids because of him, they were like, 'I got to have my own.' I am not even getting close because, I am like, 'He is going to come to Gazebo. He is going to be mine and by mine I mean he is going to be his.' He comes in and he is still crawling and his dad works at Gazebo, and he is expecting me to just pick him up. 'Well, no lad, I am not picking you up. You can crawl over here, you can crawl over there.' Very quickly he realized that I am the guy who doesn't pick him up. I'm the guy who lets him crawl, lets him do his own thing. What happens is whenever he needs help, he comes to me, because I am the guy who is actually there for him in the real sense. He comes to me. Whereas the 'picky uppy' thing is the adult's thing—which he is learning from the adult that he needs to be picked up all the time. With me he is unlearning that, and out of that he had a stronger bond with me than anyone else in Gazebo, because I am the guy saying no. Not because of anything against you Emilio, but you can walk and you can crawl. I have seen this with other children, that when you give strong boundaries within the philosophy, that builds up the trust. The clearer you are with a child, that allows the child to become clearer too. Don't pick up a child. Always come down to them. If you have a child who is crying on the ground you can always come down to them. If it's nap time when it's a little different where you can kind of scoop them up and put them in the swing, but overall it is better to get down with a child and see what is happening rather than instinctively bring them up. They can do everything themselves physically and by coming down to them you are meeting them at their level. There is no, 'I am a great teacher or I am the great adult come to me and I will solve all your problems.' It is much more I am coming to you and saying, 'Well let's work it out, let's see what's happening.' It is always good to get down to a child's level rather than picking them up to your level.

Similarly, McLeod describes,

> Adults in Gazebo have tendencies or needs of their own whereby they are sucking the energy away from a child. It feels good to hold a child as a child gives out good vibes that are pure and sacred. This is better left to the connection of others—parents, grandparents, close friends outside the Gazebo setting.

With crying, as much as soothing the child, somehow the instinct to soothe calms the nerves of the adults as well. Myers states,

> The principle was that the child needs to find their own way back, and as we lift them up, we take them off their grounding from the earth and we disempowered them in our efforts to comfort them. It doesn't mean that you wouldn't go to them, that you wouldn't empathize with them, but you wouldn't save them.

Peter Levine, trauma expert and creator of Somatic Experiencing®, and Maggie Kline, state in their book *Trauma Proofing your Kids*,

> The best antidote is to tend to your own reactions *first*. Allow time for your own bodily responses to settle rather than scolding or running anxiously toward your child, unless she is actually in danger. Experiences with our adult clients in therapy confirm that often the most frightening part of an incident experienced as a child was their parents' horror reaction! Children 'read' the facial expression of their caregivers as a barometer of how serious the danger or injury is.[1]

Similarly Douce comments,

> Part of running around is so we can have a fall and learn not to cry for attention and simply to learn; because we learn from those experiences how we can develop better human qualities by learning to deal with our momentary problems.

For me, there is a teaching within this context about learning to be alright when another person is not. This has been a very deep insight for me as a mother and mover. I learned a lot about this doing movement meditation and 5Rhythms® movement practice. I would find myself so distraught when another person was emoting during a dance. And, when my daughter cries I've had to learn to be okay when she is not. This has been a big learning for my life in terms of relationships. I think this work is valuable for adults in how they interact with others and also learning how to stay in their own experience. How do we sit with someone else's pain? How do we witness them, support them, see them, without trying to change them? How do we stay grounded and not take on another person's issues?

While I was teaching at Gazebo, Vieregge gently pointed out a situation that needed awareness. There was a certain child who had very difficult time self-regulating. He often cried and, as Handl would put it, he needed another limbic system for comfort. I would put him down for a nap, or comfort him when waking up, and I would often put him in my lap. Vieregge pointed out that while it was alright for him to be connected to me, I should try, at the very least, allow him to keep at least one of his limbs or feet connected to the earth. When I tried this, I found this helped his experience in reintegrating into the group and into his own confidence and comfort. This was a valuable lesson for me as a Gazebo teacher to reflect on the comforting the child also was somehow connecting to my own feeling of self-importance and self-esteem. Furthermore, the practice of not picking up a child, was again a metaphoric symbol of allowing the child to be attached to the earth and not only to another individual. Eizner says,

> They need to be where they need to be. Not picking them up is important because they need to be where they are. Janet used to say, 'Children don't need to be taken to a place where they are not ready to be taken.' So, if you encourage little kids to develop physically, body development, crawling, walking, balancing, that body development encourages brain development. It's important to be with them at their level rather than taking them to places that they are not ready. So, the teacher would go and sit down by the kid

and get down on their level and very gently and when the readings were appropriate the teacher would maybe put a hand on the back of the child and support the kid. Most of the time when the kids were hurt they would maybe crawl into the lap of an adult if they wanted to be held. Sometimes they would lay there and just look at their surroundings and just get up and move on, on their own. It would be going down to their level, maybe putting on a hand, and letting the kid know that you are present and you're available to them and they can make a choice of getting more support from you or not. It's giving them that choice, and when you go pick them up you are not giving them that choice. That sense of responsibility is a big one, because if you pick up a kid and something happens to you and to the kid it is not going to be on that kid, it is going to be on you. You are walking with a kid and you trip.

Frequently spoken of, and echoed through many of the wisdom keepers of Gazebo, is the idea of trusting the child's personal space and process. Yet, there is no rule of not holding a child or being there for them with comfort. In fact, many of the teachers state this is the most important aspect of relating to a child who is distraught—coming down to their level, meeting them where they are. In this way, you are not trying to change the child's experience, but rather allowing them to be where they are, with support, with presence and sending them the subliminal message that they are comforted by the earth and those around them, and that they are capable and trusted to be in their bodies.

Crying: Is it Okay to Cry?

Another area which has been a challenge for some people at Gazebo was how much the adults allowed children to cry. That is one of the places in which Gazebo is distinct from other programs and some of this is influenced by the Gestalt approach. However, I hear parents say so often, 'don't cry' (especially to boys). While this may be a cultural phenomenon, not allowing children to emote is also a social construct. Douce recalls, "With boys, if you have emotion it shows you're weak." Other sentiments we hear frequently are, "It's okay" or "Don't be sad."

For many children and adults alike, during the moments they are crying, and when they are not okay, perhaps there are way in which they need to feel these feelings? It can be constructive for a person in distress to be seen, heard, and acknowledged for what they are going through before offering feedback. The impulse to fix the problem or change the uncomfortable emotion is common. How often have you been upset and tried to talk to a friend or cry only to have that person begins to offer advise and solutions before acknowledging your feelings? Would it be more helpful first to just hear a reflection of your difficulties? "Wow, that sounds painful. That must be very hard. I can see that you are hurting." These are just a few ways that reflecting can be affirming.

Parenting expert Susan Stiffleman, author of *Parenting with Presence*, suggests that crying, even over something small and seemingly insignificant, is an opportunity to release important emotional buildup. Stiffleman says,

> When we begin taking time to slow down and be quietly present, painful emotions that have been long repressed may rise to the surface. Many of us remain in constant motion so we won't feel the pain of unresolved sorrow or grief, when in fact, feeling those feelings is what lets them move through and out. How wonderful to help our children learn that they can allow their emotions to be felt, including the difficult ones. [2]

Furthermore, parenting approaches such as those delineated in *Aware Parenting* method also encourage parents to reflect back feelings and just sit quietly with a child as a way to allow for this. One term for this is 'stay listening.' More and more brain research suggests that the prefrontal cortex part of the brain, that is in charge of emotions, needs to offload, and when it is emptied out of the emotional buildup, there is more space for learning to occur. 'Stay listening' is a newer term in the growing field of parenting, however Gazebo has been honoring the emotions of children and the need for expression since the beginning. Before allowing children to emote became more accepted in parenting and education and consequently supported by brain research, there was great resistance to it socially.

On the other hand, in my experience at Gazebo there have been many breakthroughs in creating space for tears. As a parent, I often hear people, even myself, say to a/my child, "Don't cry." I remember just after my daughter was born hearing myself say it to her and wondering to myself, 'Why I am saying this?' It was bright and new and perhaps painful and even shocking entering this world. She had more than enough reason to cry! Some of this is instinctual on a human level and other parts may be cultural and social. I remember Handl mentoring me as a parent to increase my stamina for crying when at the time I was experiencing felt like an assault on my nervous system. Thus, the adult's discomfort with a crying child may be more problematic than the crying is for the child. For the child it might even be the opposite, a way to regulate the nervous system.

On the other hand, it can be positive for children to realize their impact on the people around them, and at times take space to emote. Sometimes being separated from a group if causing disturbance may be appropriate. Yet, in my opinion, it is the baby and child's right to cry and it can sometimes be so healing for that child to just let it out and start fresh. With my daughter, I have frequently been met with judgments, nasty looks, and unfriendly treatment when she has cried in public. The world doesn't seem to understand or allow for this kind of open emoting. Jones feels that, "Holding space for a crying or screaming child honors and validates their emotion, empowering them to feel what they are feeling and move on when they are ready, in their own time."

Similarly, Baldwin describes some of the tension for outsiders viewing the philosophy at work,

It is not ignoring the children necessarily, but it is not rushing in to see what is happening and saying, 'Oh my god.' I had a boy climbing that fence and as long as you're on the inside of that fence well that is fine, but he would fall over, and it was on the inside and it is soft grass, but he would cry because he wanted me to help him up. Well, I was trying to separate from him because this was a boy who spent a lot of time with me since he was very young and there is a point where you gotta get out in the outside world where there is not going to be Neil with you all the time. I was already doing a job. I was cutting the fruit. There is a woman coming by and she comes in and tends to this child, I had to go throw her out of the Park. No, you're not seeing what you think your seeing here woman. Of course, crying you want to investigate, but if there is an adult already engaged with this child in an experimental school, and you walk past, don't just assume that I am ignoring that child. I am just doing my job here, you can just know we are doing some serious work here; you are learning to separate from me, you are learning to pick yourself up, no hurt here, if he had fallen over and hurt himself than that is different. I come over, 'Do we need first aid? Do we need the ice bunny?' But I had already been over three times and ascertained that this is something he was doing to get my attention, so there is a point I am telling him I am cutting fruit, you can come to me. I am actually engaged with this child. It's not me just ignoring the kid. There is history, there is structure, there is learning going on for the child, and it looks like when you walk by it is just a child lying on the ground and somebody ignoring them, but that is not actually what is happening.

Though this concept of allowing emotions will be explored in greater depth in the chapter on Gestalt, one principle is that through the lens of the child, we can learn to orient to the child's experience. Releasing emotions is natural, and as adults, it is helpful to bring awareness our own emotions. Do children even need to be rescued from their feelings and experiences? Do they need to be supported? What is the distinction? Where is the impulse coming from? Can crying be a valid part of their emotional and cognitive learning and development?

Physical Conflict: Is It Ever Alright to Fight?

Finally, one of the most controversial concepts that had been practiced at Gazebo is physical conflict. Many people disagreed with the idea that in the early days of Gazebo, that some level of fighting was allowed. There were rules, and for health and safety considerations, there were still parameters that prevented real injury. Regardless, this practice, in the last few decades of the program's operation, had lessened, if not stopped completely. On the other hand, I think it is worthy of exploring the context in which Lederman had allowed physical contact and consequently a deep level of physical experiences for the children.

When children appear to be fighting, sometimes they are not actually hurting each other, but rather having a somatic—of the body or physical— experience in which they are exploring their strengths and boundaries. Having a teacher tell you, "We don't do that here," or, "It is not nice to hit," is not nearly as meaningful as feeling what it is like when someone hits you or seeing their face when they are hurting. I am not advocating violence, but I am suggesting that learning through experience is much more lasting and meaningful.

In the history of early Gazebo, physical conflict was allowed. Yet, the basic ground rules were:

1. Health and Safety first

2. No biting

3. No weapons

4. Matched Energies

While Lederman felt children needed to learn through direct experience, of course health and safety are always the guiding parameters.

Matched Energies

Furthermore, the children engaging in physical conflict needed to have matched energies. This is a very important concept for Gazebo regarding how children are engaging in conflict and even in play. Matched energies wasn't necessarily related only to the physical size of the child or the age of the child. Matched energies was about how the child communicated, what was their level of confidence, if they could self-advocate. Perry Holloman, former Gazebo teacher and parent, Gestalt therapist, and Deep Bodywork® founder and teacher suggests,

> It happened differently in each and every case, but some of the basic ground rules of not allowing violence, not allowing an asymmetry to dominate the space because an older child or bigger child was in some kind of conflict with a smaller one or some kind of a sharper more verbally adept one was in some kind of a verbal conflict with a less verbally adept one.

The concept of matched energies is very much like it sounds. If human were put on an energetic balance scale, sometimes it is even, and sometimes it would tip one way or another to where one being would be energetically stronger than another. Matched energies are even and balanced. Matched energies are capable of similar physical and emotional boundaries. Even without direct conflict, through rough-and-tumble physical play, the rule of matched energies was applied. No child should be getting physically hurt, and yet there was a somatic learning and development happening for the children that was not stopped. The teachers were closely watching and observing when and how to intervene in physical conflict and play.

Wyatt describes how the physical conflict was a source of tension for her,

> It is not as easy of a crossover. The thing that happens with fighting is the physically stronger ends up winning. The strongest shall

survive. It doesn't feel very evolved. To me that is part of the *WE* where peace and harmony come in.

Nevertheless, Holloman makes the distinction that,

> Violence was a key structural point that wasn't allowed, kids weren't allowed to hit each other, or throw things at each other. Anything that could create some kind of physical injury, that was clearly not okay, but another thing that we needed to attune to was overwhelm. Overwhelm could occur in different ways. One, there could be a power differential between the kids—so one person could be relationally more powerful or physically or relational more powerful. We paid close attention to asymmetries in power—both physically and emotionally. We paid close attention to that which can lead to situations where a lot of bullying occurs and the less powerful child in the constellation becomes overwhelmed. Overwhelm is a situation where the central nervous system shuts down, and no more growth and learning can happen. When conflict arose, we were acutely aware of leveling the playing field such that overwhelming experiences wouldn't happen.

Baldwin says,

> Basically it is not about breaking the fight up unless it is one sided. It is about equal energies. The first lesson of aggression. That doesn't mean age. I have seen two-year-olds wipe the floor with four-year-olds. But if it is clearly one child with way too much energy and another one really now able to deal with it, then I intervene. The teacher has to be very aware, both of the situation at the moment, and also the history of these children. No biting. No weapons. Not interrupting, and allowing them to reach the boundary of where they are with that. It is very animalistic. We are animals. If you watch a bunch of little young foxes, these little guys they are ripping each other, they are shredding each other, and they are learning about the outside bigger world.

Baldwin continues,

> For instance, I am sitting with Bedaman (good ol Beda). We are
> reading a book, Tristan is not there, and these guys are totally oc-
> cupied. Then, Tristan is sneaking up and punching Bedaman on
> the back. I withdrew and was doing something else and watching.
> Bedaman would turn around and say, 'Stop it!' He was using his
> words. Tristan was not giving up. He was coming and going, and
> Beda is getting more and more wound up. Finally, Beda (you know
> he is a big fellow, our boy), he gives up. He has used his words. He
> has tried everything else. He goes over and just sits on Tristan.
> Tristan just wails and I'm watching and he's laughing. He is wailing
> but he's laughing. He is not actually the victim here. Bedaman is
> the victim. If you would have just walked past Gazebo you would
> have seen a huge boy looking like he is just whopping the hell out
> of a little boy, and the teacher is just kind of standing there looking
> at his rake. What school is this? But no, what was happening was
> much more complicated than what you see just walking by. This
> was about Tristan just not listening. I was standing by watching.
> This isn't about endless war. It is more like, 'Lets learn how to deal
> in the more difficult situations, so we can move on from them.' I
> might come down, I am telling them to use their words, I am not
> encouraging them to be physical with each other. I am encouraging
> them to use other directions. Unless we get serious, like it looks
> like another kid is about to come in and bite, then I am going to
> come and get between them.

Baldwin remembers the rules as,

> No biting, no weapons, no eye gouging, no using the fingernails.
> It was more about the physical. I might come in closer if I have one
> child looking for trouble, if I have a biter, if they are not matched
> energies. A biter child might be biting for whatever reason and
> needs a closer eye. This is the child's place. And so, the child also
> has to have boundaries. Which is why they don't just get to run free.

Davey reflects, "If I needed help or couldn't do something I knew I could ask for help—and I wasn't ever afraid to ask for help from the adults." On the other hand, if there was a need to release anger, one tool that children were encouraged to try was something that adults did in Gestalt process which is what we used to call as kids, "pillow pounding." For example, there was a boy that was very big for his age and very physical in his body when I was working at Gazebo as a teacher. I remember having a hard time when he would hurt his little brother even by accident. I also felt he had some unresolved anger issues and I used to redirect him toward punching the large pillows in the pony shed as an alternative to hitting another child.

In the Arf stories below, the Gestalt processes show an example of how physical conflict was redirected to investigate the feelings using an object rather than another child.

I Want to Hit Flash!

Dylan: (comes running over very upset and angry) Arfur! Arfur! Flash hit me and I hate him and want to hit him.

Arfur: Dylan, would you feel better if you hit Flash and hurt him?

Dylan: (with anger in his voice) Yeah!

Arfur: Okay! let's pretend that Flash is this big pillow.

Dylan: (perplexing look) Okay, can I kick him too?

Arfur: Sure, you can do whatever you want to the pillow.

Dylan: (starts to punch and kick the pillow, getting very angry and yelling) I hate you Flash. I don't like it when you hit me. (Dylan begins to cry and falls on the pillow and sobs).

Arfur: (allowing Dylan to feel his sadness) How are you doing Dylan?

Dylan: (the anger has left and he appears calm now) Good!

Arfur: Do you still want to hurt Flash?

Dylan: No, but I want to tell Flash not to hurt me anymore.

Arfur: Why don't you go and do that. (Dylan goes off to share his concerns with Flash)

Dylan Bit Me!

Lucy: (comes running over crying and very upset) Arfur! Arfur!, Dylan bit me!

Arfur: Where did he bite you? Lucy: (crying) On my face.

Arfur: What do you want right now?

Lucy: I want you to hold me.

Arfur: (takes Lucy in his arms and holds and comforts her).

Lucy: (starts to cry more and then after awhile begins to calm down and begins to speak)

I want to bite Dylan! (anger rises in her voice).

Arfur: Let's imagine that this teddy bear over there is Dylan? Could you bite it?

Lucy: (yells) I don't want to bite that teddy bear, I want to bite Dylan.

Arfur: Let's pretend the Teddy Bear is Dylan and see what happens when you bite the teddy bear.

Lucy: (with reluctance. Lucy goes over to the teddy bear and begins to bite it. Soon there are sounds of growling and anger and Lucy throws the bear down to the ground and stomps on it with her feet).

Arfur: (waits until Lucy is finished with her release) What's happening?

Lucy: (relieved) I feel happy now, it was fun to bite the bear.

Boundaries

Jones feels that, "Allowing children to fight enables them to develop boundaries and gives them the opportunity to learn how to go after what they want and to defend themselves." Though there are perhaps other ways to develop boundaries, some children really do find growth in putting up physical boundaries and defending themselves. These are unfortunately, skills that will serve children as they grow into adults. As a teacher at Gazebo, it takes a lot of sensitivity to weigh out matched energies and sometimes it requires supporting children in developing in new strengths. I worked on this many times with children with more timid temperaments paired with children who were very boisterous and big. There was tension in their opposing personalities and issues often arose. However, I really encouraged the more shy children to develop their boundary-setting techniques by using body language and words to create space for themselves. Responses vary in conflict depending on temperament. Perhaps there is anger in response to aggression, or an impulse to flee, or perhaps a child shrinks back. These are examples of fight, flight or freeze responses and each individual has different responses which can change depending on the situation.

In any case, working with the child to set a clear boundary in a firm and loving way teaches them that there they can keep themselves safe, and that are appropriate moments to take space or to say no. These practices help develop a skill set for children that they will inevitably need throughout their lives. Rather than jumping into a conflict and saying, "Stop, we don't do that here," a teacher might allow the conflict, physical or verbal, to play out in order for the child to work through their own process at developing the skill of setting boundaries with the support and guidance of the teacher.

Kevin Harvey, Gazebo father, shared a poignant story about how his son, Sage, learned to set boundaries at Gazebo. There was another boy named Dodge who he had been having some conflict with. At first, Sage was very timid and shy and would often run away or cry in response to Dodge's big energy in their interactions. Harvey shared how at night he would hear Sage practicing with himself before bedtime. He would put out his hand and say, "Dodge, stop!" Then, he was able to bring that work back to school and say the same words to Dodge. Their friendship flourished and Sage gained more confidence in himself that he could set a boundary, protect his personal space, and be heard by his friend. It was a very important process for me to witness as a teacher, and both Sage's family and the staff felt proud of this emotional development. Harvey says,

> "Sage turning into a child was amazing. Learning to relate to the kids and let himself be a child! He related best to adults, until one day—poof—here is this amazing wild human being, being a child, soaking in every little detail of his interactions with the universe. Taking it all in for himself. Being free. Watching Sage make friends by being himself made me feel so proud of him. So good."

Nelson recalls, "I think they really learned boundaries. I am this person."

Charles, Gestalt Facilitator and longtime Esalen community member, addressed how physical conflict and boundaries were particularly important with pre-verbal children.

> I think to emphasize that physical conflict is especially useful before they have a good command of language, because with the four-years-olds, I would encourage them to use their words. It was more for the toddlers. 'What is she saying to you? Do you see she is crying?' Then they make their own translation of it.

Douce says,

> The element of really listening to the child and supporting the child is really Gestaltian. Here is an example. One day this kid was standing there and out of the blue and this other kid came up and bit him in the face. It became a real issue. Really big issue. The child was walking around with these teeth marks on his face. Arthur said a few days before that child had been bitten by the

other child so he was waiting for revenge. So it is not that this child just came out of the blue and attacked this other one, the other one did it to him first. But then when it happened again Arthur got all the kids and we all sat there and we all talked about how biting was wrong so it wasn't me and Arthur telling this child biting was wrong. I remember Jenny Price goes, 'Oh no, that's really wrong.' Probably you and your sister, the kids were all saying, 'Oh no, that's wrong.' So the kids were the ones saying it was wrong to other ones. It wasn't us saying it, but we didn't blame the child, we educated that it was wrong. Because Arthur said he or she had been attacked a few days earlier, so they were just evening the score. Rather than make the child wrong—see the dynamic that led to it. You don't have to say it is wrong, let them say it is wrong and they will remember it more. Plus, they have already forgiven you, so they are just communicating. Also how to listen to each other, how to communicate, 'I don't want you to do that.'

As a child, I remember learning about the animals by being with them, close to them. I remember my teachers and a lot of nurturing and comfort provided by them. This was a hands-on somatic aspect of the education. This was the way in which we could have contact with the earth, ourselves and each other. I remember being in contact with other children and playing and also being very physical, wrestling, resting, being in the mud, in the paint, feeling our strength with our bodies and hands but not hurting. I remember fighting, not in any situation, but I remember the physical sensation of slobbering and touching and feeling other children and tussling over toys.

Gazebo took on a lot of the social constructs and questioned them through experimentation, and as a result many of these practices were born. Sampson Day, former Gazebo student, describes two sets of social norms in different environments.

I feel like what I remember most was, because I went back and forth from a New York school to Gazebo, was the sense that all the rules were socially constructed by other five-year-olds. There were no grand consequences of the externalities of your actions that extended beyond Gazebo, there was no sort of administrative bureaucracy. You actually had to deal with the consequences of your actions and I think that was scary at first because you didn't really have someone you could go to to complain about the minutiae of what another child was doing. In my schools in New York there was a bunch of rules I really didn't understand.

The difference at Gazebo is that the child learns through consequences rather than by adults' rules, which in the end becomes so much more about the child's experience rather than the adult's.

Who Are Children Without Their Parents?

Gazebo is a place where children explore who they are, what they can do, and how they feel – apart from parents....and in doing so discover who they are, what they can do, and how they feel ...with parents."

-JL

I Want to Go Home (Arf Story)

Jenny: (comes up to Arfur upset) I want to go home.

Arfur: How are you feeling Jenny?

Jenny: I miss my mommy. (starts to cry). I want to see her.

Arfur: Jenny, your mommy is at work and won't be here until later.

Jenny: (Starts to get angry and upset) Then I will go find her.

Arfur: Jenny, your mom wants you to stay here until she picks you up.

Jenny: (angry and frustrated) I don't care, I want to go.

Arfur: Would you do something with me? Jenny: (abruptly) What!

Arfur: Close your eyes for a moment.

Jenny: (closes her eyes) Now what?

Arfur: Imagine your mom and tell me when you see her?

Jenny: (starting to calm herself) Okay! I can see her.

Arfur: What do you want from her?

Jenny: I want her to hold me.

Arfur: Then ask her.

Jenny: (tears begin to roll down her cheeks and she begins to softly cry) Mommy hold me!

Arfur: (there is silence for a moment as Jenny is making a connection with her mommy. Jenny is looking different now) Jenny, see if it is okay to open your eyes now.

Jenny: (opens her eyes and a little smile appears on her face)

Arfur: How do you feel now?

Jenny: I want a hug.

Jenny and Arfur hug. The feeling of wanting to go now has left and Jenny goes off to play. She has found her mommy inside her home.

A big part of early education for families is the separation of the child from their guardians. Feldenkrais said,

> The child's dependence on the parents gradually diminishes. The growth of the voluntary nerve paths and their connective bundles enables the child to assume responsibility for moving and preserving her own body. Gradually, dependence shifts from the parents to other adults, and finally to society.[3]

Thus, children are learning about themselves and their autonomy at school.

While Gazebo methods can be used in the home, the role of the teacher is very different from that of a parent or guardian. Munyer states,

Leave children alone detached from parents (obsession, overprotective, shielding, codependency) and let the child explore. Parents would take themselves out, and the needs of the child became more important—greater than the needs of the adult.

Therefore, there is a social skill set being developed that initiates a new learning for the child. McLeod adds,

It is not home. It is school. A child needs to learn to be responsible and to be able to self-nurture without an adult doing it for them. And then what happens if an adult is not present to do so? Do they not focus and do anything for attention and sometimes get hurt in the process.

Furthermore, Cheda implores,

Encouraging exploration and self-determination is important. Not trying to fill the parents role, but rather teaching by example. Letting the child find her/his power by not interfering in conflicts, or attempting to rescue the child when a problem arises.

Parents begin to see through the Gazebo lens as well and see how their children might rise to the occasion of being trusted. For example, Libby Barnes, architect and Gazebo parent says,

What I think is most important is the outdoor classroom and the teaching of self-relevance. I've seen Olivia grow into a very self-confident little person. (Strong will, where did that come from?!) Self-confidence and relevance are some of the most positive and fundamental traits we can acquire.

Similarly, Gazebo parent Sarah Harvey says of her child,

A triumph for me was the day that Sage gave me a kiss, said, 'Bye Mom!' and ran into the Park at Gazebo without looking back. I knew he was becoming more independent. One thing Sage was proud of was showing us that he could get a drink out of the sink by himself without any help. Also, his first time going to Pottyville was huge because at first he didn't go potty in it, but was proud that he hung out by Pottyville and talked about going to the bathroom.

Nelson recalls,

It was easy for me as a teacher because even though I loved them they weren't my kids, so then I really noticed how it was different. I tried to do it with my daughter Gaelen, but it was clear that it wasn't working. It's o.k. to be different. The parents can go into Gazebo and do whatever they want, but then they have to leave at some point.

Lederman encouraged parents to drop off their children at the entrance to the park and let the children enter their own territory. It is true that the role of parents is different than that of teachers. What a parent might do, a teacher might not. This is unique to each situation, and both parents and teachers can apply the basic view of the child. Nevertheless, there is a distinction, because parents have different boundaries with their children; and life outside of school has a different set of needs and expectations.

Thus, the experiences, the processes, the relationship dynamics for children and adults were intentionally sculpted in a frame of trust in the child. Though it is hard to describe, there is an essential respect and equality that is not often referenced in education. Magda Gerber was once of the pioneer educators who approached education in an alternative way that was similar to Gazebo during the same. The basis of Magda's Gerber's RIE philosophy is also rooted in respect for the child and a trust in them. Magda encouraged parents and caregivers to provide more opportunities for the baby to be "an initiator, an explorer, and a self learner."[4]

Sharna Whitehand, Gazebo parent, says of her child's experience, "Gazebo gave my children the confidences to be themselves, to know what it feels like to be your authentic self. It was a solid foundation."

Fredrick Perls said,

> Often children are more mature than adults. You notice here we
> have a different equation, or rather a different formulation. We
> have not the equation: adult equates a mature person. As a matter
> of fact, the adult is very seldom a mature person. An adult is in
> my opinion a person who plays a role of an adult, and the more he
> plays the role, the more immature he often is. My formulation is
> that maturing is the transcendence from environmental support
> to self-support.[5]

Behavior

Trust and respect make love grow.

– Glen Cheda

As a reader you may be wondering by now about "classroom
management" or "behavior problems." I wasn't sure how to address
this in this book because it really does manifest very differently in
this type of environment. Firstly, the children teach each other the
culture. They naturally mentor new children or younger children the
rhetoric, the rules, and everything in between. They regulate each
other. Also, because of the environment and the great amount of
space, and the flexible timing and schedule, behavioral problems do
not manifest nearly much or in the same ways as in an indoor setting.
Not every program can create this kind of individualized study with
such a high teacher-to-student ratio. Nonetheless, issues that occur
in a program like Gazebo could be dealt with on an individual basis
by examining the need and addressing problems in a personal way.

For example, Baldwin tells the story of a boy Lederman used to
call Pockets.

> There was a boy who used to thieve all the time. Everybody's toys
> are missing. This is when Janet was still alive. She decided we
> would make him a special coat full of pockets and his nickname

was going to be Pockets. When he stole and the kids wanted to find what he stole, it would be in his pockets. That was okay. In other words, 'We are not going to stop you from doing what you are doing, because that won't work.' Janet then turned the whole thing around to where, 'You're the official thief,' You're 'Pockets.' It wasn't something that was hidden and no one said, 'You can't do that.' There wasn't something blocking it, and we could bring it out into the open a little bit more.

Gazebo was able to individualize the responses to behavior issues. Charles feels,

> That could be the first point is that we recognize their talents and abilities and intelligence and that we focus on that. We offer them a safe, yet risky enough environment for them to learn in. It is not like we are going to impart, this wisdom, these ideas, this knowledge to them, to the top of their heads and pour it in. Recognizing what they can already do, and building on that would be an important piece of it, I think. And the other is looking at communication and how they communicate, first before they have a lot of language, and then as they develop language and how to use the Gestalt language with them and support them in using it as well. Like being polite to each other and cooperating, modeling that is much more powerful than saying to them, 'Say please, say thank you.'

In Gazebo culture, people were allowed their individuality. Douce says,

> At the Gazebo, we were encouraging the children to have their feelings, we weren't interrupting them. We weren't telling them this feeling is wrong. But when it got to violence, we would step in. When it came to any excessive behavior we would step in. But basically we were supporting the natural evolution and the release of the feelings and the person that is inside.

For me personally, as an educator, I have often come across teachers who want to create the perfect classroom, with only well-behaved children. Behavior problems are real issues, even within the framework of Gazebo. Yet, I do find the Gazebo environment eliminates a lot of the usual problems of sitting still and listening. Nevertheless, I find it troubling when teachers alienate families with children who have children behavior problems by suggesting they find other programs that are a 'better fit'. I feel it is my responsibility as a teacher to find out how to reach a child. I see each being like a puzzle to unlock. What is their individual key that will allow me as a teacher to understand them and build trust with them? How do I reach them? What do they like? What are their interests and strengths? What do the problems they have stem from? There is a lot of influence from home life and there are times when given the temperament of a child, some programs work better than others for them. There are often core issues that create behavioral problems for children and it is important as an educator to feel motivated to try to connect with the children.

There is a term in the education world called "growth mind-set" or "fixed mind-set." Teachers can look at students through either of these lenses. In a growth mindset, an individual can change, grow, learn and develop. The late Seymour Carter, Gestalt therapist and long-time Esalen community member said,

> Each moment is brand new, and if the person is not confronting the moment that is brand new, there is some filter in the way, some distortion going on, or else they would recognize that new moment. The new here and now is brand new.

Openness to growth is really important in addressing behavioral issues.

And perhaps there are real emotional challenges underneath their impulse to "misbehave." Lederman used to say, "Take the focus off the focus." In this way, she approached "Pockets" in a positive light. I think of the story of the Babemba tribe in Africa that holds a special ritual when someone makes poor choices. They bring them into the center of the village and each tribal member tells them all the good things they see in them. In this way, they are held, supported, and encouraged. In the same way, I have often heard stories of how Dick Price approached adults in a psychological crisis or in a nervous breakdown as having a psychic emergency. He would coordinate community members to hold space and sit with them in presence to support them through these difficulties. It is with these kinds of practices that I would like to include children with behavior problems, and I believe that is how Gazebo was able to see each child as an individual. I would like to see all the children of the world held in community in this way, despite their challenges.

The Role of the Teacher

In the time of youth, folly is not an evil. One may succeed in spite of it, provided one finds an experienced teacher and has the right attitude toward him. This means, first of all, that the youth himself must be conscious of his lack of experience and must seek out the teacher. Without this modesty and this interest there is no guarantee that he has the necessary receptivity, which should express itself in respectful acceptance of the teacher. This is the reason why the teacher must wait to be sought out instead of offering himself. Only thus can the instruction take place at the right time and in the right way.

– *The I Ching or Book of Changes,* "Meng/Youthful Folly"

A child was going through a lot, at two years of age his parents separated, his father was incarcerated, yet he had a blessing of a grandmother who brought him to the school. He was so smart, very verbal and big for his age. I spoke with the other teachers and we decided it would be healthy for him to feel powerful and in control in his life here as we imagined his external circumstances were not feeling that way to him. He had been standing on the table one day after snack and sort of marching on top of it. Normally, I may not have encouraged getting on a table, yet I saw this as an opportunity for him to feel powerful. Yet, there were concerns about hitting and spitting at home, and at school I watched as he began to develop his emotional vocabulary. One day, he fell down, pretty hard, scraped himself and cried for daddy. He fell from a kangaroo bench rocker that was a challenging toy for him to navigate. Nevertheless, he recovered very quickly and suddenly remarked, "I'm happy now." Later, when he got up on the kangaroo bench, he wrapped his little toes on the bar of the bench and held on with all his might. He finally could have his feet on the top of the kangaroo and hands on either ear of the kangaroo. I said, "Wow you are strong, you are powerful." He seemed to delight in that moment.

*I*n the Gazebo pedagogy, the teacher is not the focal point. The child and the child's experience is the movement, the teacher follows that movement. The teacher does not dictate to the child what the child needs to know. Rather the teacher leaves space for curiosity, exploration, and growth on the child's terms and timing. Delevett remembers teachers being,

> Loving, supportive, and kind. I remember having a meltdown and the teacher was there to facilitate a mini-Gestalt session. What are you feeling? Happy? Sad? Angry? Where are you feeling it in your body? Make an *I* statement! 'I am feeling, I don't like, I want, I don't want.' Adults were around, but not intrusive. We got to learn to trust ourselves. Maybe it was Spanish, maybe it was a lesson on first aid, maybe we read a story or sang a song—but mostly they were just there, in case something larger than us came up, and often they would explain that really, we could tackle this on our own actually, with a little help.

The role of the Gazebo teacher is less of a "teacher" in the traditional sense, but more of a guide, protector, advocate, facilitator. When I say protector, I especially mean a protector of the child's wonder, innocence, curiosity and imagination. When I was a child at Gazebo, I remember my teachers being nurturing, loving, and caring. I remember their support and guidance. I remember at times wondering why they wouldn't do things that I wanted them to do. It was frustrating at times, but in the long run, I believe it made me more resourceful as a person. Delevett remembers "The grown-ups were not that important. It was us."

In this way, from the child's perspective, the energy of the Park and school was not centered around or directed by the teachers. Wolfinger reflects,

> I always felt like all my conversations were eye-to-eye contact. I always felt like I was valued, not condescended towards. I was always left to choose. I was always loved unconditionally. I always had good male and female role models that made me feel safe. They made me feel responsible for the community. I think that teachers saw me like Max (from *Where the Wild Things Are*), because I would just fly by the seat of my pants. I felt I was seen as a pioneer of discovery and creativity. I always felt like this was the first time ever. Okay kids have been doing this for years. You know like building the magic castle again. Making it waterproof with Flash putting a roof on it. Really feeling empowered. I only saw the teacher if they were doing something I was interested in. 'Oh, what are you doing? Gardening. Can I help? Sure.'

Wolfinger adds,

> The role of the teacher is to use eye-to-eye conversations, to allow the children to choose, to be loved unconditionally, to be safe, and to take responsibility for community. The role of the teacher is to provide safety, provide, resources. Teachers are not single-head authority. Conflict was self-discovery and resolution, and violence was not tolerated."

In this way, for the student, the teachers were not the focal point. Davey remembers,

> For me, the biggest difference was that the Gazebo teachers came down to eye level. The importance of eye contact and having them at my level made me feel more understood. During those few minutes when a teacher was talking to me directly, I was being listened to. The panicked feeling of not being heard didn't happen while at Gazebo. I also didn't feel so small.

Davey describes the feeling of being small in comparison and this practice of coming down to the students level is assuring the the child in many ways. Being met at their level seems to stand out for Gazebo students, and this alone is a metaphor for how the teachers approached the students in meeting them where they are. In graduate school, a professor had us do an exercise where one person acted as "teacher" and stood up on a chair, and the "student" stayed on the ground which made them about knee level to the "teacher." It was a very good exercise for gaining insight into the physical perspective a child, and how children are always looking up at people.

McLeod describes Gazebo teachers as having a complex set of roles.

> Gazebo is an education unit that provides itself with a team. The animals (pony, chickens, goats, dogs) and the greenery provide the setting for this unit. First of all the children are the number one team members, without them there would not be a game and therefore no team. The children are mostly American yet Canadian, German, French and other nationalities are often in attendance. (I am anxiously awaiting the arrival of space aliens. Gazebo will not only be international, but universal!!!) In addition to the animals, greenery and the children are other collectives that play on the team. These collectives are the Gazebo adults—Umpire or Director; Mama and Papa Gazebo; Grade Teachers; Scanner; Toddler and Baby Persons; Grandma and Grandpa Gazebo; Work Scholar one and two; Visiting Teachers; Consultants. I am basing everything

that I am writing about Gazebo from direct personal experience. What will follow are the roles that the Gazebo team plays.

During the early years, with a large staff, there were specific roles the teachers gravitated towards and were prescribed. For example, there was usually one of two teachers that felt most connected to the very young children and babies. Also, while that person focused on the young children, and perhaps others focused on the older children, one person (McLeod referred to as the "scanner") was like the 'hawk eye' and would scan the entire macro view of what was happening in the park. In those days work scholars one and two were students that lived at Esalen that could do the work portion of their program in the Gazebo. This role later evolved into the internship program at Gazebo. Moreover, within this network of roles at Gazebo, a system developed to create an organic, evolving structure.

Nevertheless, the role of the teacher at Gazebo is distinctly different than in most traditional programs. Though the Gazebo approach developed over time, it grew from the seed of experimentation and fluidity. Thompson-Clark recalls,

> Very few preconceived notions were given for the role of teacher, the role of the 'place,' or the curriculum. Janet started with the right of the child to explore the natural world. For myself, as a teacher witnessing this for the first time, I saw a unique laboratory for observing how young children acquire the information, skills and attitudes pertaining to the infinite relationships between living things on a finite planet. Stated in a different way, in context with Esalen Institute's mission, removed were preconceived notions of what a school should be, and allowed was the development of Human Potential.

What follows are different lenses that the teacher might look through and roles they could adopt, and though these roles were important in the development of the philosophy, there is the underlying sense for most children of Gazebo, that the experience was not centered around the teachers.

Teacher as Tree

To teach means to show a person that something is possible.

– Fredrick Perls

Traditionally, at Gazebo, the entry point for any adult has been through the role of the "tree." The tree role has been used for visitors, for teacher training, or any adult entry into the Gazebo Park—be it a guest observing for a day, or an intern that would be at Gazebo for three to six months, or a teacher who would be on staff for the long term. Being a tree is an opportunity for active observation while being disengaged from the children. The way one enters into being a tree is through work—raking, weeding, turning the compost, etc. Nevertheless, the intention is not necessarily to be productive, but rather to have an anchor—to be engaged with something aside from the children's activity. The signal is that the tree is not available to interact, but rather is interacting already with their work. The tree tries to situate themselves in a position that is not central to the children's activity, but rather is peripheral. Yet, it is important for the tree to be within earshot, so that they can still listen, observe and get a sense of the children's interactions. A tree is not a stump, the tree doesn't plop down in the center of the activity and mutely expect the children to not take notice and want to interact. Metaphorically, a tree is present, provides shade, strength, shelter, roots. If the tree is approached by a child, a gentle gesture or word indicating that they are not available or that they are working is enough, and the children continue with their play.

Historically, an intern may be asked to be a tree for one to three months. This is an incredible time of receptivity and learning. This can also be a difficult time. I have noticed many interns have struggled with the tree phase. Many emotions arise about feeling "part of" and accepted into the community without the social interactions. For instance, even the thoughts and emotions that arise from feeling outside of the group are important to pay attention to. This phase seems to trigger the most primal need of humans to belong. Perhaps this is genetically ingrained as we once depended on belonging for our survival. On the other hand, this intentional withdrawal from interacting is similar to when people fast or cleanse, leaving space for observation, reflection and integration. Becoming a tree, despite its challenges, is ripe with possibility.

Observation and reflection are the key components of being a tree. Observing without interaction is the first step, then the reflection on the observations is equally important. For example, stepping back and writing about interactions witnessed between children or adults or between children is crucial. Verbatim note taking is encouraged. Attempting to take notes without personal thoughts or judgments is a great exercise to filter through the active mind and see facts for what they are. The tree can then ask questions to an experienced teacher or mentor outside of the park. Mentorship is important during the tree phase. Having resources and relationships with others experienced in Gazebo ways is vital. The mentor and the tree check in frequently and the mentor is a useful guide, a touchstone for the reflections and questions that arise as a tree.

The second phase in the internship is that a tree transitions to dipping in as a teacher and beginning to consciously interact. This intermediary stage is important, yet is often skipped over. In this second stage, it is so essential that the observer's mind is still at work and that the tree has not turned on autopilot, relying on their old teaching training or ideas about education. Thus, the tree has short interactions, then pulls back, takes notes, and reflects on how the interaction went. Trees may ask questions or journal about these interactions. For example, "How was it Gazebo? How was it not Gazebo? How were my responses preconditioned or authentic in the moment? What have I learned? What am I aware of now? What is stimulated in me?" In this second phase, we began to explore this dance between action and inaction. For some, the idea of being a tree created the feeling of being root bound, or held back. Perhaps some people felt the pressure of the culturally entrenched Western value of productivity. There is a tension between "doing" and "being" and exploring this balance is part of the experience of the tree.

Eventually, within the open time period each individual's personal development, the tree transitions into being a teacher. For interns and new teachers, being a tree really was the main training that they received in Gazebo methods. It was also given as the vehicle for any observer or visitor who wanted to see what the park was about. With a little instruction on how to be a tree, someone new to Gazebo could experience it without disturbing the environment and learning community. Similar to the way the children learned, the learning for the adult was completely experiential by which they created their own curriculum based on their needs and experiences. The tree formed his/her cognitive assumptions based on their present experience. The emphasis is on "being" rather than "doing," experiencing, observing, noticing. The mentor also must allow what will unfold to be specific for each learner as tree, and the mentor must trust this process of unfolding.

The tree time is essentially a time of *unlearning;* especially for trained teachers. Trained teachers often compare their interactions at Gazebo with their training or previous experience. It was important for these teachers to reflect on the examples at Gazebo in contrast to what they may have been taught. When I worked at Gazebo, we worked hard on developing the internship program, as many professionals with high degrees came there to intern. I found sometimes it was harder for them to come with "beginner's mind" as they had many preconceived notions about what was the best way to educate children. Though their minds were open to this new paradigm, there was much unwinding to be done. It is much harder to sit and be with a crying child than it sounds! It is much harder to not engage and be apart from participating for a month or more. Though being a tree is a unique opportunity, it is embedded with potential triggers and possibilities for growth.

Here are Vieregge's instructions for being a tree:

To Be a Tree in the Park, by Penny Vieregge

Step over the hay bales

Find a grown-up rake or trowel

Scan the park. Pick a spot that has activity around it.

Keep your eyes toward the ground, your ears listening in a circle around you.

Rake or weed. Mean it—

Take in the sounds and talk around you.

Use peripheral vision to take in movement. Silently absorb everything that you touch, smell, hear.

When you are full—put your tool away. Leave the park.

Sit down in comfort. Play back everything.

Write any questions that you have. Think about your answers. Ask your staff person—

Come back again.

PS if a child speaks to you, respond directly—offer nothing but attention.

What does it mean to be a tree? A tree is grounded. A tree is strong and independent. A tree is a home to animals. A tree is breathing and living. A tree is a metaphor for a person who is willing to stand outside and observe. A tree holds wisdom, but does not share it, rather it shelters, it shades, it protects. A tree is a teacher in hibernation, in the value of each season, which has its growth and dormancy. A tree is a person who can disengage long enough to reflect on how it feels to be disengaged. A tree then gains great consciousness about his or her interactions when ready. Therefore, if it needs to come into action concerning matters of health and safety, the tree comes alive, sheds its leaves and moves and acts. Most often though, the tree is a silent listener, an observer, a worker of the land, a transformer of energy, space holder, and giver of fruit that later comes in the form of teaching.

LaVerne McLeod's interpretation of what it is to be a tree is as follows:

> Within Gazebo's culture is its own language. One such term is to be a 'tree.' This role is carried out when someone new is beginning training to work at Gazebo, to assist Gazebo workers to 'feel' out a potential 'Gazebetter;' or to allow an observer to see Gazebo functioning. I can see a tree as an observer only when—
>
> – silent
>
> – still (sitting on the borders—hay bales or logs unless the scanner directs him/her to be a moving tree as raking or pulling weeds)
>
> –allowing things to happen around him/her without doing anything.

Jones reflects on her time as a tree.

> One of the most valuable aspects of my time as a tree was learning to distinguish between my objective observations and my personal interpretations. I did this by journaling in two columns. In one I recorded events and interactions that I witnessed – documenting what happened, what was said, who was involved. In the other column I described how what I witnessed affected me – my urges, discomforts, and assumptions. Many times I was shocked by what happened and how it was handled. My impulses raged to intervene. Having to sit back and recognize my story and reactions while watching the interaction play out or be facilitated in a different way taught me so many invaluable lessons about myself and what children are capable of.

This process provides the opportunity for the "tree" to track the mind, the patterns of thinking in relationship to self, others, and beliefs about children, how they learn, thoughts about education and life itself. Former intern and educator Sharon Dvora wrote,

> The simple directive for me during these first two weeks has been: be a tree. Simply be. Rake, sweep, observe. I've raked, but not with the quiet calm of a tree—more like a whirlwind of intensity. It's one thing to rake quietly, while observing the children. It's another to tidy up the yard with fervor. On the one hand, it's very satisfying to tend to this place and get to know each pathway and planting. On the other hand, my focus drifts compulsively to the materiality of the place, driving my attention away from the simple observation of the children at play. My attention does its dance between discerning focus on beauty, order, materiality and joyful engagement with the children. Neutral observation is foreign to me. I'm not only unaccustomed to being an uninvolved bystander, I'm seriously resistant to acquiesce to the role. As I continue to explore the role of the tree, I stand to reap the benefits of being an unobtrusive witness—contributing without disruption or interference, but through silent presence alone. No positive reinforcement, no entertaining, no reassuring. Simply being present and slowing down.

Eleizer Sobel, author and Gazebo intern, reflects upon his experience as a tree at Gazebo.

> When I arrived for my first day, I was instructed simply to be a 'tree,' and not interact with the kids unless directly engaged by them. Otherwise, I was to just go about my business, doing little gardening chores on the land while observing and remaining conscious and present. I wasn't a very good tree, and I was never famous for remaining conscious and present. Janet, along with Lia Thompson and another supervisor named Cathy, had no qualms about offering 'constructive criticism,' but for whatever internal, emotional reason or interpersonal dynamic, I had a lot of difficulty simply receiving negative feedback without defending myself, especially when I thought I was being misunderstood. I see now that had I dropped my resistance, I could have been learning the fine art of letting go of ego.

Dvora remarks,

> I've been asked to be a tree. At Gazebo, if you're new to the school,
> you're asked to quietly observe rather than interact, so that the
> children are free to direct themselves in their encounters with one
> another and with the place. It's not easy being a tree. It's the perfect
> setup to discover just what it is that triggers a reaction. How can I
> say this tactfully? Well—I'm *triggered* by *boys will be boys* behavior.
> The way that guy-play can be rough, and challenging, and there's a
> level of delight that's taken in doing just the thing that gets others
> stirred up. It's so good that I'm a tree. I can feel my judgment, my
> *reactivity*, the quick nature of my mind. And I can remain neutral,
> exercise patience and wait it out. I'm noticing that others aren't so
> bothered by the same things that cause me alarm. I'm impressed
> with how children navigate themselves, jumping full-on into play
> with new friends, dancing their relatedness courageously and with
> curiosity.

Baldwin suggests,

> The first thing is for teachers to know how to be trees. For me that
> means that the teacher can withdraw easily and know there is a job
> for me. That might mean clipping, picking up a rake, it's not a big
> project because the kids are all over the place. I don't get involved
> with them unless that happens. Sometimes that does happen when
> they are doing something. That is when your own natural skill of
> getting things done comes out. Anne Seifert, my co-teacher, could
> say 'Oh, let's do this.' And the kids would say, 'Oh yeah.' I might
> have to be in the middle of my job for the kids to come to me and
> want to do it. Also, that leaves the space for them to come up with
> it themselves. Some of them will remember they have those jobs
> to do. When teachers do have skills, that is great, bring it out.

Charles says,

> The kids come over the hay bales every day without knowing a lot.
> They don't know the rules. They don't know the new intern. They
> don't know what this plant is, and so we can support them better

in their learning if we can tolerate the not knowing along with them. Now we have to know essential things, and you can just tell the interns that this in an opportunity to have more empathy for the kids and to experience their world from their viewpoint.

Thus, there is a sense that being a tree can be an acceptance of the unknown, allowing for curiosity, and attempting to filter out our personal judgments and emotional triggers. Being a tree can really lead to being in a place of receptivity that creates a very unique starting point for a Gazebo grown-up.

Teacher as Individual

Gabrielle Roth, Lucia & Jasmine
Horan, Glen Cheda

The teachers at Gazebo themselves brought very different skills, talents and personalities to their teaching. The idea that each teacher shares their own passions, gifts and sensibilities has been echoed to me by many of the senior teachers of Gazebo.

Charles shares that,

> We used to get the feedback a lot that, 'You do it differently than Lia does it,' and my response to that is, 'Yeah, welcome to Gazebo.' There are basics about the philosophy, and we all bring our own personality. That is a part of Gestalt. Fritz used to say, 'I don't want to create a whole lot of little Fritzes.' There are values of each practitioner, and each therapist is going to bring their own history, temperament and interests to their practice. Janet would say we don't want cookie cutter teachers here. One of the difficulties in public school settings, where there was one teacher and twenty five to thirty kids, is that children resonate differently with different personalities so to have a range of people being themselves and implementing the philosophy was really key.

In this way, teachers are individuals each with their own unique skill set. Carter felt, "Anyone who is a teacher has to do your own style or it's not going to be authentic, you have to do what comes out of your own creativity." Wyatt says,

> I think of my role as a guide, as a mentor, I like those words, because I think that children learn most from observing and experiencing the people around them. I think my role is to be present with myself, clear with myself, doing my work, paying attention to my judgments and what is go on with me—so that I can be a clear reflector. And I think reflection is unique in Gazebo. I think this is super valuable. I cannot be a clear reflector if I am not taking care of what is inside me. To share what I am passionate about, then a child is going to get, deeply in their being, an experience of someone's passion. It is not going to impact them as much if I am trying to impart something I am not really passionate about or I am not really behind. It is just a bunch of words and kids are super good at picking that up. They are good barometers about myself.

Most importantly, each teacher is who they are, and children naturally resonate with different personalities, yet each teacher shows up as an authentic and unique part of the fabric.

Marquis says,

> My memory of the teachers is that they were there, they were
> adults, they were very capable and were available, but they had no
> interest in controlling me. They were around. They were people
> we could talk to, relate to, and once in a while they would gather
> us together and share a slice of who they were.

Teacher as Student

One of the unique aspects of the Gazebo experience is that there
was an exchange between the children and teachers rather than the
one-way approach the that teachers are "teaching" and the students
are "learning." At Gazebo, the children were also the teachers and
there was a process in which both teacher and student could be curious
in this shared experience. This meant that teachers were not the only
ones who possessed valuable knowledge about the world, and the
teachers were not there just to impart information to the children. I
know from my personal experience with children, I learn so much
them, certainly more than they learn from me.

Douce says,

> I never assumed that I was superior to the child, that I had more
> wisdom, I just had more experience, and I had more responsibility
> to protect them. There is a thing about all schools generally, but
> preschools particularly, that the adults think they have to teach
> something to the children. Well, the Gazebo, when I worked
> there, was very much a mutual learning experience. The children
> would learn from us and we would learn from the children; not that
> we were teaching the children, it was more that we were in some
> mutual moment. We were learning how to support their feeling
> of freedom and the ability to experiment and learn without fear.
> As the adults, we were not trying to impose. We were learning
> how to be supportive of the children's energy rather than trying to
> present a thing to teach them. There was no preset thing to teach.
> If you make learning interesting and exciting they will want to do

it. That is the two-way learning. I am not the teacher and superior. So in that, it wasn't that kids were going to learn from us, it was we were learning from them.

Therefore, in this way the teacher is also a student. Douce reflects,

> Being trained by Feldenkrais, who could do things that look like a total miracle, I do things that look like a miracle too—except it is education and it comes from the work—it isn't me, it is us. Getting over the thing that you are a superior being and you have to lord over the children rather than that we are a group, and we are cooperating and we are listening to each other, and we are doing this together. It is a very different attitude than, 'I am your teacher.'

At Gazebo, there was an exchange and more reciprocating among teacher and student than in traditional programs.

Children inhabit themselves so fully in every moment. They are so honest, authentic and expressive. They are present; that alone is a gift that children teach adults. Adults forget to be in the moment and get so concerned with their to-do lists. There is so much filtered through adult's perceptions and judgments while the child is still forming theirs. The complete presence of children is what drew me to working with them. Also, children have such a way of being honest and transparent with their emotional experience in the world. They don't hide behind the many masks we learn to form as adults. When I began teaching, I liked it because I felt that I could not be too caught up in my own problems when working with children. There as no time for self-pity. The children were in the moment, in their bodies, and they would bring me right back to the moment time and time again.

As a teacher, I have adopted a different sort of guidance that is also honest. I don't see myself as having all the answers or pretend, as I think is the expectation of teachers, to know everything. I try to "teach" resourcefulness. In this way, I try to show the students that if something interests them, there are ways to find out more. At Gazebo this may have looked differently depending on the situation, but allowing space for the child to observe was the beginning. In their own time, it became apparent what they found fascinating. This was the entry point to access their inner learning. Plus, not giving the answers leads to further inquiry, which in turn leads to a process and development of ideas and knowledge. If a child came to me with a question, I returned their sense of wonder by first celebrating that wonder. Sometimes I would ask another questions in return to continue to engage in an investigation. This kind of collaborative, investigative learning is so fun and creative for both teacher and student.

In this way, Nelson suggests,

> It was really neat for me because I was always very fond of children but I was afraid of them. I gradually realized they are people; you talk to them like people, and everything is just fine and they were really good people to be around and you can learn a lot from them. That was a really strong guiding principle in those days is that you were learning as much as you were teaching. Learning how not to do the 'coochicoo' and not to talk down, or to talk baby talk to kids, was easy for me. I thought that was so great, because I when I was raised, I was the kid and with my parents, especially my mother, there was a definite separation. I liked to try to keep it more equal and to honor each other's individuality rather than treat them like some secondary person that had to do whatever I say.

Teacher as Land Steward and Park Keeper

The tools for gardening and developing the land are critical learning materials. The landscaping and surprise developments become the overall learning project for the children, the staff, and the neighbors.

-JL

One way in which the teacher supports the dynamic of the student being in the lead of the learning is by assuming the role of land steward.

Forman says,

> We didn't impose. Everyone had the space to BE, to DO. If a
> teacher started the process of tending the goats, getting lunch
> together, or working on the grounds, sparks would be ignited and
> you'd have helpers and the project would evolve.

Much like in the role of tree, a teacher who adopts the land
steward role is occupied with earth-based activities yet present to
the needs of the child. This is a multifaceted vantage point. In one
way, the teacher is inviting the children to interact, while still doing
projects on their own, and still able to witness the children's activity
nearby. Also, the teacher is actually taking care of the land, because
the Park has many needs and demands a certain amount of care. The
gardens must be watered and weeded, planted and harvested. The
leaves must be raked and carried away. Porches and rugs should be
swept off and outdoor/indoor areas need to be tended to in order to
be kept tidy and in operation. In contrast to cleaning up after children, land stewardship is a proactive way of caring for one's space.
It models this for the children as well.

One of the key elements to nature education in the Gazebo style
is the park environment and how it is tended. Baldwin stresses the
importance of the teacher's role in relationship to the land.

> A park keeper is very different from a teacher. A teacher has cur-
> riculum. We all remember parks, big and small, that we played in
> as kids. There was a certain freedom there. Whether it was a little
> town park or it was some huge park with rangers and stuff, they
> weren't out to give you something, they were just there to tend to the
> place. I was a park keeper, an English park keeper. In my overtime,
> I was a tractor driver, and I used to work in the winter and travel
> in the summer. I would work in my hometown as a park keeper.
> Little parks with a few swings and slides, a little tennis court, a
> place for kids to throw a ball. My job was not to get involved with
> the kids. My job as a park keeper was never to do anything, but
> make sure the kids were safe and contained in that park.

There is a fine line as a land steward and teacher between having a focus and being sensitive to the children and the activity around them. The teacher must adopt a state of presence. There is also the awareness of how to invite the children into the work rather than being task-oriented. The teacher can and will need to put down their work at any point to assist a student in need of support outside of the task at hand, or alternately offer ways for the children to get involved. For example, if a teacher is gardening and several students wanted to join in, they would stop, get child appropriate tools, show them how the work was being done, and adjust their pace accordingly. The role as land steward and teacher is multifaceted and ultimately modeling care of the earth and at times inviting children to get involved. For example, a teacher is working, yet they invite students to be involved in whatever land stewardship activity they are doing. Especially, if a child shows interest in joining the teacher, the teacher slows down, gets the necessary tools, and offers support to bring them into the process.

Baldwin expounds,

There is always this awareness thread of connection between you and the child and also between you and the other teachers and all the children in the Park. There is that awareness. I will look up and I see another teacher looking at me, see that we need to communicate, and it may not be with words. There is a flow there that develops. Some of the times I am cleaning a shelf, and kids can come in and help me do that if they wish and that's the curriculum. But I always have to be ready to give up the job I am doing. There is no way that 'Neil is going to do that job, so don't disturb Neil for half an hour.' Unless there is something very important. Also, it is constant awareness.

There is a saying that was posted in the pony shed, a shared space that once housed the Gazebo ponies and later became an area for cubbies, books, and a reading nook. This sign reminded teachers to slow down and involve the children:

Slow down and involve the children.

Encourage independence and self-reliance.

Slow down and involve the children.

Help children practice and develop motor skills.

Slow down and involve the children.

Give children time and space to explore the environment.

Slow down and involve the children.

Foster problem-solving, independent thinking, and conflict resolution skills.

Slow down and involve the children.

Much like the above declaration, the importance of the teacher's role as land steward was not product oriented towards getting tasks done, but rather poised to involve the children. At Gazebo, achieving a task was less important than involving the children. In this way, even as a land stewardship, "teachable" moments occurred and magic unfolded. However, there did seem be a shift over the years as the land stewardship tasks became more adult oriented with perhaps less child involvement than in the early years.

On the other hand, when the children have ownership of chores within the park environment, there are many valuable teachings within that framework. Yet for the teacher, it can be important to have a focus. While the teachers stays attuned to the children's play, they may not be directly involved in it. In this case modeling caring for the land while being attentive to the needs of the children can be a powerful tool. The teacher is not the central focal point for the children, and it gives them ownership of their domain. They have choice in creating their curriculum through their activities and play, or the choice of getting involved with what the teacher is engaging in. Accordingly, Baldwin feels,

> I think that is the important part, the space, the park, the teachers stepping a little bit back when you can, but that also relies on having

enough children. If you don't have enough children then those children are going to be more orientated towards adults because that is the way it is. Knowing where they come from doesn't have to be specific information, it can be partly intuition, partly just knowing the bigger picture.

Fatima Faria, Gazebo intern and Executive Director of Sunshine Valley Child Care Society in British Columbia notes,

Opportunities for self-mastery are repeatedly and easily thwarted in the moment, if teachers intervene or have too much of an agenda, delaying natural dynamic development. Children are exposed to the basic elements of life in the environment e.g., plant, bug, animal. Teachers serve as models of land stewardship and demonstrate the activities needed for thriving, healthy development and balance of activity; motion is critical to all living things in the environment as well as stasis.

Teacher as Facilitator

A child who is able to 'pay attention,' to attend to what he or she is doing with awareness, will be a successful learner. We teach paying attention by paying attention.

-JL

The role of teacher as facilitator supports the use of Gestalt practice in relationship. Practices of developing emotional literacy, learning conflict resolution, and setting healthy boundary setting are important tools for the facilitator to help the children learn. The facilitator is attending to the child's emotional experience and guiding and supporting it along the way. Sometimes, offering feedback may be appropriate, or sometimes sharing their own experience or feelings may assist a Gestalt process.

Handl suggests,

> Grown-ups might also offer a lens or focus, helping the child
> begin to wield their own attention towards what the natural world
> is offering in the present moment, what their peer's face or body
> might be communicating, what their body might be trying to let
> them know (wet, tired, hungry, upset, frustrated).

Therefore, the teacher can facilitate the child's learning through
presence, noticing, and sharing a conscious reflection.

Moreover, the teacher at Gazebo maintains a responsiveness to
the child without robbing them of their experience. Being attentive
to the child's cries is one way in which a teacher might attune to the
children's needs. Douce proposes,

> The whole thing was the different types of cries. A child cries, a
> child falls, but they start crying to get attention, so it is really not
> a cry for pain, it is a cry for attention. Janet taught us not to run
> to them.

Yet, ultimately, the teacher should be responsive. Eizner says,

> My experience of Gazebo is not that the teachers did not respond to
> the children, it is that they did not *rush* to respond to the children.
> Not responding would not be appropriate, but not rushing to re-
> spond is appropriate. Teachers responded, but also respected—they
> kind of like looked to see. Like Penny's concept of when you go
> 'to help' or 'for help.' Stop, look. What is going on here? You stop.
> Is it safe? Look. Like the same concept, you look at the kid and
> see what's going on. Is this a kid that wants you to support the
> emotional process or is this a kid that is going to brush their pants
> off and keep running after they fall? Why not look before reacting?
> Teachers did react, but we did so gently and approached the kids
> by respecting their emotional state and their wish.

As a teacher, parent, basically as a grown-up in our society, there
is an instinct to rescue, save, and prevent injury. It is very hard to
listen to a child cry and not try to change, distract or save them from

their pain. I can think back so many times to my work at Gazebo where myself or another teacher had to battle with our own impulses to change, distract or save a child. This happened frequently with goodbyes. At the entrance to the park, the soft hay bale boundary, many a drama played out. Naturally, children are sad and sometimes anxious to be separated from their parents and guardians. The goodbyes often are accompanied by tears. Most teachers at this point want to distract the child from this experience by getting them involved in something else. At Gazebo, a child might have cried at the gate for a long while with a teacher patting them on the back or other children coming and going to check in. This is an unusual approach and this can be a painful and difficult process sometimes for everyone – teachers and students alike.

The social messages to children are most often, "Don't cry," or, "Be careful so you don't fall." *Don't* is the operative word and way of being. In the Gazebo paradigm, it is different. Taking risks and learning through experience both emotionally and physically are part of the curriculum. I realize it is so much more meaningful and relevant to have the experience rather than hearing an adult say not to do something and why. The children are learning from the inside out. Essentially, as teachers we sometimes had to retrain ourselves not to react to our impulses and to facilitate an experience the children would learn from. The facilitator needs to really listen and pay attention to what is going on for the child and find ways to support them rather than change them.

Teacher as Inner Healer

It takes two to know one.
– Gregory Bateson

The setting at Esalen, being a center for personal growth, set the stage for personal work, healing and transformation. Being at Esalen, participating in workshops, and being a part of this growth-oriented community, encouraged people to work on themselves. Self-inquiry and personal growth were in the air. Gazebo was no exception from this. Each department at Esalen regularly practiced Gestalt group process which was simply called *process*, or had the option to participate in an "open seat" in which anyone at Esalen could join. These were opportunities for individuals to sit in awareness and to talk about issues that arose for them with supportive witnesses and a trained facilitator. At Gazebo, there were process meetings, and teachers would have the opportunity to explore their own emotional triggers either related to children or other adults. They could filter through some of the emotional charges around certain issues, and work with the energy of the emotion. Within specific interactions in the Park, often there was rich material to be unearthed in relation to the teacher's reactions and judgment to these situations. Often these stemmed from other issues they came with, and the group process was a safe space outside of the park to explore their emotional landscape.

Consequently, Gazebo teachers and interns found that the atmosphere at Gazebo activated memories, reminded them of painful experiences, or brought up issues from their own childhood. Processing these issues with awareness was an important for the teacher in the appropriate setting. In this way, Lederman felt it was important to keep adult process out of the park. When Gazebo began, there was little formal process, and Lederman would do Gestalt work with people in staff meetings. Later, this work became isolated to a group process with the Gazebo staff. Also, during these processes, conflict between staff members could be addressed away from the children. In many work environments, miscommunications may go on indefinitely and people just get used to working under difficult circumstances. The Gazebo staff had a unique opportunity for closeness and connection, and also for understanding themselves throughout these group processes.

During my time as a Gazebo teacher, my own personal experience with these group processes was profound. I have not worked in another environment that supported the emotional growth of the staff members in such a way. I found it very healing to explore assumptions, judgments, resentments, and share from the heart. I also found that sometimes other teachers were experiencing the same situation very differently and this sharing cleared up a lot of the misunderstanding and allowed me to tolerate differences better. I also found that some of the triggers I was feeling with children were actually wounds from my own childhood. I was able to see how I had been projecting issues from the past onto the moment and how it was interfering with my ability to be present with the children and my coworkers. Thus, "unpacking" some of this emotional baggage was very important for me.

Working with issues from my past, gave me the ability to be more present and less reactive with the children. Consequently, as adults, it was supportive of our work all around to be living the principles we were teaching the children by promoting authenticity, clear boundaries, and self-responsibility. Furthermore, I found the group process work to be very healing personally, and it also allowed for a closeness and deep connection with the people I worked with. Being able to witness their personal processes and grow with my colleagues was very deep, and it gave me more understanding and compassion for myself and my coworkers. With the respect for privacy, the content of these processes was not talked about outside of the process itself. Thus, the group process created a unique understanding around the group dynamic that was supportive of self-awareness, communication, and conflict resolution.

Later in the history of Gazebo, "weather reports" or morning "check-ins" were implemented. Check-in's can be a helpful practice to do at the beginning or end of the day and can be done inside or outside of the Park or even in a journal. This was a time of briefly touching in with oneself and the other staff members. The check-ins were done before or sometime after the children arrived; though waiting until the children arrived did at times present challenges. Depending on the directors, they chose different times to do this practice. If the children were present, the staff was available if an important need were to arise, yet we still met briefly with the children present and thus modeled for self-care. In any case, the teachers and staff would each take a few minutes to share mostly about how they were feeling in that very moment. If there was an illness or an important personal issue that would affect their work that day, they might also share this. The others would not respond, but rather listen until it was their turn. A few announcements might take place, but generally it was simply a short touch-in for the staff for that day.

In my personal experience working at Gazebo, not being a morning person and having severe morning sickness for the first months of my pregnancy, I practiced saying the same thing a lot. One of the interns at the time shared how she was impacted by my level of authenticity. "Still sick," or "Grumpy again," I would say. To check in with oneself about the present moment and share an honest reading is a simple practice, yet can give opportunities for the staff to stay connected and in tune. Sometimes we would offer the prompt of "What am I feeling right now?"

Additionally, in my conversations with many former staff members at Gazebo, I heard again and again how healing it was to work at Gazebo. Josef London, Gazebo teacher, Gestaltist, and long-time Esalen community member reflects on this by saying,

I have an amazing life. Gazebo was a chance to revisit my childhood memories, and see a childhood I didn't have. Gazebo is fascinating. I was completely mesmerized. It was a very healing time—the experience of what kids could be. Being a tree I could see a conversation verbatim what happened to me at three, four, five and six. I was not allowed to interact with them, and I was completely mesmerized. Eduardo would take me to the castle and let me cry my eyes out. Kids bring a lot from home. I would practice being in the present time. That's all we have. The children would include me into their world, and into an awareness of present time. It was a rich experience in every way possible. We would also do debriefing at the end of the day. What did you notice about yourself today, and we would write it down.

Under Eizner's directorship, he implemented daily journaling practice for the staff and interns. Similarly, Nelson reflected on his childhood and his parenting choices based on his time at Gazebo.

> I guess it prepared me to be a parent as I grew up being emotionally dominated by my mother. When I was ready for kids I just didn't want to dominate them or impose on them. I guess when I started parenting, at least early on, I was congratulating myself for doing it different than my own parents. It's not that I had bad parents, because I was lucky in that I had very good parents, but it was a different generation and kids were meant to be seen and not heard.

Baldwin saw the pattern of self-work as he guided interns. He says,

> Some interns were absolutely as good as teachers, and sometimes I spent more time looking after the interns than I did the kids. Again, it would always change. Part of being at Esalen was that there would be interns, not because they would be interested in the child part, but because they wanted to get into their own childhood. Those interns needed a lot more attention than those who were coming in clear.

Gazebo was never intended to be a center for healing the inner child, it was really about the children and the current moment. On the other hand, being able to clear up issues that were getting in the way of being present for the children was a gift to both teachers and students. Delevett remembers,

> ...not understanding that what teachers did was intentional, but later interning at Gazebo as an adult, learning more about the philosophy. The adults were there as compassionate witnesses, but not to place their ideas of the world onto the children. One example stands out for me—one day we heard screams coming from far out in the ocean. Roars like someone is in deep distress. It turns out a staff member was out swimming in the ocean and was having trouble get back to shore. My instinct was to whisk the children away to distract them from the something bad happening. I got scared. Eduardo pulled me aside to witness the children. They were

excited and it was an adventure full of possibility. Rather than my story that there is someone out there who is drowning and he will die it turned into, 'He is being rescued.'

Dvora describes an experience in which her own perceptions were contributing greatly to an interaction with the children in her blog post entitled *Play Nice in the Sandbox?*

So yesterday I was tickled because I stumbled into a zone of creative synchronicity with some of the children. I have a way of relaxing into the materials, the simple actions of working with my hands, the delight in discovering what unfolds.

A child's process does not always unfold gently and what emerges is not always delightful. Today started off with a lot of excitement, in part ignited by two interactions that I initiated {so much for staying out of the way!} First, I brought the hose over close to the sandbox, so that I could fill a bucket with water. T. (2 years old) and I were talking about mixing cement. E. (7 years old) came by, spotted the water being added to the sandbox and took great interest in the hose access. I gave him brief instructions on how the water could be turned on and off at the spraying end, and from there the action ensued.

More children gathered, with lots of activity and intense interest in pursuit of a variety of projects. Two of the children had begun working on a volcano scenario the day before and were intent on continuing their process. E. had ideas of his own, which involved a good deal of water. And T. and I were dissuaded from our cement mixing project, as the sandbox became an active zone of contention.

I intervened here and there as the dialogue thickened, and things almost came to blows. J. {our fearless director} sat nearby, coaching from the sidelines in her skillful way, doing the dance of stepping in as needed, and stepping back to let the children's process remain in the lead. I got caught up in my own reactivity—tightening a bit around the injustice of things, the lack of rational thinking, the unkindness that surfaced.

J. quietly drew me aside, and I was grateful for the time-out! I needed to breathe a little, remember to trust the children's process—and STAY OUT OF THE WAY!

The young clan did work things out on their own {of course}. They negotiated the turf, collectively navigated the emergent project and for quite a long time, there was a peaceful sense of accomplishment emanating from the sandbox."[1]

Foreman describes her experience as,

Gazebo was a lab for me, too, as I explored who I was and began to heal my own wounds. The mirror of Gazebo unfolded my inner child, planted seeds to her voice, and began my process of exploration and expansion. It was a long process for those seeds to blossom!!!!!

Unlearning at Gazebo

As the child attends to his or her learning, we are careful not to intrude.

-JL

Each adult who worked at Gazebo had a considerable amount of unlearning to do. Often there was inner conflict based on the training that they had received, their education and past experiences in the field of education. Also, the impulses for adult intervention are driven by cultural and social conditioning. Otis Kriegel, Gazebo intern, educator, and author of *Starting School Right* remembers,

> One of the challenges was learning to not intervene. I didn't think I did before, and I thought I was child and play-oriented. It is a process of pulling back and giving enough space. This works because the ratio is so good. It is a really crucial part of the Gazebo. Knowing that there is an adult somewhere within range, that the children will always be safe. If you were here alone you couldn't allow the same things to happen.

Gazebo teacher, and current teacher and director of Big Sur Park School, Sofia Snavely, describes her feeling of a Gazebo teacher as one who is:

> Seeing the whole being and really respecting who they are. Creating this little potion, a little remedy that is so unique for each person. I think that supports the whole development of the individual—that each child is seen so vividly as a person whatever their age. The child on the other side of the hay bales is such a different being once they are inside and their parent is gone. To be able to see that is such a gift. As a teacher embracing a new child coming in, it is like knitting an individual sweater around the child that is coming in. A whole being over the hay bales, clothes clean and clinging they are dropped and caught by support. As the teacher to really hold this new being and observe them in their pace, their texture, their color, their shade, their whole being, and just knit and create a little space, a safety blanket for them. It is not something that is restricting, it is something that is warm and safe and can be taken wherever they go. I think a big role of teachers is to model. Modeling the interest or modeling respect, either self-respect or respect for others. Focus and responsibility with the animals and the land. It comes like this mobile. Teachers are like a mobile going

around the Park and modeling particular behavior. How do you become a Gazebo teacher? It is so interpretable. Especially right now where we are all so new and we are all so young. There is a lot of this seeking—seeking that mentorship and questioning really, what is Gazebo and how it is?

Dvora shares,

> The topic has stirred a mix of internalized beliefs from my childhood that have held me back from fully embracing the rights of the child, and I'm in the process of untangling those early adopted beliefs from my current understanding.

> I'd like to give voice to some of the internal concepts that have had a hold on me:

> Children must be well behaved, especially in the presence of adults {and in particular, adults with authority, like teachers}. Children do not have a place in adult conversations. Contrary thinking and ideas are not welcome and will be met with disapproval {which, to the child, may feel like anger and a resulting belief of being unloveable}. Resistance or not conforming to the requests of adults will result in consequences {punishment}.

> These are not the beliefs that I carry forward into my teaching and encounters with young children. This is my declaration of the rights of the child:

> Children have the right to express themselves—even if their expression is loud, contrary and challenging. Children's thinking, ideas, opinions and requests are valuable, essential, valid and illuminating. Children have the right to make choices. They have the right to healthy communication—to be listened to with serious consideration. Children have the right to be received with positive, accepting and unconditionally loving responses to their presence and their expression.

Children have the right to experience the world firsthand. Children have the right to spend time outdoors, in wild and alive places. Children have the right to experiment with what they think and know—to explore their own identity and develop relationships with others. Children have the right to be heard. Children have the right to healthy air, water, food and living environments. Children have the right to be safe and protected from physical, emotional and environmental harm.

Childhood is a precious and irreplaceable developmental time in the life of a human being. Every child has the right to be free from institutional imprisonment—free of the unreasonable demands that a child is to be seated for long hours, enduring boredom and conformist training, fluorescent lighting, indoor environments that are not conducive to health and well-being and authoritative adults who take choices away from children. Children have the right to a voice and a choice about learning and schooling. Children have the right to be free of surveillance, assessment, judgment, comparisons and institutional consequences. Children have the right to be free of unreasonable requests for their attention, focus and restraint. Children have the right to develop free of encumbrances placed upon them by governmental authorities. Children have the right to become uniquely themselves—to craft their own identity and to respond to the world in their own unique ways.

I've tweaked my declaration and created this healing statement that I claim for myself {as a never-too-late correction to integrate into my core understanding of self}:

I have the right to express myself—even if my expression is loud, contrary and challenging. My thinking, ideas, opinions and requests are valuable, essential, valid and illuminating. I have the right to make my own choices. I have the right to healthy communication—to be listened to with serious consideration. I have the right to be received with positive, accepting and unconditionally loving responses to my presence and my expression. I have the right to experience the world firsthand. I have the right to spend time outdoors, in wild and alive places. I have the right to experiment with what I think and know—to explore my identity and freely develop relationships with others. I have the right to be heard. I have the right to healthy air, water, food and living environments. I have the right to be safe and protected from physical, emotional and environmental harm.

My life is precious. I have the right to become uniquely myself—to craft my own identity and to respond to the world in my own unique way.[2]

– Sharon Dvora

The unlearning process at Gazebo unfolds during the tree phase. A lot of this energy is the shift between being a leader to being the follower. So, coming from directing the children's experience to following the children's curiosity and timing is a big jump for many people. I think this was the biggest hurdle for most trained educators who came through the park. I saw trained professionals humbled by this experience. Common questions arose about conflict, communication, trust and these were up to the individual to explore. The Gazebo approach flipped so many social and cultural views on their head and turned so many preconceived notions upside down. Gazebo asked people to question why they did what they did, and how they felt doing it completely different.

Steven Harper, former Gazebo teacher and parent, Gestalt practitioner, and wilderness group-leader says,

I was used to being in the wilderness instructing. National Outdoor Leadership School® (NOLS) is very instruction based, and Gazebo was not that. For me it was the first concern taking children into the wilderness that everybody was safe. That was a lot of what my intention was, providing a *safe container* for the kids. I don't know that the Gazebo teachers at that time had the same awareness or concern around this; or maybe they just held it in a different way. They were more relaxed about that about the container of the wilderness. All of a sudden, I felt like it was me that was the one checking on kids; and maybe it was also from my NOLS background. I did learn, especially on the instructional end of things, how to get out of the way. And once we got out there, I let the kids explore. We needed to stay on the trail. We couldn't just let them roam forever. So, there it was, 'How do we create a *container?*'

Harper describes the container he created—basically the intention he set and the safety of the group and the *field*.

Keep the kids somewhat together. We are just going to walk down the backbone of the trail here, and instead of just making it, 'We're are going to walk to a place,' it was more of, 'How do we walk along with lots of stops along the way as curiosity presents itself?' Then there would be what in NOLS were called 'teaching moments.' There would be moments where we could interject something like if we came across a plant with a strong smell like a Bay tree. There weren't Bays growing on Gazebo turf, so I could crush a leaf and the kids could smell it, play with it, and get curious about it. There would be a little bit of me like dropping a pebble in a pond and then seeing where it goes. It would come up, like we would also learn what poison oak looked like. That was in the days of 'Yum' and 'Yuck.' You show this plant—poison oak. A lot of kids were verbal, but their vocabulary was not that large, so we would show them the plant and show them this was not one to touch. There were things like that, I had to learn a different way of engaging with the kids. Some of that was done through mime as much as it was through language. Because with adults I would talk about poison oak, but with kids, I would gather them around and show them the sign not to touch and point out leaves of three, and point out another plant and see the differences. 'This one they got to touch, smell, see texture, and this one was one to be left untouched.' Trying to do it in a way that was educational, but not making them afraid of poison oak.

Harper continues,

> The other piece that did draw very strongly into raising my own
> boys was this idea that babies want to put something in their mouth
> almost immediately, and rather than saying no to that, what I got
> curious about is what could I say yes to. If there was something
> they were putting in their mouth that wasn't good for them, instead
> of saying a flat no to that, there was, 'That is a Yuck, and here is a
> Yum.' It wasn't just about saying no, it was more about drawing
> attention to, 'Here is a yes.' A little bit of it is my belief, this comes
> from living with indigenous people, that evolutionarily we had to
> figure out what we could put in our mouths at a really young age
> or we wouldn't be here. We learn this though taste, or watching
> elders, mothers, fathers, uncles, aunts, or by other kids showing
> what we could eat. For example, in my neighborhood there was
> this plant called sour grass and it was not passed from adult to
> kid that this plant is edible. It was passed very clearly from kid to
> kid, this plant is edible. That was completely how it was learned.
> Similarly, an oxalis—redwood sorrel is also an oxalis, looks very
> different from the sour grass I grew up with, which wasn't a grass at
> all, but the idea is we show them what they can put in their mouth
> as opposed to what they can't, because it's such a natural thing.

(This is also an example of Lederman's tenant of "taking the focus
off the focus." By showing edible plants, or Yums, a teacher/guide
avoid any shame around the Yucks, the inedible plants.)

Being at Gazebo for any length of time—whether it was visiting
for a day, spending three months as an intern, or teaching there for
years, provided opportunities to uncover some of the beliefs, thought
patterns, and social structures that we took on throughout our lives.
Discomfort, growth, and transformation inevitably took place while
shedding old beliefs systems and adopting new ways of being with
children. It was truly a fascinating process to feel and to witness this
unfolding.

Gazebo Grandparent—Intergenerational Learning

The philosophy involves the integration of generations, the inviting of children back into society, and the re-introduction of Living into the content of learning.

– JL

Eizner says,

These kids that are establishing attachments to people, they are bonding to adults, they are relating to different generations and learning how to relate to generations in a way that most kids don't have. The extended family. Janet always wanted a grandma or a grandpa, the uncles, aunts, someone that might represent a mom or a dad for these kids, and for them to work through their issues in a safe environment. Gazebo was for them—it was their home. Kids will cry for whatever reason, conflicts, attention, you know whatever might be going on with the kids, and having the kid crawling into your arms and feeling safe. Most kids don't get that in their own homes, and especially not in schools.

As a volunteer, consultant, and mentor at Gazebo, Miller would bring stories each time she came to read to the children, she supported the teachers and interns, and she represented the grandmother role as well. Certainly, Penny Vieregge was a continual grandmother figure in the lives of so many Gazebo children. The inclusion and respect for the elders and the great wisdom they hold contributed to the magic of Gazebo. The network of school, family, farm, community, land, plants, animals, is what built the feeling of safety and connection, and the feeling of home that my daughter felt there. I do believe the integration of "life and learning" that Lederman spoke of deepens the experience of school.

First Aiders:
Penny and the Core Components of the Focus Bus Curriculum

I'd rather learn from one bird how to sing than to teach ten thousand stars how not to dance.

– e.e. cummings

Penny and Toby in Gazebo Park

*P*enny Vieregge is one of the most dynamic people I've had the pleasure to know. At any moment, she might break out in song, recite a Hafiz poem, or do an impromptu spiritual healing on you. She is an inspired human being with many talents, but one of the amazing accomplishments of her life is that she taught emergency preparedness and first aid to young children for thirty-nine years at Gazebo. Many of those years, her classroom was "the bus," an old school bus converted into a classroom. She developed an entire curriculum designed for working with young children in a subject normally only taught to adults. She empowered them to deal with emergencies with calm, to administer first-aid to each other and to adults, and she prepared them for the increased structure of kindergarten and/or the public school system. The "focus bus" as it was later called, was a vital counterbalance to the wildly unstructured Gazebo Park environment. Children made a contract, respected rules, and did academic work in an organized way. What Penny brought to Gazebo was unique and it was deeply carved into the lives of the children who experienced her teachings over the years.

Vieregge remembers how it all began.

> I got a phone call from Janet, and at that time I would not let my-self be identified with any department. I was a freewheeler. Janet calls and says I want you to work at Gazebo, name your price. She told me about what your sister, Lucia, had done when her friend had used an old-fashioned can opener and it had jumped and had slashed her arm. She said that Lucia, I think she was four or five then, immediately elevated the arm, applied direct pressure, led the adult to the sink and put on cold water. She called the ambulance and in those days the ambulance wouldn't come up. It wouldn't leave the highway. They get in the car (no seat belts because it was before seat belts) and Lucia looks at whoever the guest was who was driving and says, 'Your job is to get us safely to the highway, and my job is to control the bleeding.' I had taught her and many more intensely, but I had only been a teacher of first aid and not kindergarten prep. Janet told the story and then said, 'Name your price.'

When I would walk into the bus beside Penny, one of the first things I would notice was the line of flags with Red Cross badges with different children's names on them, most of them familiar to me—including my own. Vieregge recalls,

> I was a Red Cross instructor, so I had access to all of these Red Crosse badges and we were teaching basic first aid. They had bails of stuff and I also had the stickers we used for classes, Red Cross, my name is.... And I would write the names, we would spell the names. I would hold it up, we would read the names, and put their name stickers on their chest. The red flags were just part of participating, and since I had them we would put their names on them and hang them up. It is so great to look around and see them.

The environment of the classroom was supportive of the classroom structure. The front of the bus had a little kidney-bean shaped table with "connect the dot" name writing worksheets displayed above. By the driver's seat was a timer for cleanup. There was a little section of miniature emergency vehicles and figurines. The back of the bus had a comfortable couch with a library section with many books about health, anatomy, systems of the body. Depending on the unit of study, there might be a skeleton displayed, or another life-sized human health system hanging from the ceiling. The bus was a cozy place, but a place of discipline and structure. It was a place children either didn't pay much mind to, or greatly looked forward to, and for younger ones, something they aspired to do when they were ready.

Nevertheless, Vieregge's teachings didn't begin in the bus, nor was her curriculum confined to such a classroom.

> You can teach first aid under bushes and the kids just love it. We would use the old backboard from the ambulance, the manikins and stuff like that and would do first aid in the park or anywhere. I would set up accidents, and we would practice. I would give tests. The computer bus was phased out and given to me. This one [bus] broke down on the highway and it was given to us. It was a living bus and maintenance made it a point to take out the kitchen and the bed and turned it into a classroom. This was the second bus in place and before that I had a yurt. The yurt was called 'the reading yurt.' That is when I got into the kindergarten prep stuff. The kindergarten prep just happened. I was teaching emergency, the kids were making their own notebooks, and I discovered I could dot. My minor was primary education, and I would dot the words and the kids would connect the dots. They would make words and draw pictures. I told you that they were going to teach me! Then, they would dot, 'Breath slow check go.' It was all mixed in, it was organic. Just the way teaching led into teaching the body the systems. I am still a stochastic teacher. The stochastic model is part of the chaos theory, whereby everything is related and nothing stands alone—parts relate—one move affects everything. So, in stochastic theory everything is relative. As a stochastic teacher,

everything that was relative began to come up. We flowed into reading as reading is easier than writing. That was when we were in the yurt. Then we got into myths, then we got into myths that were developed because people wanted explanations for things they had noticed that were happening around them. Myths were early science. Then we got into scientific experimentation—making a premise and proving it.

Gregory Bateson, anthropologist and Esalen workshop leader, defined Stochastic as:

(Greek, stochazein, to shoot with a bow at a target; that is, to scatter events in a partially random manner, some of which achieve a preferred outcome). If a sequence of events combines a random component with a selective process so that only certain outcomes of the random are allowed to endure, that sequence is said to be stochastic.[1]

Bateson stated in his book *Mind and Nature*,

It is a general assumption in this book that both genetic change and the process called learning (including the somatic changes induced by habit and environment) are stochastic processes. In each case, there is, I believe, a stream of events that is random in certain aspects and in each case there is a nonrandom selective process which causes certain of the random components to 'survive' longer than others. Without the random, there can be no new thing.[2]

So, Vieregge taught arithmetic by planting bulbs, and stocking the first-aid kit. For instance, she would say,

Hand me seven Band-Aids, and then they get accustomed to numbers and how they are combined. That was the goal and seemingly random, once you start on it you see when the focus starts to develop. Circles and triangles, looking in nature. The goal was to become accustomed to circles. To have an awareness of circles. You have a goal, random movements that gradually close down closer and closer to the goal.

Furthermore, one of the touchstones Vieregge used was, "The combination of relevance, imagination along with the introduction to and development of intellectual rigor. This is for staff as well as children." I have heard Vieregge refer to these three elements many times, and this teaching became an important touchstone for the staff over the years. She created this "spiral," as she called it, while working on her Masters of Science degree.

> When I was working on my masters, I came up with this: That education was a spiral and it had three legs—relevance, imagination and intellectual rigor. What we found was in first aid, it was relevant, it appealed to their imagination, and we found that they demanded intellectual rigor. They wanted to know the right way, they wanted to know the discipline, they wanted to know the form. There it was.

Though Vieregge's curriculum developed over time, her insight as a teacher philosophically met the Gazebo methods, and added other elements which seemed to balance out the program as a whole. Vieregge says she taught kindergarten prep, first aid and emergency preparedness, and she adds that she also taught appropriate behavior.

> Esalen kids were free kids. All sorts of language was allowed at Gazebo. It was appropriate at Gazebo, but it was not appropriate when you went into kindergarten and first grade. A lot of times we were training the kids to say, 'I don't like to be called that' to a child who insulted them.

For many of the children at Esalen, the culture of was one of exploration, and sometimes the children were not learning outside social norms. "For the Gazebo/ Esalen kids and Esalen families who lived on property, lets face it, for them there was a lot of drugs a lot of sex and the children had very little idea of appropriate behavior," Vieregge says. Though this may not have been the experience of every child at Esalen, we certainly grew up in a counter-culture experience where nudity and profanity were not taboo. She sought to provide a safe container for children to experience and learn about appropriate behavior which provided perspective outside of their own experience.

Education Contracts

An important part of the bus is that the children made a contract to participate. Firstly, the staff helped them understand their commitment by using the word "focus" frequently in the Park so the children understood the meaning. The contract was a verbal agreement that the child will focus. The second part of the contract is that the child will let the teacher know when he or she doesn't want to focus any more, and then they will go back to the park. Thus, the "focus" contract began on the hay bales at the edge of the Gazebo Park where the children would gather before they crossed the street together to the bus. Vieregge would announce that she was going to begin to be available to go to the bus soon and the children who wanted to participate would join her at the hay bales. Vieregge remembers, "I would say, 'I am available to go to the bus.'" Sometimes there was a short period of liberation, but generally, the unsure students would filter out quickly. Sometimes, even with children who loved the bus, they already had something they were engaged in or something else they wanted to do. In that case, it was up to them to go or not, but they were not allowed to come in late if they chose not to go when it was time to make the contract.

The bus was an optional activity, but I always found there were some children who were very passionate about it, and who looked forward to it all week. When I worked at Gazebo, the Focus Bus was only once a week, and this gathering at the hay bales happened each time after lunch during a natural transition time. Vieregge adds,

> Part of the contract is classroom behavior, we share, we keep our voices down, appropriate behavior for the classroom. If they are not acting appropriately, they leave, and this doesn't come from just me. Sometimes the children decide that someone isn't ready to focus.

Consequently, after the contracts had been made, the group would cross the street together—which was also a strong part of the curriculum. Vieregge used to say, "Stop, look and listen." Over the years, it changed to something she and other Gazebo teachers used to say each time they crossed the road. "Look, listen, ask yourself, 'Is there anything moving? Is it <u>safe</u> for me to cross?'" In this way, even the crossing of the street towards the bus was an important element of the safety curriculum. Vieregge states,

> You notice in the bus are areas, bone area, really clean teeth, the digestive area, the science area, the orientation area with the globe. That was always the first thing in the bus is that you sit down and you wait for the teacher. Sometimes, I will deliberately not come for a while, but they can't play with anything, they can't touch anything. They wait, and I say, 'Are you ready to start the class in first aid?', and when they agree I say, 'the class in first aid has started.' We always do first aid first. Either the first aid song or owies, and this is why kids can only come to the bus at the time I am available. They can't say a half hour later, 'I wanna come to the bus,' because the bus discipline starts with the first aid lesson period. Now if a child says, 'I don't want to focus anymore,' and goes back to the park, then that child has the privilege of saying, 'I want try focus again,' and can go back to the bus. There is no, 'I didn't feel like it,' when you said you were available, but now I want to go.' The focus part starts at the hay bales and then we cross the street.

Vieregge recalls an experience of an educational contract being made.

> One of the stories is when Mahalia wanted to come over. She was very young. She was on the hay bales and she said 'focus bus— I want to go,' and we sort of talked contract. I looked at the older kids and said, 'Do you think she really understands,' and they said no. I said, 'Do you think she wants to understand,' and they said, yes. Then she is going to need teachers, she is going to need mentors, and the older boys said, 'we will mentor her.' We all crossed the street, the boys teaching her the chant. She lasted about three or four minutes, but at that time Gazebo was independent, had

money and had a good sized staff. When a younger child decided to try the bus, there was always a staff member outside raking. The second part of the contract did not just come from the child, it came from the other children. Sometimes they would say, 'You're not ready, you're not focusing and you're not ready to be in the bus, go back to the Park.' But it would come from the kids, not from me. The mentorship is a very important aspect.

Mentorship

Vieregge says,

> My basic theory, for a child growing older, is to say, 'The older you get, the more responsibility you are capable of handling.' Being four or five doesn't mean you get to stay up later or watch television. It means you also have responsibilities like cleaning up the bus. 'You do it at the Park too.' I use an egg timer, and set it twenty minutes before class ends. It goes off and its clean-up time. Frequently they will ask if they can continue, particularly if they are doing prekindergarten work. Because by this time, for the last bunch of years, I have had a list of requirements for kindergarten and they fit in here perfectly. A lot of it is self-discipline and focus. And our inner-directed kids are open to listening to an outer-directed person.

The mentorship aspect of the bus curriculum always seemed to develop naturally through the mixed-age groups. California regulations for most licensed programs do not allow mixed-ages in the same way as Gazebo did during its history. In many ways, this is a shame, as children naturally learn from each other just by observing. Children within the guidelines of the focus bus curriculum and with the education contracts, hold each other accountable for behavior and work. It is really marvelous to see how much is learned, especially by younger children learning to walk, talk and go to the toilet, through this contact with older children. Also, the older children feel great pride and responsibility in sharing what they know with the younger kids, and in being able to focus or do academic work a bit longer than their younger peers. The tasks of the older children become something for the younger children to strive for and challenges the older ones to continue to develop their skills.

Kindergarten Preparation

Vieregge recalls,

> I thought I had invented the reading method, but it turned out it had been invented by Sylvia Ashton-Warner of New Zealand. We had word boxes. We had name words, we had action words, and we had descriptions. We learned *is*, we learned *ing*, and then we wrote cards. The child would tell us an important word to him/her. I dot it out, hold it up. They read it, we name it an action word or *name* word. They had papers with the dotted words. They dotted cards and filed them in their individual boxes. Words that they had forgotten we would toss, and words they remembered we would put in their word box. As, it turns out Ashton had invented this and written a book called *Teacher*. She had worked with the Māori. I was so excited and delighted that somebody else had done it, and it was out there and it was a book and it is a great way to teach reading.

After the "work" period in the bus after the first aid unit, the children would do a block of "free choice" activity. At this time, Penny would ask the children if they wanted to listen to Mozart or Beethoven which she would play while they studied. She suggested that research had shown classical music to increase brain function and therefore learning. Oftentimes the academic work in the bus was simply practicing writing letters and numbers. The simple task of sitting at the desk and practicing the fine motor skills of using the pencil was important for young children who would transition to kindergarten. The work period was based on the child's interest. They could choose an activity from one of the learning centers, or a book that interested them, and stay with it for as long as they liked during that work period. In this way, the student-directed approach that Gazebo took, based on choice and inner direction, was also being implemented in the focus bus. The library-like environment in the back of the bus was always pleasant—with music and warm fuzzy seating and pillows.

Furthermore, the clean-up time was also an important time structure and behavior management technique that related to kindergarten preparation. Vieregge would ask that everyone help put things away—especially what the student had been using. Each item had its place in the bus, and they were required to either remember or ask a friend if they did not know where. At clean-up, children were responsible for cleaning up their own work and their shared space. Some children took pride in their organizational skills while others had challenges cleaning up, but regardless, it was an important skill and preparation for these students.

Emergency Preparedness

Critical thinking skills are an important component in how children learn about handling emergencies. For example, Vieregge suggests,

> Asking the questions, 'Is there anything moving,' rather than 'Are there any cars?,' "Is there anything moving,' and then following with the question, 'Is it safe here for me?' It's not just cars, it can be marathon runners, it can be goats, it can be ponies. It is also stand by the side of the road, look to your left going down the hill, look to your right going up the hill, but when you are coming back it's look to your left up the hill, and your right down the hill. It is so exciting when one of them suddenly gets the idea that left and right stay the same. Then they are ready for orientation, east, west, north, south, what is in front of me, what is behind me. That is why I do the orientation to get the feeling of the energy bubble that surrounds you. What is behind you, so that when I have a baseball bat or a stick and go to swing it, and somebody might be behind me, I have to be aware of what is behind me.

Vieregge taught children how to handle emergency situations by using songs, fun games, and role playing. She taught Gazebo students through real-life situations that were completely relevant to the world they lived in. Nelson tells a story of how important this ended up being for his children.

> When Tyler was three or four he was home alone with his sister because she was twelve or thirteen, and he fell down the stairs and broke his arm. She was very good and she splinted it, calmed him down, and called the gate guard. They located one or both of us and they found us fairly quickly. She was very grounded and she was trained. She was a cool cucumber, and it wasn't just because it was her brother, it was because she knew what to do. We took him in and they set his arm and it worked out pretty well.

Vieregge says, "In all the chaos and if somebody is hurt, a three-year-old can keep the sun out of a victim's eyes. A small hand stroking a forehead and a small voice saying 'the ambulance is on its way' helps." Therefore, Vieregge showed the children how to stay calm in an emergency. She taught us "emergency behavior." There are vital questions she taught children to ask in an emergency. She taught this through her playful song that starts

> Every first aider needs to know. Stop, breath slow. Then ask yourself. Is it safe here for me? Check, then go, you go *for help* or you go *to help*.' And what is the first question you ask yourself? Is it safe here for me? If it is not safe—I go *for help*. If it is safe—I might/can go *to help*.

She remembers how her important song lyrics came to her, "When it came it was so perfect. You have three questions, 'Is it safe here for me? Do I go *for help*? or Do I go *to help*?'"

Thompson-Clark says that her daughter maintains that she went into medicine because of having first aid offered at a young age and thus getting interested at a young age. Wolfinger also stated that he wanted to be a doctor because he learned first aid in the Gazebo bus.

He did become an EMT and then a teacher. His love for Vieregge's teachings of health and medicine were a strong invitation to him to learn and to teach. Wolfinger remembers learning:

> ...the nurturing discovery of all these tools for caring for community. When Penny talked to me I had so much rapport and respect for her as a child. Everything she said I held onto her golden drops of wisdom. It inspired me in my choices. I have yearned for that as an EMT and firefighter and teacher and I love all that stuff and I think she turned me on at a really early age.

She taught the students to dial 911, simple tools that might save their life or someone else's.

First Aid

Band aid application

First aid is a skill set that is useful at any age in any geographical location. For children, learning first aid can be inspiring, empowering, and even lifesaving. This can be achieved by using simple language that increases in complexity along with the age and understanding of the child. Children can surprise us with their calm and capability for handling many unique and even high-stress situations. With the right modeling and education, children are able to learn complex systems and skills that help them react to real-life situations. Particularly for children living in Big Sur, far from hospitals and doctors, these principles were highly relevant.

Vieregge taught first aid that was specific and rich with medical vocabulary. She taught the names of different kinds of wounds, and how to treat them. I remember the mantra, 'First you WASH it then you COVER it.' Barnes said, "I would love to hear from Olivia what she learned in the bus from Penny! How incredible to hear her say, at barely two, 'LA-CER-A-TION' (!)" Vieregge's first aid curriculum could be used with staged first-aid lessons or in response to real-life accidents and 'owies.' I watched Vieregge train toddlers to be experts in Band-Aid application. It was truly amazing to see the children practice first-aid on each other. Each time someone got hurt in the park, a group of children gathered around, and those who were trained offered first aid. Even an "owie" was a teachable moment.

For instance, Vieregge shares a story about first aid in the Park.

We had a kid fall off the Hot Wheels hay track and the child, the injured/victim, is permitted to choose who is going to be the first-aider. Someone would come and say, 'Can I be your first-aider? Immediately the victim has power and is given back power. It was Michael Cohen again, the child was screaming and he said 'ow.' 'What kind of owie is that?' The kid stops and looks and says, 'abrasion.' No more screaming, no more tears, no nothing. I am supervising of course, and so Michael became first-aider. That means the first-aider stays with the victim and gives orders and says, 'You go get the first-aid kit, or go get the calendula.' A child came running up with calendula, but the blossom, and while the leaves were being scrunched up I started to say, 'No just the leaves,' and then I said to myself, 'Shut up Penny,' and I watched. The kid took the blossoms, dipped them in water and used the wet blossoms to wash/caress the mud out. They were soft, gentle, pretty and effective. That is a perfect example of how the children taught me.

In this way, the children knew the possible first-aid roles for in any given situation and they knew the tasks associated with those first-aid roles. Vieregge clarifies,

You have your first-aider, the victim, and the comforter. Even with grown-up accidents, a three-year-old child can hold a jacket and keep the sun out of a victim's eyes. A three-year-old, if the area is safe (because that is the first thing I teach them is ask if the area is safe here), can have a hand on your forehead and a little voice saying 'The ambulance is coming. We have the first-aiders here and everything is going to be just fine.' With the older kids I have taught about shock and all of that because they could do it. They are good comforters. And it also gives the child the power of not running around screaming and frightened, but I have a job to do. That is my whole point, to present the tools and empower the child, and to support the child in discovery.

Baldwin recalls,

Another thing about first aid, it's all there, it's all curriculum, it's all happening as it happens. Some become helpers. The guy who hit the person can look after them, or maybe the guy who got hit doesn't want that."

It is in this way, during a physical injury, the whole learning community seems to rally around the victim and get involved in helping. I have seen this in action, and I believe that it is a way of cultivating compassion. Even during an emotional moment in which a child is crying, the children seem to care, tune in, name the facts, come close or give space depending on the needs of the situation. There is an awareness of others and an ability to read situations that increases with the knowledge of first aid.

Health

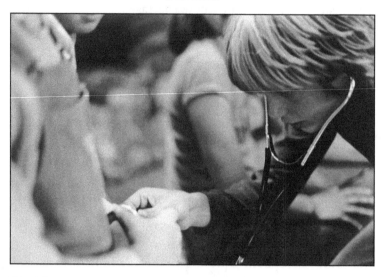

Health is an important aspect of Vieregge's curriculum. She introduced units on each one of the systems of the body. She offered supporting literature in her library in the bus where one finds books from anatomy to elimination to reproduction. Around Halloween and autumn time of each year, she tried to time the skeletal system to coincide with the skeletons in people's decorations. The chant, "Them bones, them bones, them dry bones, and the neck bones connected to the shoulder bone," and so on was a favorite at Gazebo.

Based on a unit of study, a current event in the Park, or simply a student's curiosity, Vieregge might pull out her medical bag and show children some of the instruments. She had a stethoscope hanging on the hook on the wall of the bus. Children would find their own heartbeat and they loved this hands-on real-life application of learning. When I was pregnant with my daughter and working at Gazebo, some of the students loved to use the stethoscope to try to listen to the baby's heartbeat. The children at Gazebo had a comfort and confidence with themselves and the human body; partially, I imagine, from understanding it so well through Vieregge's curriculum.

I feel like it was such a gift for me to be able to witness Vieregge teach later in my life after I had become a teacher. I saw how much she held the children accountable, and she didn't limit their capabilities, completely trusting their limits. Wolfinger stated, "I remember when she took us to the hospital when I was a kid and everyone thought maybe I shouldn't go, but Penny said, 'He will be fine.' The hospital was amazing for me."

Vieregge also tells the story about the visit to the emergency room.

> I took the Gazebo kids to the emergency room at Community Hospital of Monterey. At lunch, the staff at the ER sent a thank-you note to the kids. An ambulance arrived and the kids moved against the wall to get out of the way. It was appropriate behavior. Dylan [Wolfinger] wore a blue blazer. At one point we were in the atrium and Michael Cohen was running around, and Dylan or Flash said to him, 'Michael, that is not appropriate behavior.' He sat down. 'You know what is appropriate.'

Davey, Vieregge's granddaughter and former student shares,

> Now that I am an adult and I look back on what Nana has been able to teach so many generations of children I am filled with an immense sense of pride. I believe her experience has shown that we are constantly, as adults, underestimating the minds and capabilities of young children. Children are thirsty for experience and answers—for the tools to take care of themselves and each other. One of my favorite lessons is when she would have the kids close their eyes and run their hands down the spine of the skeleton in the bus. We would then all walk over to the goats and she would calmly hold the animal while the kids all closed their eyes and ran their hands down its spine—realizing that these structures are similar! 'Feel your ribs expand as you take deep breaths! Then feel his ribs expand as he takes deep breaths!' Animals and humans aren't that different and therefore we are all sharing the Park and the world. First aid has been an area of comfort for me because of Nana. She instilled in me a sense of calm in chaos that I carry with me to this day. Her songs about slowing down and breathing and taking in what is happening around you. Asking the question, 'Is

this safe for me?' has come in handy. I have been able to evaluate scary situations (a stranger having a seizure, a coworker slicing their hand, being the first person to come across a car accident, and natural disasters. (Big Sur is a wild place!) I feel grounded and I know that I have been anchored to this idea since I was so small, that if this is safe for me than I can handle this. I can help. Penny is able to still view the world through the eyes of a child. She can match the child's wonder and excitement. She remembers that the life of a three-year-old is full of 'firsts' and that discovery and the desire to understand is 'fuel to the fire' of life and education. BE EXCITED when a child discovers and understands something! Share the thrill. Being raised with this as my experience has been invaluable and I am forever grateful for her excitement in my wonder.

Davey continues,

I believe that I am a rare and lucky person in that my grandmother has taught at Gazebo for much longer than I have been alive. What I know about the philosophy, I know from the ways in which my 'Nana' treated my brother and me. Everything is an experience with a purpose. For example, if we were to garden with Nana, my brother and I would dig the holes, we would plant the seeds, we would be responsible to water and maintain the beds, we would nourish the plants until we got to enjoy and share the strawberries. We were able to understand the whole process and gain an understanding that our actions (that we can do on our own) can have a beneficial impact on our world around us. By doing and understanding we become capable and conscientious.

Marquis says,

I think I've always been caring, nurturing, empathetic. I don't think Gazebo made me that way, but it encouraged it. I realized there were tools for that and that you could help someone with first aid and that you could help your friends. Penny and the bus made me love medicine from an early age—made me confident I could care for someone if something went wrong. Made me aware of the plants around me—that they could hurt me or heal me. The Yums and Yucks. I think about the bus often, about her enthusiasm for working with kids, with me, and how much I loved it.

"It is such fun. It is such a delight! You know, and Janet just encouraged me and let me play no matter what," says Vieregge. While Vieregge developed her curriculum based on health, first aid, emergency preparedness, appropriate behavior and kindergarten preparation, she implemented the same respect for the child's capabilities that Gazebo practiced. The two counterbalancing components of the unstructured Gazebo Park, and the first aid Focus Bus, provided both freedom and a safe container for the children. As Vieregge puts it, "Complete freedom, complete choice."

Vieregge is an amazing teacher, and anyone can see how she connects with children. She treats them as equals, as capable and intelligent beings. Yet, her humility and understanding of her own goals and the depth of Gazebo-style education, makes her realize the focal point is the student and not the teacher. Vieregge recalls being asked about her goal as an educator. She responded,

> To become obsolete. I know they have stars in their eyes when they are young, but by the time they are three, four, five-years-old, I would hope that I would become just another reference.

When it becomes about the children, their learning, their wonder, their excitement and curiosity, something extraordinary happens. Her suggestion that teachers can "become obsolete," however challenging an approach to maintain in today's education systems, is a rare and profound perspective. In this way, her aim is for the students to become so engaged in the learning that the teacher can step aside as a witness.

Gestalt Practice

Learning integrates and incorporates

mind	*thinking*
body	*doing*
spirit	*reflecting*
	FEELING

– JL

In Gestalt Therapy, we are working for something else.
We are here to promote the growth process and develop
the human potential.

– Fritz Perls

*I*n most schools, children are taught to be polite and ask nicely, rather than speak their truth. At the Gazebo Park School, children were taught different skills about being authentic in their emotional and social communication. Children learned to express their feelings, and conflict resolution was very intentional through facilitation and deliberate communication in an individual or group setting.

Gestalt Practice in education can help children develop interpersonal and intrapersonal skills through language and somatic awareness. Gestalt Practice invites participants to connect the present moment— including sensations in the body, give specific language to the states of being, take responsibility, and set and respect boundaries. Gestalt Practice, in essence, invites individual or group process and allows for witnessing to take place. Furthermore these processes cultivate compassion through authentic awareness of self and other.

The key practices can be applied in any stage of life—from early childhood, to adolescence, to adulthood—and are useful for both students and teachers, children and parents in attuning to emotional needs and modeling direct communication. Gestalt Practice is an important construct to education in relation to a child's development, cognitively, physically and emotionally. Gazebo Park School is a model of a school that had used these methods for forty years.

Gestalt History/Context

As a center for human potential and growth, Esalen Institute was home to Gazebo Park School for 40 years. In 1977, Gazebo Park School began a progressive and unique outdoor-based learning center. As one of the original core values of Esalen Institute, Gestalt became part of the early childhood education at Gazebo. Gestalt had been practiced in all of the departments at Esalen as a form of therapy, a practice, and a way of being.

Fredrick Perls began practicing "Gestalt Therapy" at Esalen in the early 1960s. Later Esalen founder Dick Price and his wife Christine Price, adapted this method to include more Eastern philosophy— creating the more holistic "Gestalt Practice." Christine

Price later refined this more into "Gestalt Awareness Practice," and Dorothy Charles focuses on "Relational Gestalt Practice." Many Gestalt practitioners such as Fritz Perls, Dick and Christine Price, Dorothy Charles, Claudio Naranjo, Julian Silverman, Robert Hall, Will Schutz, Mariah Fenton Gladis, and Seymour Carter, to name a few, have utilized this practice in the Esalen community through open seats, departmental process, and individual sessions as it has developed.

Lederman, incorporated Gestalt methodology into the curriculum and moral fiber of the Gazebo learning community. Lederman believed that experience was the greatest teacher. In this sense, Esalen provided a rich cultural context that deepened the learning in their adult offerings. Gestalt extended into the lives of its children through the use of Gestalt Practice with children via Lederman's vision of incorporating Gestalt into education in experimental and experiential ways.

Gestalt Practice

Gestalt Practice is a exercise in being in the present, being open to growth, and allowing feelings and the environment to exist as they are rather than as you wish them to be. In this way children, with encouragement, can find ways to experience and express the full spectrum of human emotions with honesty rather than judgment.

Thompson-Clark notes that Gestalt awareness is:

Breath

Witness

Taking Responsibility (*Response-Ability*)

Respecting Boundaries (own, other, earth)

Contacting one's own authentic voice

Sensing, Naming, Reflecting

In this way, the teacher's task is to model and coach the students in awareness, expression, and skillful communication. Thus, within this application there is the intrapersonal—the child's relationship to their own feelings, and the interpersonal – their relationships within the learning community; and we can extend this to the terrapersonal or the child's relationship to the environment and the earth. Through experimentation and experience, teachers and students may find principles that deepen any learning process.

Vieregge, says that based on Dick Price's teachings, guidelines for Gestalt are to "Trust the process. Follow that process. Stay out of the way. Except when it comes to health and safety." Her addendum was the last sentence. In addition, Harper expounds on this teaching in saying that Dick Price's three guidelines for facilitators are to:

1. Trust the process

2. Support process (stay present with process, allow process)

3. Get out of the way

Addendum – If in doubt: Do less.

Harper also distinguished the role shift from therapist and client which followed the pathology paradigm to the roles of *initiator* and *reflector.* These language and role shifts changed Gestalt Therapy to Gestalt Practice during Dick Price's era. This, according to Harper, put the power back in the hands of the initiator and thus shifted the role of the therapist into more of a responsive reflector role. (Reflectors can also be referred to as facilitators or Gestalt practitioners.)

Thus, in working with children and Gestalt, facilitators/teachers encourage the child to work with their feelings—both pleasant and unpleasant, and empower them to make appropriate choices in response to them. Consequently, life offers the opportunity for communication through conflict, and teachers and students alike may find skillful ways to handle these situations by using Gestalt Practice.

Price-Waldrip shares that,

> For me, Gestalt Practice has been a huge part of my life. I so appreciate how some of the values were passed on to children as well. For me, Gestalt Practice encourages beings to meet their feelings and emotions fully, to learn where they are embodied, to not push them away or try to change them, but to give them space, time, and breath. Giving a child this opportunity can be transformative. To be able to act out a behavior or emotion in a safe and supportive environment instead of being asked to change, I see that as a gift. And especially as a child, being able to integrate all parts of the self at a young age can be incredibly beneficial for the growth process. Allowing natural human processes to flourish instead of capping them, I think that's part of what made Gazebo special. The sooner one can be in touch with their feelings, the more they can learn about themselves and how they want to interact with the world.

Furthermore, Perls recognized the value of witnessing or group process, which became one of the foundations of Gestalt process, and additionally differentiated the form from other types of self-inquiry. Regardless of whether there is an inner or outer conflict, the learning can be a shared experience. Although there are times that require more privacy, group process, or the witnessing of individual process in an educational setting, can be valuable for the whole learning community. Moreover, students both involved or witnessing conflict interactions are learning compassion, empathy and self-awareness. In this way, Gestalt Practice provides a contact point for both inner wisdom and valuable reflections from witnesses and can create a culture of understanding through a common language.

Gestalt and Somatics—Following Cues from the Body

My Tummee Hurts (Arfur's Gestalt Stories)

Arfur: (Lucy is lying on the ground next to the pony stable looking like she would like some attention)
Hi Lucy, How are you feeling?

Lucy: (in an upset voice) I don't feel good!

Arfur: What doesn't feel good?

Lucy: (putting her hand on her stomach) My tummee hurts!

Arfur: Would you like to do something about your tummee pain?

Lucy: Ah! Huh!

Arfur: Would you like to play a game with your pain?

Lucy: (with eyes that are searching for guidance and support) Okay!

Arfur: Close your eyes. What do you see?

Lucy: (Lucy closes her eyes) Dark!!

Arfur: Do you see any light around?

Lucy: (spends a moment to look around inside) Yeaaah! I do see a little light!

Arfur: See if you can go to towards the light and tell me when you get there.

Lucy: Okay! (moment later with eyes still closed) I'm there!

Arfur: What do you see?

Lucy: I see a sun and it's warm.

Arfur: Lucy... would you travel to your tummee?

Lucy: How would I do that?

Arfur: Well.... take a look around to see where you are now!

Lucy: I'm by my heart!

Arfur: Okay! now your tummee is below your heart so let's travel down to your tummee.

Lucy: I can't, I don't know how to.

Arfur: What could you use to help your self down to your tummee?

Lucy: (thinks for a moment) I could use a rope and climb down!

Arfur: That's great Lucy use your rope.

Lucy: (feeling good about her choice, begins her journey)

Arfur: What do you see as you are climbing down?

Lucy: (concerned) I see red and colors.

Arfur: How do you feel Lucy?

Lucy: I feel a little scared (sadness comes over her face and tears begin to well up in her eyes)

Arfur: Is there a place you could rest for a moment?

Lucy: (Softly) Yeah.

Arfur: Go to that place.

Arfur: Are you there Lucy?

Lucy: Yes.

Arfur: What do you feel scared about?

Lucy: I miss my mommy (tears begin to pour out and crying starts as Lucy lets go of her feelings)

Arfur: (watches as Lucy begins to stop crying, a feeling of joy comes over her and a smile begins to form on her spirit). What's happening now Lucy?

Lucy: (opens her eyes) I don't feel scared anymore!

Arfur: How's your tummee?

Lucy: (big smile) It doesn't hurt anymore (Lucy runs off to play)

Munyer articulates some of the ways somatic learning meets language with these questions,

> How does that feel in your body, stay away from WHY. How is that important? Where do you feel that in your body? Not everywhere. Specifically. Where do you feel that in your body?" He adds, "It was always about the feelings. What happens in the adult world is that they think things, but it's not about story, it's about the sensation that is created inside your body. That it's important—what is your body saying?

Gabrielle Roth, dancer, author, and founder of 5Rhythms® said,

> Feelings are real. They are not ideas that can be turned off. They are not abstractions. They are physical manifestations of energy, uniting body and mind and bringing them to the moment. Unexpressed, repressed, or suppressed, this energy becomes toxic. Without release, it surfaces in lumps, clots, tumors, spasms, migraine headaches, and other symptoms of physical distress.

Roth's teachings embodied movement and dance as the basis for emotional expression. She said,

> The basic emotions are vital to our survival and total well-being. The challenge is not to transcend them, but to transform our relationship to them. We need to befriend and express our feelings with purity and directness and in the moment.[1]

Somatics is the holistic study of the body through the use of different body-oriented forms of movement, physical expression and body-awareness practices. Somatic practices bridge the mind-body connection and are key to experiential learning. Some of the early somatic therapists, such as Wilhelm Reich and Charlotte Selver, began to make these connection between the sensory experience and how we hold onto or process our experiences of the world. Later somatic practitioners and many of the teachers that were part of the Human

Potential Movement contributed to ideas and concepts such as mind-body that were sowed at Esalen. In particular, Gestalt Practice was one form that connects to somatic awareness. In this way, children learn through somatic experiences stimulated by their environment, their interactions, and their experience of the world in each moment.

The environment at Gazebo consists of terrain that requires fine and gross motor skills, and the education is play-based, and is full of exploratory, outdoor learning. The environment itself requires risk-taking, and within the play-based learning, there is an incredibly physical experience occurring— therefore a somatic education takes place. Accordingly, early childhood center design, especially in an outdoor environment, is an important aspect of somatic education. One of the highlights for children over the years has been riding Hot Wheels down the hill. Munyer, says he specifically "built the big hill with the bikes which helped them to orientate their physical bodies. Speed or movement is simple neurological and biological information that can activate the adrenaline. Then the children could ride into a transition, a slow long and calming movement, into stillness."

At Gazebo children were invited into an outdoor park environment that is highly physically stimulating. London calls it, "Pure feeling—pure sensory awareness." In calculating risks, climbing trees, digging in the dirt and using hands-on and full-body movements, children are getting in touch with their bodies. Thus, the education at Gazebo is a somatic experience that connects mind and body and aids in development of the whole child.

Delevett remembers,

> I loved that experience preceded cognition—that we just got to be. That's what I understand Gestalt to be like as well. What are you noticing now? What are you sensing? Warm sun on bare arms, grass under feet, some warm patches of dirt, the smell of eucalyptus, ocean air, the sound of blue jays and hummingbirds. Grounded in experience first. Then what do you make of that? What story do you tell yourself about that? When have you felt that before?

What's the earliest memory you have of that? What else do you notice? I love the sense of presence the approach teaches—being grounded in your experience, being grounded in the moment. Fully embodied. I am laughter. I am love. I am joy. I am safe. I am lucky. I am held. Life is good. Making 'I' statements and if I have a meltdown, I go sit on the hay bails. Boundaries are another way of getting back to self, being centered, calming down. Boundaries are important. Rules are to be broken. Rebels raised us, and broke rules so that we could experience something new. Awareness of present, trust the process, let go, and see what happens.

Somatic awareness is a key factor in practicing Gestalt within education. Munyer articulates that,

> It was always about the feelings and sensations. What happens in the adult world is that they have been educated into thinking in stories. It's not about stories, it's about the feelings and sensations in children that are created inside of their physical bodies. What is your physical body saying? This is one of the focuses of Gazebo and Janet Lederman's vision of early childhood development.

Holloman feels that play, music, and touch are all ways in which children express themselves and process emotionally and cognitively. He says,

> Touch is a big one, and it is not just interpersonal touch, but it is contact with the environment itself, such that very young children and infants who are just beginning to transition to crawling, and toddling and standing. They grab a hold of the bark of a tree when they are trying to help themselves to stand up, and notice there is a difference between the density and coarseness. They can't understand this intellectually. It is completely a bodily experience, but they learn that they are softer than tree bark, they are not just learning about tree and tree bark, they are learning about themselves in relationship to.

Holloman continues, saying,

> Part of the concept of Gazebo was developmentally, at all stages
> from birth to the five to six age range, that children would learn
> not just about the environment, but about themselves. They would
> stick their hands in the cold water from the tub, they learn that
> that water is colder than they are. They are not just learning that
> the water is cold, but they are learning about me in relationship
> to. Whereas tree bark is denser than physical body, body is a lot
> denser than water in tub. There is all of this difference that children
> are experiencing in flat ground and steep ground, and climbing
> up stairs and no stairs, and rocks as opposed to grass. There is an
> organizing and a development of the identity of self in relationship
> to environment that is learned through these types of differences,
> that are mediated through the body, primarily through touch.

Likewise, Lederman viewed child development primarily through
her belief that experience precedes cognitive learning. In this way,
experiential learning happens with bringing awareness to the somatic experience. Similarly, Gestalt Practice focuses on experiencing
through the somatic reference points through the awareness of body
and breath. Christine Price describes this relationship between Gestalt
Practice and somatics: "The embodiment aspect of Gestalt practice.
What it means to be in a body. To have a life. Deep delving into
physical awareness." This aspect of Gestalt is inherent to all humans
and particularly to the experience of children.

Children are naturally experiencing life on a somatic level as
learning begins with movement, touch, and sound and evolves
into language and more advanced small and large motor skills and
movements. In this way, a Gestalt facilitator might ask, "Where do
you feel that in your body?" Thus teachers are inviting descriptions
about the student's somatic experience. Teachers can also rely on their
observations of body language, the student's breath, their movement,
and gestures as indications of their states of being. Though somatics

is an entry point, teachers also begin to explore the use of language in Gestalt Practice. Price-Waldrip suggests,

> You can encourage the foreground, 'I see that your breathing looks shallow. Can you breathe deeply?' I tend to pay a lot of attention to body gestures, people's breathing, the color of skin, small gestures that might not be complete. That doesn't mean I don't also pay attention to language, language is also very important. Use this phrase, 'Now, I'm aware of.....' begin to pick out from the foreground what you are paying attention to and not paying attention to.

The foreground may shift to what is coming up in the moment, and a Gestalt process may turn towards the new moment with attention and awareness.

Gestalt Language—Ownership, Naming, Reflecting, Speaking from the Heart

The language instinct is the simplest form of the social expression of the child. Hence, it is a great, perhaps the greatest of all, educational resources.

– John Dewey

Importantly, the use of Gestalt Practice in education requires a closer look at language, as there are many subtle language shifts within the Gestalt methods. Christine Price explores the language aspect of Gestalt Practice by saying,

> Gestalt Practice is a descriptive rather than analytical exploration of what is in the moment rather than an explanation of what it is. Moving towards direct contact with the experience rather than explaining the experience.

Specifically, in Gestalt language, "you" and "it" become "I" statements and suggest self-awareness and self-responsibility. By using

"I" statements, teachers or students are more in contact with their own direct experience. Teachers model Gestalt language by using "I" statements and are more explicit in their demands on children in relation to their own experience. In Gestalt language, the "abstract" becomes "concrete" and the "implicit" becomes "explicit." For example, "I don't want you to hit because...," rather than, "We don't hit here" or "It's against the rules to hit." When using Gestalt language it is useful for the *initiator* to name the issue and to be specific about their needs. Therefore, by using Gestalt language, an individual may find it helpful to identify, name, and take ownership of their emotions.

Wyatt called Gestalt language 'responsible language' when she took it out in the world. She felt that based on her experience with Gestalt, the key was to take responsibility. She says,

> Making 'I' statements, being clear that this is my view, my thought, my feeling and 'you are you' and 'I am me' and being clear about that. Using 'could' instead of 'should' and instead of asking a question make a statement. We are going to lunch and Jonny is in the sandbox. Rather than saying, 'Do you want to wash your hands?' (He is going to say no) Say, 'I would like you to wash your hands, it is lunch time, let's go together.' Always phrasing it to draw attention to what I want to see happen, or what I want to highlight instead of what I don't want. When a child hears 'don't,' they tune out everything afterward.

She suggests keeping the language slanted towards the positive. Instead of, 'Don't climb the fence,' you might ask the child to 'Keep your feet on the ground.' If, for example, someone is climbing the fence, you can make requests by offering parameters. Handl shares that,

> For me, the biggest challenge is using precise language that takes ownership of my own feelings and experience while honoring the other(s) feelings and experience. It's a struggle for me to keep firm boundaries between [self and other] especially when I am 'over'

empathizing with fellow teachers and children. At the basis, as I understand it, is mutual respect, clear communication, responsible communication, and allowing space for all feelings. Also a huge trust in the body as part of the communication of self to self and to others. All of these things resonate with my experiences with children over twenty-five years of time.

The language shifts in Gestalt practice were not imposed dramatically on the children at Gazebo, but are woven in the ways of being with them. Again, this experiential learning provides tools to empower their communication as they practice what is modeled for them. On the other hand, Gestalt language is principally direct and in support of ownership of one's feelings with an emphasis on personal responsibility. Miller suggests, "The language is less directive. During conflict resolutions, children are given more opportunities to do it themselves." Consequently, these subtle wording shifts build a common rhetoric for students to describe and support their experience. The use of Gestalt language subtly encourages a deeper sense of self-responsibility, authenticity, honesty, and clarity of communication.

Within Gestalt, a curiosity is brought to the experience of the moment, and to the language and communication. For example, the 'why' becomes 'how,' so in an educational setting instead of asking, "Why are you doing that?" a teacher might instead ask, "How will this work? How is that for you?" Wyatt describes,

> How to form the 'how' statements? Why aren't you coming to lunch?
> An example is, see what was going on, and kids in transition are not
> ready to go, honoring that and paying attention. 'Wow, what are
> you building? How fast can you run to the lunch table? It doesn't
> get into 'why.' He doesn't want to go and that is his business in
> a way, and they probably react to that in a way when it feels like
> needling, like you are trying to get a justification. The 'why' often
> has that feeling for me.

Wyatt continues,

> Gestalt is responsible language. You know how sometimes you can
> feel the statement behind the question.'Do you want to wash the
> dishes?', 'I want you to' is taking ownership over whatever it is that
> spurred the question. The questions comes from something so it is
> getting to that source place and naming that first as a way to take
> responsibility. The question feels like it is just throwing responsibil-
> ity out on you. Is there as statement behind that question? 'Why'
> becomes 'how' because 'why' is kind of useless and irrelevant and
> personal and none of your business. When you ask 'why' you can
> always get, 'Because I want to,' and that can be really true. It is also
> there is something about 'why,' and I know it can be coming from
> a real curious place but, it is also a bit like explain yourself from a
> justify yourself place, and the 'how' is more accepting and curious.

Davey speaks to Gestalt language in this statement,

> The idea of being completely present in the task/experience at hand.
> 'How are you feeling? Angry? What is that anger about? What are
> you going to do to relieve the anger? What has to be done now?
> Did you hurt yourself? What is that hurt? What will make this
> feel better?' Conversely, being present with your peers and active
> listening. When learning, I try to be committed to the present and
> focusing on the experience as a whole. I can remember things more
> clearly if I think about all of the senses and experiences. Asking
> myself questions.

When asked, "What tools were you given to describe or process
emotions? Did this help you in your later life?," Davey replied that,

> Gazebo and the teachers taught me to communicate more clearly
> and owning the feelings as my own and being able to categorize
> them. They gave me simple prompts like, 'I feel angry because....',
> or 'I feel happy because...' Owning the emotions as my own and
> being able to communicate them (because someone was listening)
> has been invaluable in my relationships.

This may seem like a lot of constructs to follow, but on the other hand the framework of language can be a support and doesn't have to be complex. Baldwin feels,

> The great thing about Gestalt is the simplicity and clarity of the language. The 'I' statements make life easier in our communications with each other and come in at a very early age. It is speaking, having a child speak for themselves, more and more of that simpleness is coming into the big picture. Rather than saying stuff for them, it is encouraging them to make their 'I' statements and to speak for themselves.

This curiosity in Gestalt and the language allows the child to stay in their experience and the teacher to support them without changing it. Curiosity brings greater awareness, and allows teacher and student to notice what is going on for them and others. For example, London felt the importance of modeling the use of language with questions like,

> How is that for you? I don't like it when..... Can you see their eyes are red, pale, crying? Do you see how he is crying? What you did, that is the impact? I understand you're angry. This has an impact on her.

One important question in Gestalt is, "What are you noticing right now?" It is such a simple question, but can bring about so much more inquiry into the entire experience.

When given the time and space to experience them, children begin to identify feelings and name them. In this way, children take their own emotional temperature and mirror each other's feelings with astute neutrality that is clear and not loaded with any judgment. For example, one day at Gazebo there was a girl named Naima, who was so sad all day because she missed her mommy. It was one of the first days in which she was without her. Naima had come with her best friend Olivia, who had been coming to the school for some time already, and was very independent. Naima cried and cried and the only thing she wanted was to be cuddled by a teacher and to have them read to her. Olivia was playing independently and watched her friend from a distance. Then, from time to time Olivia would move in, during calm moments and say, "You're not crying." Naima said, "I'm not crying, but I'm a little bit sad." Olivia would look at the teacher and restate this as a literal observation of feelings. There was no qualification as she was just commenting on what she saw. This was such an honest interaction between these two young people that involved an expression of different emotions and a sincere noticing. In this way, simply naming the feelings is a foundation as it takes getting in touch with them first to begin to make observations and statements about them.

Reflecting feelings is an important aspect of Gestalt language. The ability to notice the feelings of another person and *reflect* them back to them without qualifications and judgments is a profound practice. This can be done by simply naming what emotion you notice in the other person as demonstrated in the previous story. "You seem sad," or "I notice you seem angry." Also, being a *reflector* can be done by simply saying back to the person what they said in their words or in your own. For instance, "I hear you saying that...," or "What I understand from what you said is that..." This practice has been used in other forms of therapy dialogue such as Nonviolent Communication. Thus, reflecting back can filter out the judgments of the witness, as they reflect what they notice or think, which sometimes differs from what the the other is really experiencing. The reflector isn't trying to fix, change or put a value on their statements, they simply reflect back what the initiator is expressing. Holloman shares,

> The other way that is important is it is important that teachers can find a way to explore so they can be what Dick [Price] called reflectors of an experience. For teachers, being there in such a way that space is held for someone or something to express itself, because everything that is expressed in a game has meaning. It means something, and if we can help that meaning reveal itself, the potential for learning growth and development goes way up.

Essentially that is what Gestalt is about—it is an awareness practice that prioritizes the development of awareness, because the idea is the more aware we are the more likely we are to gather information and learn and grow and develop.

Charles emphasizes the use of the word "appropriate" as a touchstone for behavior. The word "appropriate" may have different connotations depending on the developmental stage of the child, but it provides a benchmark in language in which the child and adult may use as a reference for their choices. For instance, Charles states, "From four to five we really encouraged dialogue instead of physical expression of the conflict." Therefore as children begin to develop their language, they can begin to increasingly apply Gestalt language.

Application with Children—Gestalt Approaches to Conflict Resolution

Lucy's Rock (Arfur's Gestalt Stories)

Lucy: (runs over with great frustration and excitement on her face) Arfur!… Dylan won't give me my rock.

Arfur: Tell Dylan.

Lucy: I did and he still won't give it to me.

Arfur: What do you want me to do?

Lucy: Get the rock from Dylan!

Arfur: I will go over with you and work with both of you, will that be okay with you?

Lucy: Okay! (We found Dylan and he's feeling like something is going to happen. Lucy runs to him and demands her rock)

Lucy: Dylan give me my rock.

Dylan: No!

Lucy: (begins to raise her arm to hit Dylan).

Arfur: (quickly announces) Lucy stop! My fear is that you want to hit Dylan. Is that true?

Lucy: Yes!, I do (lowers her arm and turns toward Arfur).

Lucy: See, he won't give me my rock.

Arfur: Dylan is that Lucy's rock?

Dylan: Yeah!

Arfur: How come you don't want to give Lucy her rock?

Dylan: Because.

Arfur: Well guys how would you like to settle this rock drama?

Lucy: I know, let's look for a rock for Dylan.

Arfur: What about that Dylan, would you like to look for another rock and give that rock back to Lucy?

Dylan: Okay!

(Dylan hands the rock over to Lucy and he takes her other hand and they go off together in search of a rock for Dylan.)

According to the Gestalt value of keeping the past and future in perspective, teachers using Gestalt Practice are mindful about their role in conflict situations. The teachers at Gazebo did not interrupt conflicts based on expectations and values about behavior, but rather let the children's behavior be the guide; while still ensuring everyone's physically safety. A fundamental Gestalt principle that the student, or initiator, is the expert on their own experience.

London says, "I trust what they [the children] are saying is pure, pristine feeling that they express. What is the impact on me?" Classen also suggests that,

> One of the components of conflict resolution for me is, first, that adults don't have a set expectation of how it needs to be completed. Our sense of justice or fairness doesn't need to be imposed on the conflict because it's about the process and not about the resolution.

Having the people in the conflict get in touch with their feelings and be seen, and to get in touch with themselves, and hopefully have them in some way feel acknowledged.

Additionally, when examining the conflict before choosing to engage in it, Gazebo staff members used the meter that if students have matched energies, then the conflict is allowed to progress. This does not always mean equal in size, but equal in energy both physically and emotionally. Regardless, teachers move closer to any potential conflict and provide a safety in proximity, and implement a practice referred to at Esalen as *holding space*.

So, the choice for a teacher in any conflict is, "Should I step in and get involved?" The answer is entirely intuitive, depending on the individual and situation, as to when to step in, though it is useful to closely watch the children's reactions. For example, if two students are throwing dirt at each other but laughing, the teacher might stay back. Conversely, if a student is crying or showing signs that a situation is not okay with them, then the teacher can move closer and begin to facilitate a process to support the students. Regardless, teachers learn to stop themselves from preventing conflicts that are not problematic for the children or those that can be resolved by children independently. Cheda feels that,

When children learned to resolve their own conflicts, they moved on more quickly. When adults get involved, they often tend to extend the conflict. The hurt feelings seem to last longer between those directly involved.

Using Gestalt Practice methods, the teacher becomes the facilitator. This means coaching students through their conflicts and allowing them to steer the problem-solving process. Cheda says about Gestalt and conflict resolution,

I loved the idea of having the children first attempt to resolve their issues without the interference of adult teachers. Simple rules: no biting and no weapons. When instructors did get involved, we often asked the child to reflect on what the other in the conflict was feeling. Their motivation, or reasoning in the conflict.

In this way, students begin to learn self-awareness and empathy through conflict and the conflict becomes a teacher rather than a hindrance to be avoided. Kevin Harvey says,

> Learning to communicate effectively is an entirely necessary skill for humans of all ages. Most adults I know are still learning this skill, and learning to apply it to conflict resolution will help all relationships, be them personal or work. I can only imagine how wonderful it would be if our society engrained this information at such a young age. We could learn to respect each other.

Though conflict is not encouraged, it occurs naturally within everyday human interactions and an openness and common language can make conflict a learning experience rather than a negative interface. Charles says, "In those relationships where I have conflicts that move through them fully, a lot of trust is built and it is bonding." In this way, Gestalt Practice offers entry points to engage in human emotions that are often denied. Thus conflict can be illuminating, if handled skillfully. Holloman feels that,

> Conflict can be productive if it is dialogically-based [based in dialogue]—meaning if the two people in conflict are as clear as they can be about where it is they are coming from but also care about the learning of the other. For instance, if I am in conflict with you if I am just bullying my way through the conflict, I don't care about what you learn or how your behavior shifts and changes. I just want to be right and exercise my power within the field and to heck with you and that conflict never is resolved in that case. If conflict is dailogically-based then I want you to learn and grow and develop because of the potential for us to work together. For me to understand where you are coming from and for me to potentially learn something from you goes way up and our synergy can then

create a whole that is greater than the sum of the two parts. The potential for lifelong use is there, if they have an example and a heartfelt sense of the efficacy of that example.

Kevin Harvey reports that,

The Gazebo staff teaches us through their own living example and sharing effective communication tools with us. I love watching as each of our family members struggle and utilize Gazebo's respect and appreciation of the child's needs to formulate an approach of meeting everyone's needs with the least intrusion on the individuals.

Barnes shares,

I love the emphasis on conflict resolution—having this be an integral element of Gazebo makes me more aware of it as a parent and take these lessons into the home. Having a continuum from school, to come to community is so important. Being here has made me more aware of how I parent, that we are mirrors to our children. I've adjusted how I speak to Olivia, how to foster her own problem-solving, how to step back and not try to control everything. I like how I've become more conscious of HOW I talk to Olivia, how we communicate as a family.

If choosing to interact in a conflict, Wyatt suggests that,

Getting down on the kids' level and having the kids talk to each other about it. In any conflicts, I would place my body in between them, not directly but I wouldn't place towards one or the other, and I wouldn't stand over them because I am the authority figure and they are going to want me to solve it for them, so it is more about getting down and a process of getting closer. If I notice conflict is growing over there, I would get down low, and sometimes my presence is enough, if not then I am right there. I am not there to police them, because you see sometimes conflict started and they see an adult and go, 'It's his fault, it wasn't me.' Then it's about hearing and supporting each child to speak their truth and for the other to hear it.

Subsequently, supporting a dialogue with self and others is an important aspect of a Gestalt process. In this way, as conflict arises, facilitators move in close, approach at the student's level, and support a dialogue that maintains a safe environment. Teachers engage in questions that point students towards noticing themselves and others such as, "How is that working for you? I imagine that hurts. What might work better? What other choices do you have? I see that you are crying. Would you like to talk about it or do you need space?"

However, with preverbal students, the teacher might encourage a hand gesture to indicate a feeling or suggest a child move away from a stressful situation to get space depending on their needs. With respect to what is age appropriate, teachers guide the process rather than lead it and offer support for a healthy dialogue. From this safety students develop "response-ability" when given the accountability in problem-solving. Charles indicates the physical cue in preverbal children,

> I think to emphasize that before they have a good command of language, because with the four-year-olds, I would encourage them to use their words. It was more for the toddlers. What is she saying to you? Do you see she is crying? They make their own translation of it.

The teacher's role in conflict situations is in support of the children in being near, present and available, by providing alternative choices and language, or by simply offering comfort and acknowledgment. Forman says,

> The children had the space to work things out together, to learn to solve conflicts, to learn that they could take care of many of their needs, and that there was a subtle yet very present circle surrounding them and there for them. When conflicts arose, they could be played out, observed by teachers paying attention that no harm was done. The children weren't rescued from their moments, their emotions weren't snatched away. They did their walking or crawling, and had their time to cry. There was always a teacher nearby, a lap to crawl into, arms to wrap around them.

As a result, students know an adult is there to support them. Eizner shares,

> I think children do not know how to deal with conflict because they are exposed to different types of parenting. One is those parents who have different types of inappropriate relationships that involve domestic violence and aggression during conflict and those who avoid conflict. Most parents do not know how to deal with conflict. Exposing children and allowing them to deal with conflict is what is going to help them in the long run. To know what to do and to be assertive when it comes to resolving conflict. Avoiding conflict is not a lesson. Dealing with conflict inappropriately is not the answer. I think children need to be exposed to experiences so they will know how to deal with those as they grow older, at their age, and then as they grow up.

In addition, with Gestalt Practice, children learn to navigate intrapersonal and interpersonal awareness by noticing both their own direct experience and how they affect others. Interpersonal skills for students include learning to set their own boundaries, and respect other people's boundaries. In this way, a teacher might offer a child support in voicing their feelings about how another child's behavior affects them. They might present them with some language such as "I don't like that," or "Stop it, that hurts," or they may simply show them a gesture they can use that represents "No" or "Stop." Then, the teacher might invite the other child to notice the consequences of their behavior and facilitate some sort of communication or acknowledgement of the other's feelings.

Though the Gazebo philosophy leans towards students engaging in independent problem-solving, the teacher acts as a witness and a mirror to the process that is unfolding. For example, the teacher may say, "She is crying. What is she saying? You seem/look/sound upset. What do you want to do? What do you feel when….? Can you tell them that?" Healthy boundaries are encouraged and a facilitator can assist children to create them simply by inviting them to notice themselves and others in these situations or suggesting appropriate choices. With Gestalt Practice, students have permission to fully explore their many states of being and they are invited to notice how they impact others around them. Holloman says,

> We would bring a great deal of attention to what each child was experiencing, often these things would take some time, we would be in a conflict situation with a couple of kids for thirty-forty minutes. We would act in certain ways as mediators unlike what happens in mediation situations with adults, but we would do our best to bring attention to the one child. 'You know when you called the other one a 'stupid dummy' the other one began to cry. What do you notice, and did you want that? How does that affect you when you notice that?' Often it was quite difficult to get children to self-reflect in a certain way where they would actually begin to become more cognizant of the affect of their behavior on each other. In conflict, what we didn't do was distract from or take it away. What we did do was create as best we could a situation that was safe and that was symmetrical, such that at least the potential for some kind of learning or information gathering could happen between kids.

Classen reports,

> The same is true for the way Gazebo works with conflict, they need a safe space to work through conflict. One of the things I think is really important is that the space plays a role in it. Also, there is so much less conflict because there is so much more space and because the children have the freedom to move and eat and be how they want to be. One thing that I noticed is different in other schools is that because they don't want to do what they are told to do at that time, but they are being required to go against their wishes and body and do it anyhow, that's when a lot of conflict arises. Conflict at Gazebo takes out that idea. Then conflict that occurs is between kids, and what that is is them learning how to interact socially and communicate. It is common that there can be

hitting and biting, as that is part of what they need to do to learn how to get their needs met and get the connection that they want. Conflict is treated as a totally normal healthy part of learning. There is no shame in being sad or angry or exuberant. We are not going to praise the hell out of them for being super sweet and we are not going to frown on them if they are yelling a lot. Instead I would use, 'I' statements, teach by doing, and by pointing out. Also a part of this is that they can eat, drink, sleep, or be where they want to be, and this is helping them get more in touch with their bodies. If they are getting fussy offer them something to eat, teach them that part of their emotional life is learning how to care for their bodies.

Application with Adults—Self-Inquiry in Relationship

We work on ourselves in order to help others, but also we help others in order to work on ourselves. The whole path seems to be about developing curiosity, about looking out and taking an interest in all the details of our lives and in our immediate environment.

– Pema Chödrön

It is important to consider how teachers can use Gestalt Practice for their own self-inquiry and how it provided support for the Gazebo staff members in their own conflict resolution. There were several processes that provided a framework for teachers and staff to develop and grow through the use of Gestalt such as daily check-ins and Gestalt process groups. There were also organic ways in which Gestalt was applied throughout the day in terms of self-reflection and/or communication with students or other teachers.

For teachers, it may be important to examine their own impulses to interfere, as to avoid *projections* from their past, shadowing the student's experience. Wyatt suggests,

> "I don't know how anyone being put in an environment with children cannot have thoughts or remembrances about their own childhood. But that could be problematic and there is something about being too caught up in the past and 'back there' and it is my belief that it is the past and all lifetimes and I have the opportunity to address anything in the present moment, all of that is there."

Traditionally, Gazebo teachers were encouraged to notice what children they had difficulties with, if they might be triggered in ways that were connected to their personal life or past, and to be present with those feelings. Thompson-Clark asks, "What are our beliefs about how children learn? How does Gestalt inform the teacher/facilitator as they allow each child to develop their own consciousness?" In this way, Gazebo teachers might reflect about their intentions for involvement in conflict, or their desire for teaching outcomes, and if these might be a projection of their own issues rather than being about the child or the situation. Wyatt says,

> I think the issue that I am passionate about at Gazebo are issues that I needed to address or heal in myself. The empowerment issue and self-esteem were a big learning and growth for me in Gazebo. Giving myself what I give the kids and that was a healing a growth for me.

Handl shares,

> I also appreciate the process time with other teachers, outside of the Park—our monthly sessions with Dorothy [Charles]. Though they can be full of emotion, they help to bridge conflict and understanding. I also like the model of weather report/check-ins with teachers, and the idea that most adult conversation either needs to include the children or be taken out of the Park (I still fail at this pretty regularly). I do feel like we need to speak with, not about the children, even when conversing with their parents, as we would with any adult.

There are reports that Lederman mandated that adult personal process was kept out of the school routines in order to keep the children's needs first. Teacher self-inquiry was encouraged, but it was recommended that a teacher's issues are better addressed during individual or group process. Because Esalen is a place of exploration and healing, many of the Gazebo staff members used Gestalt Practice in their lives outside of teaching. Naturally, Gazebo staff and interns often came to Esalen for healing, and often they found Gestalt Practice opened their awareness of not just the children, but of themselves. Holloman remembers,

> Janet would meet with us every week and we would talk about the challenges that we faced and she would work with us. She would help us discover what was arising in us as teachers that was keeping us from being in as nonjudgmental a place as possible without sacrificing our seat as teachers or our capacity or our ability to keep the space safe and appropriate. How could she help us gain insight into our own *reactivity* that would come up around the children's behavior? Because kids are very provocative, they say things and do things that adults don't give themselves space to express. In order for us to keep the space safe and appropriate to the emerging capacities of the kids, which were very sensed very felt very physical and very expressive, what was it that we needed

to look at in ourselves in order to be appropriate, effective space holders for kids (while at the same time assuring that there was safety and appropriateness within the space)? Janet would meet with us and sometimes we would have a real reactivity from something we witnessed, and it was important for us to discover what are the barriers that we carry that make us less effective as teachers. Having a Gestalt-based structure for helping us understand our experiences as teachers is a very important aspect of what is going on in the entire learning field. It is not just the children that are learning, but the children interacting with the environment and with teachers, and that is creating the quality of the experiencing and the potential learning in the '*field*' as a whole.

Holloman infers that there is an energetic "field" in the learning environment. The idea of the "field" is also a Gestalt-based concept that each one of us is part of a bigger system and affect each other in seen and unseen ways constantly. Douce describes this concept at Gazebo as the Park being the field. "It is a field and that is often not looked at. If you punish a child it creates an effect on the whole field." The suggestion is that the teachers and students are learning together within a space where growth and development are occurring simultaneously both individually and as a group. There are opportunities to learn about one's self in relationship to others, in observation of our *reactivities*, in relationship to the field; it is often in relationship we learn about ourselves.

Charles, who both worked at Gazebo as a teacher and also as a Gestalt facilitator for the Gazebo staff over the years, states that,

> Confluence is one of the barriers to contact in the Gestalt model, think of two rivers that flow together, that is a relationship that doesn't tolerate differences. If I think it is not okay to hit so and so, I am not going to tolerate any place in you where you want to defend yourself or explain. It is just black and white, or right or wrong, and I am the grown-up, and because I said so. That helps someone to develop in such a way. How we learn about who we are is that we have caregivers who are curious and interested.

In this way, coming to the experience of being triggered by a child or a game, first the teacher may need to identify their own feelings and the charge around the incident. Then, after working through that in the appropriate context, the teacher can then come to the same or similar situation with less judgment and personal charge around the situation and therefore more curiosity and space to allow the child's process.

"Gestalt is relevant to the teacher in two ways," says Holloman,

> One, the experientially-based orientation in terms of how we deal with each individual child, and group of kids, it is just an orientation that recognizes the fullness of the capacity of the different levels of the nervous system. So as a teacher, one needs to understand the experiential basis of all learning. If that is in place, then more abstract learning like learning about numbers and quantity and learning to read falls into place more quickly if the foundation, the experiential foundation of life itself, is there. There is a trust that develops in the process of learning itself, if it is connected to play, if it is connected to an organic interest.

Charles adds, "How do I learn *how* to learn? I think that is another thing the philosophy really supports."

Relational Response-Ability and Awareness

"When experience and learning are partners, resourcefulness follows."

– JL

At Gazebo, the students were given a great deal of responsibility in their own choices and that empowered them to learn through experience rather than being "taught." Vivian Danzer, original Gazebo teacher, further describes the teacher's role in conflict resolution by saying,

> The adult facilitator, with such a vantage point, has the opportunity to sensitively move in closer to potentially 'track' the child

at opportune moments, reflecting the child's experience back to him, holding the space, creating a container for safe expression of struggle within or struggle with another.

Of course, the teacher's form of facilitation may differ depending on the student's developmental ages and stages.

A child's emotional process can often be an internal struggle that requires intrapersonal skills. As a result, facilitators try to create a space where both student's thinking mind and feeling mind can be heard and respected. Children are individuals with different emotional needs and they carry their own set of emotional issues from their life experience. Teachers can notice the manifestations of anger or frustration and offer the child choices such as asking for space, moving away, releasing their feelings by crying or hitting a soft pillow or ball rather than another child. On the other hand, a teacher may see that a student is sad or alone and needs nurturing and may offer them their company.

In Lederman's book *Anger in the Rocking Chair*, she showed the importance of being responsive to children's individual needs depending on different situations. In one example she says to a student, "I take your hand. You let me. You do not pull away. Together we walk over to the rocking chair. You sit on my lap. We talk."[2] On the contrary, in another situation she says, "Children, you can yell at this rocking chair. You can kick it."[3] The openness to experiment is an important concept for teachers using Gestalt Practice as a tool to respond to student's emotional needs.

In this way, McLeod states, "Gestalt methods at Gazebo meant letting a child rid themselves of their emotional pain and their frustrations. For me this meant an allowing of whatever they were processing to come forth." Hence, a child's feelings are given space yet different approaches to expression are necessary depending on the child and their needs and the situation.

For example, it may be that a child needs their words to be heard and validated, or they may want to be alone, or they may need to channel their aggression in a way that is not hurtful to themselves or others. With awareness and mindfulness, teachers navigate how to help the child with their expression. Most importantly, teachers give permission for students to inhabit all of the feelings that may arise in their body and offer them tools for deepened awareness of their intrapersonal and interpersonal states of being. Douce feels,

> If you can't scream or you can't cry or you can't show your frustration, you're educating the children for the internal health problems they are going to have blocking all those things. The Gestalt really fit into everything, supporting the feelings, listening.

Munyer says,

> It was about being authentic. I now use my language and intelligence working with humans and horses. I know that's the option. Will Schutz taught me that we have choices. To be responsible for choices is part of Gestalt. You can use anything as an opportunity to learn something. If something doesn't happen the way you want it, then I think this is a great opportunity for me, I can learn something about myself, and I learn something about others.

Learning Healthy Boundaries

When my daughter was about three-years-old, we were on the Esalen lawn playing with friends and another little boy her age. He was coming in to take a bite of food off of her plate, and she firmly, yet gently put her hand up in a stop position. The woman who was sitting with us was very moved at my daughter's ability to set a personal physical boundary that was loving yet firm. I think this, in many ways, is the goal of healthy boundaries—to be able to communicate your personal needs in a loving way, without a lot of emotional charge, but with clarity.

On the other hand, there are emotional boundaries that arise for children and these become more relationally complex. Price-Waldrip remarks,

> I still work with my empathy boundaries and how much I take on other people's pain. I was with the kids, watching something happening, and someone would be swinging or going down the hill. I would think, 'That person is going to get hurt and I know that they are going to end up crying.' I would get mad at the adults because they weren't stopping it. 'I know that that person is going

to end up upset,' and was thinking, 'Nobody is stopping them. They are going to end up crying,' and I would be like, 'Oh no, I have to watch you cry.'

Consequently, when learning empathy, it can be helpful to learn empathy boundaries. At Gazebo, children collectively or individually tuned into each other's emotions. So, it became not only about the child who was upset, but how the situation could have potential for growth and learning for everyone. Children develop empathy by noticing if another child is upset and often many kids begin to gather and develop a building concern for a distressed child. Conversely, the upset child might need their personal space and set a boundary for the other children not to get involved. Children sometimes sense this or boundaries might need to be set, but there is a collective sensitivity to the emotional context.

Wyatt suggests, "To see where they are. To know where I am. That Gestalt—that shuttling, to see where they are, to know where I am, and obviously not putting where I am on them." Accordingly, over-empathizing with another can take an individual out of their own experience. Charles states that,

> When I work, one of the predominant things I work with in my groups and individually is that Esalen is filled with people that have an accusative pattern, they have learned to see their lives not through their own center and experiencing, but through other people's eyes. The result of that is often shame. It comes up as a theme over and over again, so what I have thought about, is that lots of people come here because their personal relationships aren't going well, or they need to come and reinvent themselves because their lives are unsatisfying. Those two things are outcomes of not having a strong and connected sense of self. We develop in relationship. Gregory Bateson said, 'It takes two to know one.' And if my limited research study of thirty years now has any merit, it is really important to be empathic and to care about other people and to be

able to see situations from other people's perspectives. What I can tell you is that I look at the groups of people that I work with who are having trouble and struggling, and that is not their *growing edge*, their growing edge is to stay with their own experiencing and that is what Gazebo taught or modeled or supported so beautifully. There was an acknowledgment of the relationship, and the other kids, and the health and safety, and taking turns, and there was also at first that sense of, 'I am a separate person with boundaries and I have a right to be with you.' It is harder to do it backwards. My business thrives on the fact that it is harder to go the other way. Gazebo is an antidote to that.

Regardless of the situation, there seems to be a genuine flow of energy between the children and their interest in each other's emotions—an energetic "field" of awareness. In a sense, this is part of the physical and emotional boundaries in both being able to give space around emotional upset, or understanding of what is yours and what belongs to someone else. Eizner states that,

> If you are working with kids then I like to think of preventive psychology. Maybe because of my profession working with people with difficulties with confidence and low self-esteem with violence and lack of respect or boundaries. A child having a temper tantrum and the child maybe wanting someone who could be WITH the child and be present with the kids without judging them, and be supportive of their emotional state without telling them to stop crying or screaming or changing their experience. Providing a space where it is okay for them to process and for them to be themselves and to be unhappy.

Being sensitive to others, being supportive to a friend, and honoring your personal needs are all part of learning about healthy boundaries. There is no right or wrong within these contexts, it is about creating a balance between boundaries, empathy, and a trust in the process.

Experiential Learning and Life Skills—Bridging Past and Future

Esalen is a community that has been on the leading edge in psychology, self-inquiry, massage therapy, somatic studies, Gestalt—and it was the birthplace of Gazebo. Thompson-Clark says,

> I saw a unique laboratory for observing how young children acquire the information, skills and attitudes pertaining to the infinite relationships between living things on a finite planet. Or stated in different way, in context with Esalen Institute's mission, removed were preconceived notions of what a school should be, and allowed was the development of human potential.

Esalen provided a resource for Gazebo and a network of individuals familiar with Gestalt concepts—a culture that supported the use of Gestalt Practice with children. Gazebo Park is a special setting ripe for adapting Gestalt principles, yet there is no formula for the application of Gestalt Practice in an educational setting. Gazebo Park School has evolved in response to social and cultural norms, changing global needs and population it has served.

Lucia Horan Drummond, former Gazebo student, 5Rhythms® teacher, and my sister, shares about being a Gazebo student by saying,

> Kids were learning to be in touch with their emotions and slow down and express them. We, as Esalen kids, learned good behaviors because we learned how to be in touch with emotions and feel our emotions; we grew up learning skills that other people had to relearn as adults.

Rather than avoiding difficult feelings and situations, Gestalt Practice in education can be used to experience and express the full spectrum of emotions, allow for productive conflict and communication, and to grow through self-awareness and skillful dialogue.

Gazebo students were lucky to have an outdoor lab for a classroom that was a virtual child-size adventure land. Without the limitations that too often exist at other schools, Gazebo provided an excellent teacher-student ratio, and an outdoor environment for children that allowed for full somatic experience. Also, Gazebo was different from other early childhood settings in that, aside from natural transitions of the day, (snack, lunch, naps) there are no strict timetables for the children. Gazebo was a rare and radical program with Esalen Institute as its grounds for growth.

Lederman says in *Anger in the Rocking Chair*,

> Children, you live in a chaotic world. Your world can expand beyond your chaos. The first step in this process is for you to touch your chaos. You must touch your chaos; you must live through your chaotic experiences in the classroom. You must not avoid these experiences. So often the superstructure of school does not permit this kind of contact. Here and now you are free; you are free to come into contact with your chaos.[4]

Instead of adopting the cultural norm of, "Don't cry and it will be okay," Lederman saw that using Gestalt in education honors all feelings and offers methods of their expression that will benefit students as they move through life. Handl conveys,

> I also think the values of care, consciousness and relationship are enhanced when there is freedom to explore what is happening internally with what is happening externally. To find our own points of connection, fear, wonder, joy, sadness, and love.

Gestalt Practice is a way of being in the world where past and future become here and now, implicit becomes explicit, where general becomes specific, and where children develop life skills for authentic communication.

The challenge is applying Gestalt Practice and making it relevant and appropriate for each individual learning community. In doing so, it is important to look at each person and situation with curiosity, with new eyes, as unique. In sharing these stories and essential principles, the invitation is to embody the ideas in a way that is appropriate for each child and situation. Lederman used to say, "All you ever teach is your own style," as she described the act of different personalities creating different approaches to teaching in the same setting. It is also vital to see the child as unique in his or her needs and even in their desire for learning. Through exploration and discovery, children can be seen as individuals and allowed their own journeys in their education.

In essence, the application of Gestalt Practice in education is intuitive and full of possibilities. There are many opportunities to learn Gestalt practice. Gestalt workshops are still offered at Esalen and there are Gestalt Institutes around the world. Christine Price and Dorothy Charles have a center in California called Tribal Ground in which they share this work. Teachers/facilitators may find that simple awareness is a gift to their own learning and the way they hold space for children. While, conflict is inevitable, it can be a valuable part of the learning process. As conflict arises, teachers may draw upon tools such as choosing to stay distant or move close, reflecting, or encouraging children to listen and to reflect back, to set healthy boundaries, asking the children to speak from their hearts.

Dick Price used to say to take the elevator down from the head to the heart, and in many ways, this is what the teachers at Gazebo were asking of the students and each other; even in conflict. Munyer says,

> I carried Lucia in my arms when she was born. We did a whole ceremony when Lucia was born. Those are the things that touched hearts, and we cried. I now see this consciousness. Ceremony is a living Gestalt. That is heart. Gestalt is from the heart.

Gestalt Practice is about the experience, through the present moment, through breath and dialogue, through witnessing, reflecting, assuming responsibility, respecting boundaries, and allowing what exists to exist. It is also a practice in being–in being present, authentic, and aware of mind and body. Essentially from that place of awareness, people of all ages can communicate from the heart.

Nature Education/Outdoor Education

Have reverence for all living things.

– Selig Morgenrath (1909-1977) Designer, Architect and Builder,
Esalen Institute and Gazebo Park

Gazebo Park at Esalen Institute

Rollie Pollies, Snails and Worms

Children have a fascination with insects. I have spent whole
mornings looking for rollie pollies [pill bugs] with toddlers
at Gazebo. It is an absolute exploration and when they are
found, there is a lot of learning getting to know these little
bugs. Inevitably, as children let the rollie pollies crawl around

on their hands and arms, we engage in conversations about why they might roll into a ball, and why they may not at any given time. The conversation can lead into their shape, their exoskeleton, and their adaptations and eating habits. Similarly, with worm exploration, the compost can become the fertile classroom as children begin to ask questions about what worms eat and what they poop. The cycle of composting and decomposition emerges through these conversations; not to mention a little worm tickling. Often the children want to hunt for snails, and when we talk about what they eat, they gain an understanding that they eat our good garden plants. So, as an alternative, the children create snail habitats or mini terrariums in which they choose edibles and housing for the snails. These animal explorations can be super fun and engaging for children and they show amazing focus in their interest in learning about the natural world. It is a joy to spend a morning along for the ride on an animal journey and offer books or materials to support their joy in learning.

Being outside I had the space to be a child and to run wild and free, to learn with living things around me. In the outdoor environment, children learn physical skill such as balance and muscular growth, yet they also learn awareness of surroundings. While listening to birds and wind, watching the sky change, feeling the texture of the dirt under their toes, their entire system is engaged in a learning through their sensory experience. As children at Gazebo, we were given the chance to be in touch with our bodies. We could feel the sun or wind on our bodies and we learned how to listen to those bodies, to understand what it means to take care of those bodies. I was able to learn about water by getting wet, and what being wet meant to my body. By responding to a sensation of cold or hot by getting a jacket, moving to the shade, or saying aloud to a teacher that you feel those things so you can get help in getting what you need. This resourcefulness supported connection to the earth and to ourselves. Gazebo was a place in which children had the space to explore this connection.

In my experience outside of Gazebo, I found myself looking for preschool programs for my daughter, and what I saw was plastic toys and play structures; and often not one living thing to water, climb on, or interact with. This worried me and it felt like a big loss. In many preschools today, and certainly into the elementary and upper grades, I feel the loss of the ability to move while learning. For young children, being able to physically explore—experience privacy, hiding places, playing in open spaces, learning to walk up and down on uneven ground, crawling around on big hills, feeling shade from trees, and digging in dirt—engages them in life in a fuller way. Playing in the dirt may sound simple, but more and more research supports outdoor education as being healthy for a child's development.

Being in nature has so many benefits for all ages groups. Sarah Harvey suggests,

> Having reverence for the outdoors instills wisdom in children that can only come from contact with nature. Taking time to think about respect for others and yourself comes from being grounded, which for me also comes from nature. All of these elements—emotional literacy, conflict resolution, work hand in hand to create this awareness in humanity for the world around us.

Likewise, eco-literacy, beginning at a young age, brings children awareness of our earth, and teaches how to be a land steward, becoming a naturalist, an early ecologist and conservationist, or even an environmental activist. Understanding there is a connection between all living systems is the first step to knowing your impact. By caring about nature and the environment, children become empowered to make changes for the better, and to be more respectful of all forms of life. Delevett, feels "The connection to nature was really important. There is some correlation to learning to take care of nature to life matters." In this way, I believe nature education is also peace education in bringing awareness to ourselves and our relationships to the earth and its fragile ecology.

Miller describes her view of nature education at Gazebo,

> What I see happening at the Gazebo is adults and children live together on the earth and how people take care of the earth and each other. The adults take care of the environment, and children are part of the environment. The adults are working with animals and plants. Part of that is because you're not specifically trying to teach cognitive skills, but they are learning to be curious, sage and caring about the world and each other and that is more important than learning colors and numbers and they will get that if they feel safe. They are learning how to live together.

There are many possibilities for developing curriculum related to the environment. There are countless benefits of being in nature—mental, physical and spiritual. Whether you call it nature education or outdoor education, whether you approach it as a science class or as a rite of passage, whether it is in a park, an urban street, or a wilderness area, the fundamentals are simply an openness to be outside and to get to know the earth.

Fostering a healthy connection with the earth provides an opportunity for learning about respecting life, the cycles of life, and caring for the earth with reverence. Respect and responsibility are learned through work and play. However, it is not just outdoor play on a playground or park, but the free play within unstructured environments that gives the imagination space to grow. Children love to be outside, and they love dramatic play. When those two elements are combined there is no limit to the fun! The learning that can occur through self-directed play is more relevant and intrinsic than being told when and what to learn. Early childhood environments often rely on activities that are led by a teacher yet students instinctually resist the control of adults. In an outdoor environment, if created for the children, the need for adult intervention is curtailed and the simplicity of play provides rich experiential learning for children. By allowing students to explore and play, adults such as parents and teachers offer children choice and a freedom that young children desire and long for but are often not given.

Emergent curriculum will be discussed more in the chapter about play, but essentially the design is centered around inquiry-based learning. The teacher follows the child's interest and provides resources to support their learning. This is how the curriculum develops and evolves in the moment in the outdoor setting. For instance, when a student shows an interest, the teacher provides resources for that student's interest. In this way, if a child loves to search for rollie pollie bugs, a Gazebo teacher might offer the child a scientific book showing illustrations of the bugs. If the child's curiosity continues, teachers could help them by reading aloud to learn the names of the insects. Then they might take a pen and pad and draw the species with the child. Later, the child might teach their friends about these insects on subsequent adventures.

The Environment

The environment is there to maximize the body experiences....it has slopes grades, terraces, and many textures to give a varied body experience from moment to moment. It is an environment that Rewards the child for every movement.

– JL

Eco-literacy, eco-education, eco-curriculum, sustainability, going green, reclaiming, re-using, forest schools, adventure schools, outdoor education. These are current trends that Gazebo had been practicing decades ahead of the curve. Lederman said that life is not separate from the learning, and life on the farm, in nature, in the outdoors can set the stage for the innovation that creates a different kind of classroom for children. She also said that the environment was the primary teacher. It is the environment we learn from and from our interactions with it.

Designing and nurturing an environment in which children can explore and be free to have choice in their activities is an important element. Furthermore, responsibilities on the land are also anchors for the children. On the contrary, there are different approaches to outdoor education available depending on what your community has access to. It doesn't have to look one way, or be set in a magical park, it could be going for walks in urban areas and observing the birds, the wind, and the trees, and tuning into what life cycles are present in that environment. Creating an outdoor classroom that has a farm/park focus in the main way in which Gazebo utilized outdoor education, and the curriculum was naturally born from this space. The teachings came about organically within the environment. Adventure outdoor education is another approach that can be applied in different locations—from parks to the wilderness areas. While Gazebo was a place-based environment in which children are oriented towards a park and farm space, nature education can look differently as there are many possible ways to be outside. Peggy Horan remembers,

> Gazebo, the childcare Mecca for parents in the '70s at Esalen. We had a magical place where children were encouraged to explore the natural surroundings supported by loving teachers who allowed them to discover a world of wonder, where all things were sized for them. A staff of aware and loving teachers were there to guide the children, but not to interfere with their exploration of interactions with each other. The children were taught how to create a boundary by saying 'no,' how to relate to nature by planting a garden, taking care of a pony or goats, how to explore the gentle landscape that had been created for them.

Faria describes the teachings of the place as,

> At Gazebo the environment is not static for very long, a little log appears in front of a doorway, the child notices and hops over it easily and deftly navigates the environment. In a typical daycare or preschool setting the terrain may be static for months and obstacles

are not found on the path very often, so much is considered a hazard that the child needs protection from. When not given the natural out-of-doors course of chaos, the child is stymied by the order of things when they are shifted, they are readily frustrated and give up quickly. In this natural space, there are no flat spaces. There are lots of nooks and crannies and many uneven levels of landscape, incredible for acquiring balance as a toddler or adult! A natural, not over cautious, determined stepping into the world is developed by the child's own pace which is likely a lot slower than what many adults might consider time well spent. When this pace is embraced the child develops an inner balance and joy at experiencing the environment and challenging their own limits.

The Gazebo Park belonged to the children! The importance of chores and daily work within the Park creates routine, ritual and daily touchstones for the children. The ownership of the work belonged to the children and they learned about responsibilities through care of the land and the animals. Though routines may change seasonally, there were also daily activities such as feeding and watering the chickens and goats and letting them out to pasture, turning compost, raking, watering the gardens, and weeding. Foreman remarks,

> The environment was the learning lab that included daily chores of tending the garden as well as feeding the animals and cleaning their spaces. Projects evolved and were worked on individually (lots of construction), in pairs (watering the garden, making mud pies), or groups (forts, planting seeds). The children learned life cycles through the garden, planting seeds, watering them, watching the plants grow, sprouting seeds, tending fruit trees or vegetables, eating their harvests. The same went for our animals: tending baby goats, feeding them, watching them grow, having mama goat die. The children learned from their teachers how to use tools, how to be around the pony, and water safety. They were encouraged to trust their instincts, to nurture independence and develop a sense of freedom in a safe environment.

The work of farm life is an element of Gazebo that both connects children to the natural rhythms of life and death, but it also provides the opportunities for responsibility and feeling empowered to care for the world around them. The benefits of learning this at a young age is this skill that is important when caring for personal space as the children become young adults, but also caring for the earth and the processes that are important for keeping the earth healthy. Miller feels that,

> It is nature and living in the outdoor space. Part of what makes it work is that there is so much space. Nature is healthy for children to be outside, and when they have the space to run off and go do something else they have time and space to resolve things that they would not have in other programs. There is always something interesting to do. Like what we are doing with lavender, making something with it, using it, modeling.

Miller referred to a project harvesting lavender with a group of children from which we created bath salts to sell at a benefit for the school. The children were involved in each part of the process from harvesting, to taking the lavender off the stalk, to mixing the salts and putting them in jars, and creating labels for the sale. This particular activity was project-based, yet projects and themes emerged and came to life because of the environment. For example, the use of natural materials inspired counting games using stones or acorns as manipulatives, and art projects often stemmed from found objects. Although outcomes were often positive, the orientation of the curriculum was not outcome based.

There are also important changing cycles throughout the month and year that allow children and adults to tune into nature in different ways. Eizner shares that,

> Nature influences curriculum because as nature changes the experience changes and the learning changes and the kids adapt and adjust to the changes in nature. In wintertime the kids like to go out and get in the rain and get wet and get in the mud and experience

different things that don't happen in the summertime, and in the summertime they will run and experience the sun on their naked bodies and the freedom that the summer and the weather allow, and in the winter of course the children might not want to do that. As nature changes the kids have the experiences of nature.

Furthermore, curriculum in nature is organic and driven by curiosity and exploration. McLeod remembers,

> Janet taught me that everything can be curriculum and a lesson can be created from anything in graduated levels. I found this particularly true with nature. I recall one child giving me a dead butterfly that had only one wing. We talked about it and he told me where he found it and got as much information about butterflies as we could verbally as other kids looked at it too as I asked them to take a twig and point to some parts of the butterfly—eyes, back, wings, etc. Luckily I was able to find a book about butterflies as there was a Monarch butterfly siting in an area of the eucalyptus bordering the Gazebo. Everyone that wanted to say something about butterflies did and those that wanted to drew their rendition of a butterfly and colored them.

Thus, interactions with our environment result in investigations that are relevant and meaningful because of the intrinsic curiosity and investment in learning. Similarly, having the environment be designed by the children is one concept many of the Gazebo elders stressed to me. McLeod stressed this by saying,

> I just love it when I see artwork actually created by children rather than displays created by adults. It is so obvious that adult art, though colorful and playful in nature, is not the work of a preschooler or totally some of the older children, for that age group haven't yet developed those motor skills. As an artist myself (textile/oil painting and crafts), I am appalled at these displays for I am afraid that kids may reject their own creative work because they can't make it look like an adult version.

Being in the outdoors is an opportunity for children to live as children outside the concerns of adults. Douce recalls,

> That is another thing about Gazebo, rather than kids who were always clean, always white, they were encouraged to play in the dirt, because you develop all of these immunities from the soil. We encouraged that, and they didn't have to be clean all of the time. I used to come in, this is maybe when I was nine or ten, I would come in from playing in the swamps, from rolling down the dirt hills, I would come in completely filthy, and I remember my mom shaking her head and going what a nightmare. It was normal.

Dirty, hands-on work, in an outdoor school is an experience that can be so positive for children. Delevett remembers,

> Being immersed in nature, respect for everything living, tress, grass, rollie pollies. flowers, people, birds and butterflies, goats and ponies. Joy is essential whether it's riding Hot Wheels, face painting, playing dress up, gardening, feeding the horse, giving milk to baby goat. Follow your instinct, your curiosity, your bliss, trust in the process, trust in the unfolding of life.

Land Stewards/Park Keepers

Land stewardship refers to the ways in which children and adults alike create connections to a particular piece of land and ultimately care for it and tend to it, in whatever way it may need. Teachers and children can be land stewards and park keepers. By modeling healthy care-taking of the land, and involving the children in activities related to nature—from planting to harvesting, to learning about the compost—children learn through daily activities and seasonal activities. The trees, the grass, the animals, the plants and gardens, the stones, the branches, the fences, the hay bales, and the water are aspects that need care-taking. Much like the Dr. Seuss's Lorax who speaks for the trees, a land steward represents the earth and seeks to speak for it when it cannot speak for itself. A land steward asks himself, "What is needed here for the land and the earth to be healthy?"

Similarly, the position of caretaker can also be described as park manager. The adult takes care of the grounds, but does not interfere with the children's play. The adult sees to it that the space is safe, tidy, and provides possibilities for the use of imagination, including little nooks and crannies for privacy and hiding. The park keeper models a deep care for the space and respect for the surrounding that translates to children both through observation and in their efforts to get involved with caring for the park. One aspect of the teacher's participation in nature education is to model this land stewardship. Depending on the environment, this can be done in different ways. If it is a farm or park space, the teachers tend to the land by working the land. In this way, they are modeling how to care for the land while allowing the children to participate or to think creatively about their options in other applications. Being a land steward sets the intention to nurture the earth and the life it sustains. Classen elaborates,

> We are here because that is part of what we want to do. Taking care of the land and being good to it. Having the land here for the children. We don't have to talk about it as much because it is all here—adults model getting pleasure from working the land and being stewards of the land.

Thompson-Clark identifies that,

> Another of Janet's core principles or values or tenets that exemplify the Gazebo approach is evidenced in the structuring of the environment. Her vision for the environment was to liken it to a 'Park'. This notion is a fundamental one: it is not the size of the school, or the layout, or structures that matter, but rather the understanding that the natural world is the primary teacher. The optimal age for beginning to learn about the natural world with the support of adults as role models in taking care of the park, is when crawling and interest in exploring begins, about six to twelve months. In allowing them to make sense of their world by taking

part in the daily life of environmental caretakers, their living and learning evolved into a sense of ownership of the place. It was a safe place, filled with opportunities to discover and learn about the natural world, their own bodies, and their multidimensional relationships with others. The environment evolved organically along with the pedagogy. Each day a primary curriculum had the basics of engaging children in daily chores of taking care of the grounds and animals and routines of eating, exploring, and sleeping. In the 21st century we recognize this educational principle as eco-literacy: the understanding of the organizing principles that ecosystems have developed to sustain the web of life.

Baldwin stresses,

It is easier to explain to people the difference between being a park keeper and being a schoolteacher. In Gazebo you're both. It's not that you should be one or the other. The park keeper is so different from the normal idea of teaching. The teacher is supposed to be involved. I get the substitutes coming through my school. They have all got these cute little voices that they have with the children, and they are great, but it is not what we are talking about here. What we are talking about is allowing the kids to grow. It's like we are watering the kids, but they really come through like a plant. I water this plant, but I don't do anything to make the bulb. I don't press buttons or fit things in, it just does it. That is the point of having a child in a park, they grow. They might be a weed one day and a gorgeous sunflower the next—or every five minutes. They change from different place from different ways of being. They can be all sitting around a table doing an intense project, and then five minutes later they can be scattered everywhere.

Agrarian Lifestyle—Plant and Animal Connections

A farm and garden environment provides opportunities for ancient ways of learning. In this way, those with more experience share their knowledge as they teach younger people how to grow food and medicines and care for plants and animals. The young ones then develop a connection to their food sources. Agricultural activities also provide opportunities, much like on a traditional farm, children learn not only about their food, but about life and death. The children look for chicken eggs each day, and they eat the eggs they gather at lunch. And if the chickens are not put away to roost at night, they learn animals like coyotes and bobcats also get hungry. Children witness the life cycle of plants and animals from growth to dying back, to birth, life and death again. From harvesting food to eating snacks from the garden, children follow the food process from start to finish. They learn knowledge of medicinal plants from their wild native plants and they grow a medicine garden. They can harvest medicinal herbs and make products (such as healing salves) out of them to use as part of their first-aid kit. If someone gets hurt, they go for the first-aid kit and they go to the medicine garden with the knowledge to treat owies from both sources.

The agrarian lifestyle was a big part of the curriculum at Gazebo and the farm-school model is growing in popularity. Animal-human reciprocity is also an important aspect in that it provides connection and a sense of responsibility, care and love. Price-Waldrip feels that,

> Animals have always been a vital part of my life. Peyote [the Gazebo pony] is one of my most cherished memories. I loved her size. She was calm around me and I felt safe to interact with her. It let me be in contact with a being that was much bigger than me. She was big enough that I felt held but not too big that it felt scary. Kevin [the Gazebo dog] was also a huge part of my Gazebo experience. He was one of the sweetest dogs I've met. He felt like our Gazebo mascot and I loved his sweet, consistent presence. I was so attached to him and was incredibly sad when he died. The interaction with animals at Gazebo felt natural to me, not contrived. We were taught to respect them and give them space. They were so well integrated into the park.

These animals, as well as many goats and chickens and even dogs and cats have been part of children's lives at Gazebo.

Eizner recalls,

> The goats—we used to take them out, and the kids would take
> them out. The kids were not unsupervised with the goats. When
> we had behavioral problems, we used to take the goats out so the
> children can work out some of their energy and we would be holding
> the rope at the end. It's not like we would just let the goats drag
> the kids. The animals helped them to learn about power, about
> confidence, about bigger and smaller, and what to do when you

encounter somebody or something that is bigger and stronger, how to be safe in the world, and what are the situations you might want to deal with or avoid. I think, and Janet's thing was, most of the learnings we need are in nature, with nature, and when we start taking away nature, we start creating these superficial environments that are not really helping the kids to deal with the realities of life. With animals and birth, the kids saw the animals being born, and fed them, and the whole process is just priceless. I think that people went from this type of environment and concept and to the sterile 'you need to be careful,' to the fear based, liability based. I think it takes the experience away from kids. I think that's the main issue that preschools encounter today—there is no edge to their experience.

Marquis remembers her connection to plants and animals,

I think I'm different because I grew up next to the food that was growing for me. My best friend's parents ran the farm. There was an obvious connection in the cycle of food from seed to compost that I was immersed in. I knew the chickens that laid the eggs we ate. I picked strawberries off the vine. This shouldn't be a luxury as it is now. We have a messed up relationship with food as a society. Growing up like this, with gardens, farms, an unseparated relationship to nature, would help. Knowing what wild foods you can eat is empowering.

Marquis continues,

Having animals is great too. For learning how to care for them, for having other beings to connect to, for understanding the world is full of more than just humans. When Superdog died, we had a funeral that enough of us came back for that it was kind of a party. The kids could experience death, to know the loss of a beloved, and share that sadness together. I think having other animals and having community creatures that we all raise, having shared animals that we love, and to watch them die and let them go and have a group to share those things with through life, it was important. We don't have that, unless you have a nuclear family, it is hard to share with a group of people. The animals became friends and connectors.

Similarly, Delevett remembers that,

Learning to care about nature—taking care of Peyote [the Gazebo pony], learning to brush mane, clean hooves, feed, was learning respect for nature. It was powerful to treat with care, and to be treated carefully. It was fun, exciting, alive!

This process of working with the animals and in the gardens was not about productivity and the work itself, but for the children it was an area of interest. Eizner maintains,

Kids were excited to go pick up the pony poop. They wanted to do that. They wanted to go get in the goat pen and go feed the babies, bring the food, get in the compost, take out the compost. Again it goes back to responsibility for the environment, responsibility for themselves, routines, structure. That they were involved in a fun way. Teaching kids structure and routine in a fun way is the best way to teach them rather than imposing it on them. Telling them that they have to do that like they do in many preschools.

Therefore, there is a responsibility in caring for the land and the animals, but it is also accompanied by an intrinsic motivation for being involved with life through these activities. Eizner says,

Janet used to talk about kids on the farm growing up knowing that if they don't feed the chickens they are not going to have eggs. It is part of the self-responsibility and the learning that didn't come from being forced by the teachers, it just became part of what we did. It's like waking up in the morning and having breakfast. It is not forced—you wake up and you want to eat and you eat and then you go out and play. Well, that's what we did, we took care of the environment. Teachers knew and were aware of what we needed to do in order to relate to the environment and have a healthy environment and the children were learning from us, from watching us. It wasn't forced.

The animals brought many lessons about life and loss. Eizner continues,

> One of the things I deal with in my practice is kids might have to deal with grief and death and losses. One of the things the animals teach the kids is about birth, death, responsibility. I remember experiences with the kids, 'For instance, one time they found a dead bird. Somebody said, 'It's dead, what does that mean?' I started to, actually they started to have a conversation, facilitated, as I was involved, about what it means to die. Then, the questions was, 'What would you like to do now? What would you do?' 'Well, we just want to bury it.' We bury the bird. And the next one was like, 'What do you want to do now?' And then one says, 'I want to bring flowers, or 'I want to sing a song.' It became this natural process presented by life. There is not much that adults need to do rather than just be with the kids and their experience.

In the same way, Classen says,

> One thing is for sure, the way children related to death because they were around it all the time, the animals dying, the pelicans walking into the school and dying, to the compost – then when someone in your life dies, like a part of the community, they had more understanding and tools for coping.

The Japanese word "wabi-sabi" refers to an acceptance of imperfection much like the experience of finding beauty within the cycles of life of death, and finding peace within the challenges. These are the kinds of life lessons that emerge when the natural world is the classroom. Baldwin shares his wisdom on gardening with children,

> Gazebo is more than just land. Gazebo is the place. When it came to the gardening and the grounds and the planting of the

vegetables, as a gardener just gardening. Gardening is a job you get lost in. You sit there in your flower bed, you don't look at your watch, you don't count how many weeds you got to pull, you just sit down and get yourself comfy and you have the right tool, and you just pull weeds. Your head will go wherever it wants to—often quite wonderful places. Well, school gardening is the exact opposite of that. For a professional gardener, it is actually hard to just come in and say, 'I am going to get into this garden. Oh, I've got to watch the kids.' You never actually get anything done. You have to let go of the gardener bit, and you are there available for the kids, with the flow.

Baldwin adds,

For instance, if I am down there digging in the beds, I would get some tools, invite children that want to come. It may be that some want to come, so we go and get our tools—we have our section of big tools and small tools. We get our tools, we go down there and after two minutes some of those guys they are going to be finished and that's fine. There is no time orientation or whatever, as long as either they give their tool to another kids who is coming in, because that is quite usual. Just as your leaving, here comes another kid, 'Oh do you want to use his spade?' Then they are free to go, they can go wash their hands. If they are actually finishing, then they need to put their tool away, or at least put it in a place so it is contained rather than just leaving it and running off. That part of Gazebo, it is participating, but then there is the completion. That completion is that you don't have to have done half an hour of gardening at this level, it is more that you have done whatever you want to do, and your attention level is gone. It is a park, not a school, so you have every right to go as long as you are consistent with putting your stuff away and moving on. It is health and safety to start with. Like any gardener you put your tools away when you finish, you may have to clean them. We are talking about real professional development here. That's what every gardener learns on his first day of work. For them it is right from the start that they have the freedom to participate, it is organized, there is safety. You have to wear shoes. Then they would do the job and as soon as they finish, and again they decide when they are finished. They can leave as long as it's consistent with putting the tool away and checking in, rather than just going. It is all about communication, it is all about boundaries, it is all about safety which is always important to know.

Baldwin continues,

> With the gardening, it is organic. I have a little collection of books we can look at before or after that show seeds being planted. Then you got the seeds. We can start with seeds in the greenhouse. You can get your seeds, and plant them. You got magnifying glasses if you want to look at the seeds close up. 'Wow, have you ever seen seeds close up?' They are all very involved. They are not just bits of things, they have all sorts of patterns. They get to learn differences. Some seeds are big, some are small, some are round. They are all different shapes. It is not like I am saying, 'It is shape time. What shapes are these?' It is all just coming through. That's where the teacher comes in, pointing out, 'What shape is the sunflower seed? Is it round? It is sort of round.' Then they may just rush off and do free play, because unless it is lunch time or a certain time where you got something happening, free play is the run of the Park. That is the point of a park, that is the bottom line. It is a place where they can come in and just decide what they want to do.

Baldwin says,

> As a gardener, I just have to accept that this isn't about me pro-ducing an incredible flower bed, it is about me participating in the job with the children in a full way. For instance, I remember once planting in one of those little beds and we got all these little lettuce seedlings the garden gave us in the black tray, and we get them all out and we plant them. There are maybe about eight kids doing all of this, and they are all planting, not in lines necessarily. I come back about twenty minutes later and in one of the beds, there were two, two-and-half year olds, and they had pulled out

every one and they have turned every one upside down. They have the roots sticking out, and they did it so well had this been the job. 'You know guys you have to turn the plants around.' No, it wasn't wrong, it wasn't like, 'You screwed up the blooming plants.' It was more like, 'Hey guys this is what roots are, how roots go in the ground to suck the water, how the green stuff takes the sunlight.' And again I am not going to be to complicated, just getting the roots to go in the ground, but they are learning that roots go in the ground by having them out of the ground. So often learning is, education is, to educe, to bring out. They are natural gardeners, they just haven't learned some of the basic rules yet, so it is to bring out that to encourage that.

Baldwin offers an example,

I had one boy come in and he goes to the one of the rose geraniums and he is not shredding them but he is pulling off bits. He has a whole group of kids and they are not trashing the plant, so I am not going to intervene. I think maybe his granny had showed him as he is just taking bits off. He goes up to the Gazebo, there is a nice little bed with nothing in it and he starts sticking these bits of geranium in the ground, and the other kids are too. They are watering, and this has nothing to do with me, they are watering away and they leave it, and for the next couple years we have a whole bunch of rose geraniums growing there. That is curriculum that is totally created by them. I am watching. 'Are they trashing these geraniums?' No. I could easily go step in and say, 'Don't trash the blooming plants,' which is easy to do because they will rip them to shreds sometimes. It is just a little step back. That is the whole point, take that little bit of a step back. Stepping back but still being there. It is allowing them to fill the space because it is their park. This is their park. I am here as to serve them. I am here to see what they need and make sure it is safe.

The medicine garden is a wonderful tool as well. It encourages the children's independence and ownership in that they know where it is and how to use it for first aid in the park. It also provides education around medicinal plants and native plants and builds naturalist skills. Vieregge remembers,

> I started the medicinal garden at one time. The medical garden and the first-aid kit they can use both. The calendula is an antiseptic, and so you crush them in water and you can use them to wash the owie. Particularly with the abrasions, the scrapes that have mud in them.

The medicine garden at Gazebo was an extension of the curriculum Vieregge taught in the bus. It reinforced the first aiders abilities to respond to emergency and offer first aid to each other. Getting to know the local medicinal plants is also important for children. Kimmerer, citizen of Potawatomi Nation says, "Our indigenous herbalists say to pay attention to when plants come to you; they're bringing you something you need to learn."[1] I created medicine gardens for other school programs, sometimes with older children, and it was a good experience for the children and always seemed relevant; particularly when they are able to apply principles of local medicinal plants.

Similarly, the wild plants around Gazebo were a source of amusement and imaginative play. For example, the passion flower vines always held a sweet mystery. You can turn the flower around, check for bees, and if clear, suck the sweet nectar from the stem. As a young child, I believed that the fairy queen had her bed high above the Gazebo in the passion vines. These vines provided hiding places and fairy kingdoms in which the children hung bells and ribbons. The vines were available for making wreaths and crowns along with the morning glory vines. We learned about "yums and yucks," that is which were edible and which were poisonous plants. Fennel was also a delicious snack that we used to enjoy. As children, we were encouraged to know the plants and ask a teacher before sampling to stay safe. We knew the poisonous plants. For example, it was at Gazebo I learned what poison hemlock looked like and to stay away from it.

The wild animals were present in the children's lives as Big Sur has it's fair share of wildlife. A fox would often come very close to the farmhouse. In fact, they may have been responsible for the loss of several chickens. Dvora wrote in her blog post entitled, "The Grey Fox, The Tree and other Wild Things" which was written from the Gazebo farmhouse,

> The grey fox is out and about tonight, wandering the upper deck while I'm typing by moonlight. He's searching for a few scraps of dinner, and I'm seeking words to highlight the activities of the day. The grey fox found some good treats now, and he's off. Me too. I'm grateful for this day—let the wild rumpus begin![2]

Becoming a naturalist happens organically when children are in nature. Activities like bird watching and animal and plant recognition emerge each moment as the children explore their environment. Their curiosity moves them to wonder about what mushroom this is, and it is the teachers role to guide them and offer suggestions about "yums" and "yucks," provide a mushroom book to determine if the specimen is safe before touching, and encourage students towards viewing nature with reverence rather than fear. Birds fly above and call. A crow sits atop the same tree each morning and caws. The children begin to learn its sounds and attempt to make that sound too. They know it is different from the blue jays who are all too interested in their snacks. They create a song about the blue jays to sing at snack time. The learning is embedded in their day. I remember the constant chatter of blue jays and how they used to come around especially at snack and lunch time in the Park. Handl, the director at the time, created a song to the blue jays to the common nursery rhyme melody of "Twinkle Twinkle Little Star." The children knew the patterns of the blue jays, and the jays also knew the children's patterns; especially the meal times. We also explored our relationship to the animal kingdom. One of the things we liked to do at Gazebo was that the children could choose an animal call and we would use it as a call and response—especially if anyone was out of sight. We would use this call and response to communicate inside the park.

At Gazebo, our learning about plants and animals were according to their life cycles, the times of year and the activities related to them. In the fall, harvest is an important element as well as preparing for winter. In the winter, there is much pruning and cutting back the old dead growth. In the spring when everything shoots up again, there is much weeding, watering, and planting to be done. In this way, Baldwin recalls,

> It is basically just using everything around us. If it's October we are down at the creek looking for crawdaddies. If it is butterfly time, we go and see the butterflies. I used to have my own sustainable eucalyptus forest up there which is what we would use for all the fencing. The children would help me saw it down. It was a sapling growing out of a stump so the children would look for the right sapling, the children knew where it was going, it's time for fixing fences. It may not be seasonal but always looking at jobs we can all do together. When it is windy, we rake. When it is really really windy and raining, we got all these great big pieces of eucalyptus, and so we can paint the leaves and bark. It is not only cleaning and sweeping and keeping the place clean, but also it is to make a pile of leaves and kick them everywhere, and then clean them up again. Again, that is, 'We are here to clean the leaves up, and we are here to kick the leaves all over the place, and we are here to clean the leaves up.'

Seasonal activities are a way for children to connect to and learn from the earth's cycles and to be in tune with nature. These activities are intuitive, based on what is going on around them, so they are teaching them to slow down and listen and watch and observe their environment with sensitivity—a skill many adults have not mastered. Seasonal activities are implemented in more traditional indoor schools as well, yet outdoor schools have a much more integrated curriculum because the seasonal activities are part of the fiber of life and work on the land. Though the seasons were important elements to how we learned about the earth cycles, the daily rituals inside of a park environment were also important.

Rituals, Routines, Rhythms—Daily, Seasonal, Yearly

The daily rituals and routines are wonderful touchstones for children, anchoring them into the space much like children in a Montessori classroom might connect to the activities and objects in their environment, though perhaps with more inevitable changes in the outdoor classroom. Wolfinger recalls that the traditions in the Park, however changing, provided some leadership. He says,

> You did certain things with the animals in the morning, there was lunch time we sung songs together, and just those traditions were a really great way of building the community and so it was not only being free all the time but it also brought us all together with commonality and common interests for the animals and the environment.

The children's ownership and responsibility is important as much as play and choice are important for children, there is also a sense of accomplishment and pride in caring for the animals, and the environment. Baldwin emphasized that,

> Working with the farm, you arrange with the farm when is planting time. Animals are our daily touchstones. We had the pony, we had pigs, we even had a wild boar at one time. We didn't have small animals apart from the chickens.

These routines of caring for the animals become anchors or a routine-rich environment. People from more structured educational backgrounds would come to Gazebo and perceive a lack of routines. On the contrary, the routines at Gazebo or in any outdoor environment are naturally allied with life cycles, seasonal cycles, and daily tasks and rituals. The more intuitive learning in this is the ability to understand the needs of nature and the land based on what is happening in the present time. For example, if leaves are falling in the autumn, we notice it is time to rake. On the other hand, responsibilities keep the children anchored to predictable daily routines. Thus, in their orientation towards seasonal or daily activities, the children have responsibility and ownership in caring for the land. Baldwin expresses,

> I was here a few weeks ago, giving a little talk and observing. There was this really sweet guy. I think he was an intern. It was time to get the goats, and his words were, 'Anyone want to tag along with me while I go get the goats.' Well, no–the children and the goats are both more important than you are. The children run the school, and they are their goats. You need to word that in a different way. 'What time is it? Is there anything we need to do now?' See if any of the kids know that. Then, if the kids want to go with you, then they go get the goats, and you tag along with them. If none of the kids want to get the goats, then you the teacher goes and gets them. No, this isn't a place where you tag along with me while I get the goats. This was a lovely guy, but he hadn't seen it. When I explained to him, he suddenly saw the whole difference of wording. It suddenly becomes, 'What time is it? What do we do now? I think there is something we need to do. Does somebody know what time it is? Let's see who knows?' With that, you often will get enthusiasm. Some days they don't want to get the goats, but feeding animals has to be done. I found there are always kids who always want to feed the animals. I might keep an eye out for those that don't always. Once in a while I might end up feeding the animals myself because they are all so involved with doing another thing. That is not what it's about, it's about if I can get them to participate.

A Gazebo expression is, "Slow down and involve the children." Thus, work is not done simply for the outcome of the project, but it stimulates motivation by inviting the children to participate in each job. If there is a job that can't be done with the children, it should be done outside of school hours. In other words, all work is the children's work. What does it mean to clear the path of bark and leaves after the storm in the winter? Why might this be important? If California is in a drought, so why is water awareness important? How can teachers teach through doing and show children with their work why they turn the water off and use the sink drainage to water a nearby plant.

As a child, I remember eating peas and carrots out of the garden, and picking apples from the tree. Gazebo had snacks out to eat at any time I was hungry. I remember being able to help cut up the food, like slicing bananas on little cutting boards with butter knives. After helping the prepare the food, and enjoying eating it, we put food in the compost and learned about the cycle of life as our food went into the compost bins. Sometimes we would get in the compost with shovels and turn the earth with our little rain boots on and look at the worms. The compost is a strong teaching tool for the life cycle.

Composting has been an important element of Gazebo from the start; and it also provides great fertilizer for the garden. Some traditional classrooms are now using worm bins for indoor use, but being able to have a complete outdoor compost is an amazing experience for children. Children can have so much more contact with where their food comes from, from growing it, to preparing it, to eating it. Many children don't understand that their food comes from somewhere beside the supermarket. The life cycle demonstrated through the composting curriculum is in fact profound, and composting is very fun; especially when it comes to worm bins! Yet, it is also a vital part of food preparation and snack as children learn to use the compost bucket at a very early age. They add food scraps, they dump the compost in the big bin each day, they turn the compost and observe the worms, they take the rich compost to the garden to grow more food, they harvest the food and again see the waste go into the bins again. They are involved in each step in the process. Children add paper or cardboard, and water the compost as needed to check the balance of green, brown and wet. In this process, the discussion of worm castings as fertilization comes up naturally. Many children love to touch and hold the worms as they turn the compost, they like to watch them wiggle and this sensory activity is also part of their learning process. Composting is truly a wonderful hands-on activity that connects children with their food and understanding of life. Davey says,

> I have so much compassion and feel so connected to the land. I am thankful for the bounty it provides in beauty and in nourishment. My respect for the system as a whole, and my place within it, has always been a part of me because of Gazebo. When I was at Captain Cooper [the local elementary school] even I could see that we were throwing so much away. The hot lunches would be sent down from town, and they were indiscernible pizzas in boxes. When I went to the middle school and became friends with kids from town and saw how the households were run, it seemed too sterile. I see myself within the earthly cycle, not above it.

The daily rhythms also create safety within routines that children can rely on and can feel safe within. From animal care, taking care of the park space, cleaning up materials, composting, watering, and weeding, there is a regularity of routine, yet also the possibility for many discoveries within this routine. During any of these "chores" another wonder may arise, such as finding interesting insects, tracking the movement and responses of these insects, to noticing the fluttering of butterflies which may lead to learning about butterfly life cycles. Collecting feathers from the ground may lead to learning about the birds. Building with wood can teach about termites and how they are in the world. By watching natural patterns, how animals react and act, like blue jays at the snack table, children make connections. Teachers offer resources to these children based on their interests, and the sparks of their curiosity are ignited by learning. Teachers in the outdoor classroom have resources and tools such as Audubon field guides, terrariums, seed tables, nature tables with collection jars, owl pellets, spiders, mushroom kits, wildflowers, birds nests and feathers.

Teachers may plant butterfly gardens, use animal calls, or watch for tracks and scat to know the happenings of the area. A walk to the beach leads a child to wonder about sea life from watching whales, otters, dolphins, and sea lions, listening to seals call and recognizing the formation in which pelicans fly. A walk to the creek offers opportunities for learning about the watershed and it's ecosystem and habitat. Storybooks and songs can support the curriculum that emerges, and excite young children's interest. Banana Slug String band, friends of Esalen and Gazebo used to come perform and held workshops on weekend in the Park have a number of wonderful songs about children and ecology. Harper says about nature education,

At the easiest level is the agricultural level, or the Gazebo Park model, where there is lots of nature coming in and out whether you want it to or not. The language issue is a real issue because I am using language as if we are separate from nature. We aren't. That is the same dualism. We are nature. We are nature and we can not separate ourselves from nature. That is what has gotten us in trouble. Even if we are sitting in a classroom that is completely brick walled and no windows, we are nature. Then I make a distinction between wild nature and nature and there are some varying degrees of that. Wild nature being that area which is the least impacted by humans as possible, because if we actually measure very tightly, there are probably very few, if no places on the earth, that we humans haven't impacted. So it is a relative thing. Along that kind of scope or spectrum, there is the indoor classroom. We are still nature, we are human animals, and I think it is really important for teachers to remember that we are animals. We somehow do this thing where we are separate from the animal kingdom and we are separate from nature. Even in a bricked off classroom, I have seen teachers do a good job to remind kids that they have bodies, that they have all these capacities. So, moving across the spectrum, we would then come to recess. Kids getting to be outdoors is a no-brainer in my opinion. Literally parents and teachers are having to go to school boards and show the science that says recess is necessary for a healthy developing human. To me it is outright scary that we have come to that kind of place. Then, we move to a place on the spectrum further over, I will put pretty far over, Gazebo. It is over towards the wild end of things, because birds can come and go, there is a garden, there are worms, insects, bees that can sting, there are yellow jackets, there are a lot of wild critters and plants are coming and going within that somewhat human-scaped area of the park. Then, there is the agricultural place, where humans are turning over the soil and engaging in the soil, and beginning to grow things. We pretty much grow things that we humans have developed over tens of thousands of years, or at least thousands of years, that we have developed. We are growing things like carrots, broccoli, and lettuces. But again this is engaging kids in all of their senses while they are doing that. And then further over the spectrum, would be into the realm of where we humans are having very little impact, and we are engaging. Maybe there is an analogy here, we are going into wilderness and becoming trees, and let the kids become trees. Like we are the kids at Gazebo Park and the adults are there as trees in the background letting the kids lead. When taking kids into the wilderness, I think there is a way in which we can all, including the kids, become trees and see if we can listen and let wilderness lead.

Adventure / Wilderness Programs

There is a trend in outdoor education that is more minimalist by nature. These programs focus on survival skills and being in the outdoors but sometimes in different locations and without the upkeep of the agrarian lifestyle. These are more about being in the wilderness, observing without disturbing, and oftentimes adventuring on a journey. The anchors in these programs are different. The routines depend even more on the rhythms and cycles of the earth than that of humans. Survival skills, tracking, first aid, wilderness training, bird language, and other naturalist skills such as plant identification are alive for these kinds of programs. In this way, nature exploration in the wilderness is another way to access outdoor education.

Educator Jon Young is a pioneer in the nature education movement and has developed programs that focus on nature connection and mentorship called the 8shields® model—which many outdoor schools have adopted. These programs are designed in an effort to learn about ecosystems without disturbing them. One of the teaching tools that Young uses is what is called, "the zone of awareness" and the "zone of disturbance." These are models designed to teach being in nature without disturbing the fragile balance and which heighten the ability for observation. He also talks about "sit spots" as places to return to that create a quiet space for children to listen to bird language at different times of day and year in the same location. The bird language curriculum is a valuable source of information. With the three kinds of bird language from song, to call, to alarm, birds provide much information about the natural world and offer an immense resource for young people to learn about the environment. Young also fosters mentorship and nature connection as a tools for activating underutilized senses and our capacity for relationship with the natural world.

Initially, the practice of simply being more quiet than usual is a great starting point for being in nature. In my experience applying some of these principles with first and second graders, children had a hard time remaining silent long enough to listen and hear the birds without turning songs into alarms very quickly. So, we played a game called, "silence stamina." We timed the children on how long they could stay silent and it became a very interesting practice for our outdoor education days in the forest. With older second graders especially, we would practice silence stamina, working on being in silence as a group for longer periods. We would break our own records: twenty-two minutes was the longest for that class from forest to bus, to classroom, and to a meditation circle! On the other hand, in a park environment like Gazebo, young children can experience being loud and even yelling in the outdoors when it is appropriate.

Even in a more traditional program, outdoor education can be implemented through field trip adventures or nature walks. Journaling is another great tool, even for the preliterate, with sketches and group poems recorded by the adult. Nature walks or adventures can be a brilliant way to cultivate nature awareness and stimulate children's learning. Keeping an adventure journal can help children log what they see, either in writing or logging observations, making leaf prints, or sketches of plants, trees or insects. Collecting things they find (provided that it is appropriate to remove the objects from the land) can be added later to a nature table or an altar in the classroom. Objects collected could also become part of an organic art project or be used for counting and sorting later. Observations on the trail can change depending on the time of day and the season and this provides new learning opportunities, even if that same path is taken on each walk. Adventures into the forest, journaling and collecting natural treasures, and creating organic art are all ways children can tune into the magic of life all around.

In this way, Gazebo led outings to explore the land around the Park from the farm at Esalen or the canyon and creek or beach. One of the magical adventures was going up Hot Springs Canyon along the creek bed. The children could find salamanders under rocks, crawdads, and explore among ferns and redwoods. This was a magical site for this kind of adventure, but even in a backyard or a playground the orientation can be shifted to notice nature in a deep way. I find that all it takes is modeling, perhaps the adult saying out loud, "Did you hear that bird? What kind do you think it is?" or "Wow, look at this plant," or "What pattern is that? A spiral!" I recognize that many typical classrooms do biology and earth science with terrariums, compost bins, butterfly hatcheries etc., but there is a great advantage to getting children outdoors—the full-bodied sensory experience that provides the body and brain with so much information, sensory stimulation, and learning.

Harper remembers the adventures he took the children on at Gazebo.

> I would take kids up the canyon, at least the kids that wanted to or were able to, because obviously there were younger ones. A full time Gazebo teacher would come with me, and we would go up the canyon and I would do everything from show the kids some edibles that they could eat, to stop and play in the canyon, and creek, in the water, build a dam, less of me doing something then me getting them up the canyon keeping them safe and following their interest. I would pick plants that had fragrance so they could smell them, I would offer up things curiosity wise, things to taste, smell, things to look at, and also a lot of it was just following them.

When I lead nature-based summer camps, I would have the students practice what it was like to take turns being the leader of the line, to be the first on the trail. I have learned and shared with them that being the first on the trail requires much awareness and focus, which is why we take turns. The first on the trail will confront spiderwebs, snakes, or other wild animals and must be the first to receive the information, and choose how to respond. Being the leader is a responsibility. I find young children into the kindergarten and early grades are often very concerned with being the first in line. It is fascinating to me that the shared leadership is also a wonderful opportunity to establish how they are in relationship. Some children are naturally very confident. Some are very perceptive and quiet while others stumble forward. For some children, also depending on their placement with their siblings, this exercise can be a rare opportunity for holding space for others as a leader. This practice, as well as the practice of periods of silence, build both confidence and character.

Dvora shares one of her Gazebo adventures in the following blog post:

Sucking Nectar from a Passionflower

We went on an adventure today with the toddlers. It was a relaxed journey to the lodge, pausing to savor the smells and sights along the way. One of my favorite moments was our encounter with the beautiful red flowers that cover the hillside along the road to the lodge. I've been admiring the qualities of this magnificent plant, with it's spiraling tendrils, spiky circle of purple hairs, long vibrant petals with soft pads of yellow pollen poking upward.

S., a Gazebo teacher, invited us to suck the nectar of the passion-flower. It was so delicious. Bees must be navigating intoxicated from the sweetness they collect along the way. We pulled carrots from the ground, fed the tops to the chickens, gazed contentedly at a group of community members tending the compost pile and shared lunch on the lawn.

Gazebo is a magical place—the simplicity of moving slowly through the activities of the day is a gift. I had anticipated that filling seven hours of outdoor time with children would be a challenge. But the time moves gently, and the days are long—a summertime rhythm that's wonderfully in tune with the cadence of childhood.[3]

Observation and Awareness

Here-now creativeness is dependent on this kind of ability to forget about the future, to improvise in the present, to give full attention to the present, e.g., to be able to fully to listen or to observe.

– Abraham Maslow

Children are more and more connected to Internet and TV and other devices and further away from being connected to nature. While technology has its place in society, the overuse of technology limits sensory and somatic experience and awareness which improve neurological development and function. Babies and children need small and large motor skill activities. The outdoors provides more somatic information to process and more sensory stimulation is naturally available in the outdoors. Instead, children have lost vital movements that use the whole body and apply its vast array of sensorial functions. While the flick of a finger gives a child all the information on the Internet, it does not teach them how to move, to listen, to hear, to balance, to feel, or to be aware of what is going on around them. In fact, the overuse of technology encourages indoor activities, and steers children away from the awareness and mindfulness that being in nature provides. The absence of being in nature is a great loss in the world today, and in my opinion, and is leading to higher rates of ADHD. Richard Louv, author of *Last Child Left in the Woods: Saving Our Children From Nature-Deficit Disorder*, coined nature-deficit disorder which he believes plagues this country.

Yet, Louv believes nature is curative and can be an antidote to using medication in diagnoses such as ADHD and other hyperactivity disorders. He believes nature is both restorative and healing, and necessary for all children. Though rates of medicating children are skyrocketing, an antidote is available right outside the door. Being in a technological era, children need alternative activities to engage their bodies and senses. The beauty of nature education is that it doesn't have to be a prescribed curriculum, and it doesn't have to be in a national park. How we are in the world and in the outdoors is organic and unique to each individual. Simply to walk out the door and spend time outside can offer each of us healing and can bring a sense of deep calm and inner peace. Harper suggests,

> Coming back to a Fritz Perls thing, the importance of awareness. Fritz had a line in *Gestalt Therapy Verbatim* that, 'Awareness in and of itself is curative,' and I change that because curative isn't as logical of a model as, 'Awareness by and of itself is whole-making.' Because we go back to the word healing, healing is to make whole, so awareness is whole-making. I think one of the things that kids learn out in nature is this greater awareness of all their senses and that makes for a greater whole. I think the same for teachers (and what I mean by teachers is adults in the roles of adults being

responsible for the well-being and well-doing of younger ones) that without being aware moment to moment, I can't make good judgment calls for younger ones. My role then is not to stop their learning, but to bring awareness to what they are doing. Like, 'You sure made it up that tree, I am wondering how you are going to make it back down? I am aware that you made it really far up that tree, and I am aware that I am wondering how you are going to come back down.' So, it is just interjecting this possibility in the child's mind that 'I am up here and I also have a journey down.'

Harper continues,

Nature, being in wild nature, so much is going on, it demands our organism to listen. It is not just a request, it demands. Observing is half of what an artist learns. The other half is, for example with painting, 'How now do I learn the craft of taking the paint and putting it down on the canvas so it represents what I am hoping it to represent whether it be photo-real or abstract?' It is really clear to me when I have taken art classes out into nature, there are a lot of people who spend most of the time learning to observe, and it is more than just observe visually. An artist is also observing with ears. In the classic sense, the old natural historians, would draw plants they came across, but they would also describe how they smell, how they are to touch, how they tasted. They would use all of the senses to describe a new animal or plant. So it is more than just the visual. In Western culture we have gotten so that the visual sense has become almost fascist. It have taken over the other senses.

As we spend time in nature, the emphasis on observation and awareness in the sensory-rich environment builds our sense capacities and thus develops students' cognitive skills and neurological function. We can begin with bringing a curiosity to how we are in nature, how to not disturb the environment, noticing changes in the weather, environment, terrain or botany and our own effect and footprint on the natural world. Then, the more contemplative quality of nature gives students a portal into "how" to be in the natural world through observation, listening, and attuning. American psychologist, Howard Gardner, developed the theory of Multiple Intelligence, to which he has continued to add new categories including naturalist intelligence. His theory is helpful in supporting differences in learning styles, and validates that naturalist skills are important to the 'whole-making' of a human being.

Simply put, being in nature teaches awareness skills and awareness amplifies learning and development. When children attune to the natural patterns and cycles in nature, they form relationships to plants and animals and a strong bond to the natural world. Understanding the botany and ecology of the area in which you live, helps form a bond to the land and therefore the earth. This is the terra-personal intelligence in which we as humans begin to tune into life and our understanding of the interconnectedness of all living things. We form a bond with the earth and within that bond a reciprocity exists. The act of being in awareness and observing is where this relationship begins. Listening to and noticing bird calls, and paying attention to what wild plants grow in the area, indicates an attunement to the environment. Consequently, observation and awareness are funda-mental to children learning in the outdoors. Harper says,

> I think actually that early regular contact with wild nature, and of course there is a spectrum, is one of the things that made some of the kids that have grown-up at Gazebo so healthy. I mean 'so healthy' in many measures, healthy if they have chosen and wanted to be academic. Then, they have had that capacity and choice for them and it wasn't like it was cut off for them. Some didn't choose that. I would say a lot of them [Gazebo graduates] have overall a higher emotional intelligence– awareness of emotions and capac-ity to say what it is that they are feeling. That is what I mean by emotional intelligence, because that word gets thrown around a lot, so by that I mean, awareness of what I am feeling and my capacity to communicate that.

Neural Somatics in Nature

*The Gazebo is designed with the educational goal of maximizing the
FULL use of the child's growing body and unfolding intelligence.*

– JL

Neural somatics refers to the connection between brain/nervous system and the body. Neural somatic education in the outdoors relates to how the outdoor environment stimulates the brain/nervous system and the body and supports growth and development in both areas. While outdoor play on a playground or park environment is of value, free play within an unstructured environment allows for a truly profound somatic learning experience. In particular, for a young child learning to crawl and walk in Gazebo Park is a very somatic and kinesthetic experience that connects the child to the earth and to their own bodies. This experience is so unlike being held by an adult, learning to walk on a flat surface such as hard flooring or concrete, or being in a classroom. Lederman, said, "The environment is there to maximize the body experience...it has slopes grades, terraces, and many textures to a varied body experience from moment to moment. It is an environment that <u>Rewards</u> the child for every movement." Lederman felt that it was very important for children to keep their contact with the earth and she discouraged teachers from carrying the children. Of course, the teachers offered comfort and offered attention and often got close to the earth to hold the children in a lap. On the other hand, they allowed them their ability to learn through their own experience and their contact with the earth. Harper states,

> It is clearly known that we can come into this world and learn any language in the world without any kind of any accent when we come into the world. Even these percussion accents that have a lot of nasal tonality to them that are very subtle, but we can learn them, but by five years old certain synapses have closed. Those doorways have closed, so it is almost impossible to learn that

same language without any hint of an accent. Even if you spent your whole lifetime studying it, you would still have some hint of an accent where a natural born speaker can hear that. I think we can take that same equivalent to language to nature and nature literacy. If we have been raised in a humanized environment from zero-five, we have maybe lost some of our capacity to literally speak the language of nature, just like we've lost the capacity to learn the language without an accent. We can go back and learn a lot of that, but the fluency may never be there. When that door or window closes, we may not have that capacity to know where we live and how we as a body, a human animal, engage with that human environment in the same way we could if we were a native born speaker of wilderness. Because language is a two-way street, because language is the capacity to speak, but it is also having the capacity to listen. So it opens up this interesting question of, 'What are we not hearing when we are out in nature?' We can't hear the subtleties of the speaker speaking a language. Let's take French, we can't even sometime hear the difference between a French pronunciation, and we think we are pronouncing it correctly, but a native born speaker can tell. So, it opens up this question, what are we missing, what am I missing. I saw this when I lived with the Masai in Africa. When I got close enough to them, and spent enough time in the bush, my world opened up in a huge way. I also got that I would never be able to see perceive and live in the world the way that they saw and perceived the world because those doors had already been shut to me. Even if I spent the whole rest of my lifetime there, I could get really close, but there would be a distance there.

Nature education both supports foundations of neurodevelopment and is restorative and healing. As Louv suggests, outdoor education is actually a healing remedy for many of the labels and disorders that are emerging through traditional "sit-down and learn" classrooms. Wyatt describes the importance of the outdoor environment and connection to nature as,

Nature is healing. Direct connection to source. Pure Gazebo is just being out there with the kids, and the animals, and the bugs, and the plants, and the climate and the weather, and the water, and the dirt and grass. And there is everything you need for stimulation, exploration, learning, growth, care, there is everything you need out there. So it is a great place for kids to be in terms of their openness.

Simple things like feeling the breeze on your face, smelling a flower, or digging in the dirt are simple joys, and through the senses they stimulate nueral development and thus learning. Barnes says,

> How does the outdoors affect learning differently? The sunlight, the changing temperatures, the shifting clouds, all the sounds of the trees, birds, animals make us more aware and sensitive to our environment. Here kids have a wide reaching 'cadre'/frame/ physical and psychological boundary in which they can explore. Enclosed classrooms don't provide this breadth of freedom. In such a constrained and schedule-oriented society, a physical and safe environment such as Gazebo is rare and beautiful.

Michael Changaris, Psy. D, and author of *Touch: The Neurobiology of Health, Healing, and Human Connection*, states,

> The brain controls how we breathe, our feelings of stress, our movement, our sleep, and even how we catch a ball. However, the body changes the brain. Each movement and emotion sculpts the brain. There is a complex dance between the brain, the body, and the environment.[4]

In essence, children learning in nature supports neurological and cognitive function through somatic and sensory stimulation and full body movement, which builds the groundwork for cognitive function. The early years of learning occur through simply experiencing life on a very physical level, through movement and contact with the environment through touch. Learning through exploration—especially in the outdoors utilizing the senses through direct experience— these are the pathways which stimulate physiological development cultivate growth in the child's neurological foundation. Harper suggests,

> So, there has been tons and tons of research why it [bringing kids in nature] is needed, and neuroscience to back it up. It shows how disconnected we are to nature, and wild nature if we need to have neuroscience back up what we already know. There is science to back up what I think we already know is evolutionary. We have spent way, way, way more time in wild environments than we have in human-controlled environments—just even over 200,000 years, or to be more conservative 100,000 years of homosapiens or human-like animals being on earth. Especially for the last 10,000 years, we began agriculture, as least how we think of agricultural now, and I pause there because there are some fuzzy boundaries around when agriculture began, but certainly back to hunter-gatherer groups, our organism knows this. We know the wild environment almost more at an animal level, a physiological level, than we do these urban environments we have created. There are scientists who study the senses for a very long time. In school we learn the five classic senses, but even way back from 1950s early 1960s the scientists that study this had already added way more than five. Even today, it is really unfortunate that we are only being taught five, whereas the scientists' studies have way more than that. So, for development, for any child developing to be waking up the senses, developing our sensorial world, is the only way to know the outside world through our sense portals. Through sight, through hearing, through sound, through our kinesthetic sense, which engages our vestibular system, through our proprioceptive sense. I am naming some of the others that aren't in the classic five. So, one of the primary senses that's acknowledged by all was the sum lumped together, kinesthetic sense, undivided the vestibular sense and proprioceptive sense. Our vestibular sense is our relationship to our body and gravity so literally our balance. There are some wonderful things about Gazebo. There are so many places that nothing was level. Kids were always engaging their vestibular

systems, their relationship to gravity, at all times as well as their proprioceptive sense—that is the capacity to know our body in relationship to itself. Even with our eyes closed, we have to know where our hand is, so to be in an environment where everything is not level, that engages balance, that engages knowing where our body is. But even just going back to the classic five [senses], when we are in wild nature, wilderness, we are inundated with it, and we are hooking up at the neurological physiological level. Young kids' brains are just open to be wired, and we are hooking up all sorts of synapses. There is one period around five years where they begin to close. There is another period in our early twenties where another wave of synapses begin to close down. That early early time in as wild of nature environment as you can get, I think, is critical to the development of the brain in how we know the world and literally how we know ourselves. Of course there are the classic ones, smell, sight, touch. Touch is so important. So often in classroom settings they take kids outside and they are told not to touch anything. Touch is so important. Our skin is not only our largest sense organ, it is actually the largest organ in the body. So to get kids out in wilderness where they are touching the ground, touching the earth, touching water, splashing water, getting their face in the water, all of that is activating and waking up the skin.

Despite the fact that certain neurological pathways are formed in the early years of life, there is more and more research on neuroplasticity that supports the ideas that the brain is plastic and can be changed through life with touch, movement, meditation. Michael Merzenich, Ph.D., neuroscientist, and author of *Soft-Wired: How The New Science Of Brain Plasticity Can Change Your Life*, has introduced important research on neuroplasticity and how the brain can be modified throughout life. Merzenich says,

> Whatever the circumstances of a child's early life, and whatever the history and current state of that child, every human has the built-in power to improve, to change for the better, to significantly restore and often to recover. Tomorrow, that person you see in the

mirror can be a stronger, more capable, livelier, more powerfully centered, and still-growing person.[5]

Consequently, rewiring after neurological health problems such as strokes is one example of how the body-brain is resilient. Daniel J. Siegel, M.D. speaks to the concept of neuroplasticity by saying,

> ...we create neural firing patterns that permit previously separated areas to become linked and integrated. The synaptic linkages are strengthened, the brain becomes more interconnected, and the mind becomes more adaptive.[6]

In this way, educators can support the developing child establish the wiring in brain and nervous system in a healthy way, however resilience is still possible for both children and adults. Changaris says, "Play and touch stimulate factors that increase the rate of brain plasticity—the rate a brain can remodel itself to learn new skills."[7] Touch is an important element in how we learn. Changaris relates that

> Research into the importance of touch has proven that it is vital for childhood development. In studies of both humans and animals, the quality and quantity of touch impacts the rates of physical growth and brain development.[8]

Touch is one of the many ways in which nature stimulates learning as it provides such sensory-rich experience. The natural world offers sensory stimulation through touch in each moment—from the feeling of wet grass on the feet, to the wind, or the feeling on the skin when the sun is covered by a cloud, playing in a sink or feeling the rough bark of a tree. Furthermore, additional sensory information such as the cry of a hawk, or the movement when the squirrel dashing up a tree, a bird's song in the morning, or even the silence after trees rustle is supplied unceasingly. Nature is all important when the child is learning to touch, listen, to feel, to sense and smell, and taste what the world is presenting.

Moreover, movement is an important aspect of neurological and physiological development and is of great importance to the mind-body connection.

Linda Hartley, author and Mind-Body Centering ® practitioner, says,

> The movement is coordinated by the brain and central nervous system with sensory information from the other areas of the body and from the environment as perceived through the senses. Movement is performed with the greatest ease and clarity when the most direct nerve pathway to and from the brain area is activated.[9]

In nature, children have the capacity and encouragement to move freely and ample sensory stimulus both of which contribute to the neural pathways remaining open for optimal neurological and physiological development. Harper continues,

> There is a dialogue that is going on on an unconscious level when we take a child out in nature. Who knows what is going on with a really young child who is preverbal. At the adult age, we know there are all sorts of dialogues going on on the organismic level—where every mitochondria of my body is aligning with gravity in every moment. Or that when we come together as a group in a room or outside, within the first few minutes, we have all already sniffed each other out. We have literally sniffed each other out, and we have sometimes already made assumptions about whether we like or dislike people in the group or a single person in the group by sniffing them out. And we did it on such an unconscious level, we weren't even aware of it. This is just one example, and I could go through all of the senses and give examples of ways in which our body was attending and we had no idea on a conscious level. I do believe that hooking up those full range of synapses gives us a fuller range of possibility as we go further in our life.

Harper adds that,

> I think letting young babies all the way up to young adults have as much contact with wild nature as possible, and really as much possibilities for activating and firing of neurons in a wide range of ways, actually helps develop a more whole brain. So, if we are just sitting in a classroom and sitting still, we are only going to use the visual. We are really severely limiting our mind body capacity. Our somatic capacity has just been completely left out. Our eyes are able to move. We are supposed to look at the chalkboard. We are supposed to be back and forth between teacher, or looking at writing a word or looking at a teacher. Of course there is hand-eye coordination, using a pencil, using a ball, things like that, but that is such a limited scope of what the human body can do.

With the digital world having such a strong influence on children today, outdoor education provides an important balance to learning through sensory awareness. Being close to nature and the earth allows children hands-on learning by furnishing ample stimulus for touch and movement. This sensory experiences helps make connections and form synapses in the a child's brain. With this stimuli, children gather information about the world, deduce and cognize, and ultimately learn. So, learning in the outdoors provides a sensory-rich environment, and thus opportunities to build awareness, and the ability to move and have full use of the body—an overall stimulating experience developmentally.

This sensory experience prepares the mind and body to be more aware about the world and how it works. The environment is a powerful place for academic connections such as science and literacy, and basically any of the academic content areas can be implemented or adapted to the outdoor classroom. Many parents and educators looks at academic learning as the scale for intelligence as it is based on performance, but in early education, the physical explorations are setting the groundwork for successful academic learning. So, it is possible that cognitive function in the later years is increased when a child's neurological and physiological development is nourished in the outdoors in the early years of life.

The Child's Perspective

The creation of a thousand forests is in one acorn.
– Ralph Waldo Emerson

An unstructured outdoor environment truly gives the imagination space to grow. I remember being a child and the greenhouse was so amazing to us that it was like a spaceship. It was warm and being inside with the plants and seeds and friends was a sweet memory for me. It was also a place where natural objects were on display along with a few microscopes and it was where we dried seeds in baskets and dried plants. The way the imagination is able to work when there are less props and prescribed toys and rather a connection with ever-changing surroundings of nature is pure magic. Delevett remembers,

> The butterflies and blue jays, the scent of eucalyptus, sage, ocean, cacula grass and other grass, the taste of honeysuckle and pas-sion flower nectar, calendula flowers and nasturtiums, picking fresh carrots in the garden (nothing tastes as good to me as fresh carrots), the scent of jasmine. Mostly my memories are very vivid sensations, being embodied, very different from many people who have no memories of their childhood. I think that's what made Gazebo special. Lying on the land, feeling the love for the land, for the people, the land the people the experience are all interwoven together.

Gazebo was a sort of utopia and the Park itself was designed in a way that children had a limitless freedom for their imaginations and interactions with nature. Davi remembers,

> My goodness—it is the most stunning paradise. I remember find-ing worms for the compost and learning how they are good for the gardens—that the worms are great friends. I remember warm

honeysuckle nectar. I remember the signs that Nana had us make "YUCKY" and "YUMMY" for the poisonous or edible plants. Walks to the garden, eating carrots from the ground. Hunting for bugs and finding a king snake by the road with its black and white rings.

Marquis reflects that,

Here's what I know. Now that I'm grown, working in a career I stumbled into which I love and enjoy, I know that one giant piece of me is missing. I miss being outdoors. I miss the air and the sunshine. I miss looking at the ocean. I miss having a direct relationship with nature, with my food, with the dirt under my nails. New York is dirty, but not with real dirt. I miss real dirt. I try and be eco-conscious. I recycle. I don't eat meat. I try and eat organic as much as life allows—just outside the boundaries of convenience and budget. But knowing this place is here, knowing every inch of it. Knowing the smell of the trees, the sweetness of the nectar in the flowers and the dampness of the greenhouse on a warm day—it's all in me. It's my sense memory palace. The way my young breath felt against the jacket of a teacher, the way the grass pressed into my cheeks when I lay on the ground. You know the full cycle of food. I remember the inner city kids coming here and saying, 'What! Carrots grow in the ground?' They were sort of horrified and amazed, and we were like, 'Yeah strawberries grow on bushes' and 'Yeah that's where food comes from.' It tends to be a recurring theme for me of feeling really thankful knowing that a seed goes in the ground or grows into a tree and you grow the plant and that someone grows the plant and we would cut them and eat them and poop them out. Or the food would get turned into fertilizer. Knowing the full cycle I think for me connects me to the ground and to the earth and to food. Even now in New York where I am so disconnected from everything, I still know where my lettuce comes from. It is such a nice thing that I am very thankful for.

Nature and Self-Reliance

Outdoor education provides many opportunities for self-reliance in children as they learn. Whitehand says, "Gazebo promotes independence and exploration as opposed to the structure that comes with being indoors." It goes back to the environment being the primary teacher. Children learn cause and effect in profound ways when in the outdoors. Davey remembers that environment as,

> The Park seemed gigantic—and each of the sections of the Park seemed like different lands. The entrance by the road was always the sunniest and warmest area— where the Big Wheels came down the hill to the hay bails. There was action there. The art barn seemed like a sacred place to me—I was never sure what I could or couldn't touch so I usually just browsed and poked around. The Library Boat seemed like it was its own country—playing on the deck or inside the boat with the musty smell of books. Everything about Gazebo helped me learn—how to be independent and curious.

Wolfinger feels the things that stuck with him from his nature education are his love for plants, animals, bugs, how to build strong immunity through exposure to dirt, but even more so a respect for life. He says,

> I now have spent the last ten years of my life teaching about our planet. The Gazebo Park has so many choices of micro-environments to grow from. Chores were to clean up after ourselves. Then other responsibilities were by choice. Gazebo taught me to be responsible for my actions and the environment. Gazebo gave me tools of self-reflection, strong, verbal communication, and a heightened ability to discern what is important to put my energy into.

When I asked Harper how nature teaches self-reliance and self-responsibility, he replied,

> How does it not? Every turn of the way, turn it back to: Where does nature not teach those skills? I can't think of a way in which nature—wild nature—doesn't teach those skills. And we get such immediate feedback with it too, there is often not very long for feedback. There could be with poison oak, or something like that where we got into it, and we didn't know it, and we didn't know what the cause was until forty-eight hours later. But, a lot of things in nature there is a pretty quick feedback loop into my learning curve. What could you name that you don't think supports that?"

My response was that "teachers" can sometimes get in the way of learning self-accountability, but ideally, especially within the principles demonstrated in the previous chapters, teachers might "get out of the way."

The elements of respect and responsibility are naturally present in an outdoor environment that belongs to children; whether it be a park environment, or a farm and garden setting, the children can take ownership and learn to care for the land and its inhabitants. If it is the children who care for the animals by bringing them to pasture, they learn about their needs. When they assist in watering the gardens, planting and harvesting, they learn about the process of growing, seeding, blooming. They can turn the compost and in doing so investigate the worms in the process and learn about decomposition. A park or a farm-like environment is perfect for children to learn as it offers jobs that they can take seriously and from this they learn their own importance within the rhythms of the day and in the cycle of the seasons. Furthermore, teachers model land stewardship as they work within the environment. Particularly, if the movement in the park is student-directed, the teachers have more freedom to care for the land, model this work, and always involve the children in their process.

Hannah Reese, Gazebo parent, reflects on her son Walter's experience at Gazebo,

> Empowering the child where the child is at. The most wonderful people are the teachers and interns at Gazebo. Beautiful, highly trained, peaceful, loving people surround our children and care for our children. Giving them tools to help themselves safely in the open air with butterflies and flowers. Walter is at an age where he needs/desires control for his world and the teachers understand this and give him choices to make his own decision. He is very empowered by this and I'm so thankful he has the opportunity and SPACE to grow here at Gazebo.

Calculated Risk and Unstructured Environment

Nature education is not without its risks, but when tended to with attention and mindfulness, the risks can be so rewarding. There are great rewards for children in learning to coordinate their bodies on uneven surfaces as an infant begins crawling in the grass and grows into a toddler falling and getting up to stand and eventually walk. In this way, children are building muscle patterns of movement in a nonlinear environment that allows for fuller development. Learning to walk on hills and bumps, over stones and leaves, dry sand or mud, perhaps even with bare feet, and becoming mobile through this with a connection to the earth requires a heightened kinesthetic awareness. The stimulation provided from the outdoors is entirely different than a child who learning to walk on flooring and concrete in an indoor environment. Though some cultures keep babies off the ground, a baby who is held most of the time by adults and not allowed contact with the earth has a different kinesthetic experience. There is always risk in life, and perhaps even greater risk with children climbing trees, but calculated risk is the key concept here.

Children rise to challenges. As Vieregge states, they demand the challenge of relevance and intellectual rigor. They also grow tremendously within a physically challenging environment. Children's love of calculated risk and their joy when fear is triumphed can be worth the chances. Of course, health and safety are first, but if handled with caution and respect, the responsibilities of using sharp tools and even learning to cross the road when guided by a caring adult, can become so empowering for young people. Tracking the weather and learning the potential dangers of sun, cold, wind, lightning. Understanding the risks of snakes, poison plants, and mushrooms, are all important in learning how to be safe in the natural world.

Harper says,

> I use that word 'calculated risk.' We have made our playgrounds so safe that in the possibilities of learning to take risks, there is no consequences of a fall, except maybe a little bit of a bump and your back up and going. I really believe there is this need to take calculated risks so that we learn. It is a learned thing. How do I learn to step out of what I know into what is unknown? And if I don't learn that, than I am not learning how to learn. I think calculated risk is a really important piece of that, because there is no way to learn if I don't take some type of risk. Even if it is a math problem, I try this

it didn't work. That was a risk I took to try a particular formula, and it didn't work, and I learned that and I learned to take a risk. So, all the way from the physical to the mental, and then I would include the emotional too—to be in a relationship, or to be a parent, is learning to take calculated emotional risks daily. I think that is one of the most critical things that a child or adult can learn, and if I am interested in it, I will be able to learn because I learn how to learn. I haven't limited myself, in that sense of the language, and have given myself a fairly full capacity that allows that capacity to be a continual learner. Calculated risk is really important. When Kai [my son] was at Gazebo and transferred into Captain Cooper [the local elementary school], he got a write-up for climbing a tree. He was just shocked. One, to get a wright-up and scolded as he wasn't used to that, and two, for climbing a tree! It was so natural for him, coming from Gazebo, he could not put the two together. Picture me as an irate parent going into Captain Cooper and going, 'This is not going to work. I get maybe you can't do trees, but how this was handled, this is not going to work.' An example of a kid making the transition from Gazebo to a playground where trees are not allowed because they are too risky.

Indigenous Wisdom

Mother Earth is the foundation of life. Without her we would not be here. All people know this, but all people do not respect it. Since children are the next generation of caretakers of Mother Earth, we must teach them the respect from an early age.

– Tsolagui M.A. RuizRazo

Wisdom traditions connect us to earth-based teachings. Seeking knowledge from indigenous elders and from ancient ways can help children see their impact on ecosystems and understand their interactions with the earth; so they can ultimately better understand the fragile web of life. In many Native American tribes, there are teachings about harvesting with respect. Robin Wall Kimmerer, scientist and author of *Braiding Sweetgrass*, describes her people's teachings of the concept of the "Honorable Harvest." Asking permission to use the plant before harvesting, respecting the answer, offering something in return, only taking what you need, only take what is given, and using all of what you take are important elements of honoring the earth.[10] There is an exchange in this way. Working with children on how to harvest plants with respect and reverence is a tool that has always felt right to me. I point out to children to look and not to harvest if there is only one flower on the plant, to ask permission and let the plant know the intention of your use, to offer some thanks. In this way, children learn about being in relationship with plants and it cultivates a deeper respect for their environment and the earth. Handl used to hear the call of the crows and call back, "Hello cousin crow." I used to wonder about this and thought it was curious at the time, but I look back on it now and have begun to say the same to my own daughter when I hear crows. Much like the Native American principle of "All My Relations," calling the crow cousin brought in the interconnection of all of the life forms.

I have always been drawn to Native American ways, as native people honor the earth and are connected to it, spiritually as well as physically. I see that we receive our life through the food, the plants, the animals and all that are around us. I do not belong to a Native tribe. Furthermore, being myself white and privileged, I am careful about offering traditional ancient indigenous teachings and would like to see this curriculum offered in an authentic way. Nevertheless, I acknowledge that indigenous wisdom is powerful and there is a deep well of teachings that children can benefit from. I feel I can responsibly work with these teachings in only a small ways in my work with children, by sharing my own beliefs—a strong connection to and reverence for the earth.

Nevertheless, sharing of indigenous wisdom can support the children and their understanding of the earth. We can do this by bringing indigenous people to share these teachings with the children. Connecting children to First Nation's people is a way to both honor people who have lost so much, while at the same time illustrating the resilience and perseverance of Native peoples today who work to revitalize their traditions. Acknowledging Native peoples as part of our community is important in seeing Native people for how they live today while connecting children to the crucial teachings that indigenous culture offers; especially around our relationship to the earth. There are meaningful children's books that can support this kind of learning. Sharing about the ways of the people who came before us can open children's minds to other ways of life and how people lived off the land at one time.

At the same time, it is important to avoid stereotypes that all Native peoples live off the land or on reservations and also view native peoples in their present circumstances as large numbers of Native people now live in metropolitan areas. There is a sad history of persecution and continued systematic oppression of Native people. Sometimes, these issues are challenging to address, and there are not always clear solutions on how to remedy the injustices of both the past and present. Nevertheless, investigations of indigenous rights and environmental justice can give children insight to the connection all human beings have to the earth. Understanding the ways of Native people illuminates the importance of conservation of the environment and of cultural traditions. Learning from the teachings of Native people and indigenous practices can help us come into balance with nature. Simply being in nature with awareness and respect for the earth as a teacher is powerful. Seeing the earth for its intricate web of life and all its interdependency bridges the cultural teachings and children learning in nature.

The Web of Life

Nelson says about his own children, "At some point in their lives I think they will appreciate the transformative and contemplative value of being in nature. I think it is instilled in them and Gazebo was certainly a part of that." Another Japanese word that seems to echo the benefits of the outdoors is "shinrin-yoku" which means forest bathing. Shinrin-yoku is to enter nature or the forest with the intention of silence, peace and realization. In this way, nature is healing, and has a tranquility that affects even spiritual and emotional elements of the human psyche.

Tsolagui M.A. RuizRazo, Cherokee Elder and traditional healer, shared in *Tomorrow's Children—A Cherokee Elder's Guide to Parenting*, "It is just as important to demonstrably love your child and nurture her spirit beyond the years of toddlerhood. This you can do by sustaining her contact with nature."[11] A connection to nature has a quiet and self-reflective element. For children, learning to tune into the environment and themselves in it is a skill that connects them to nature and to themselves. The first thing I do when bringing children into nature is to discuss how to be in awareness, without disturbing the environment—not leaving a trace. We can notice more by being in a state of awareness when we are not disturbing the environment and ecosystems. Learning through observation, listening, seeing, smelling, touching, are only a few of the senses that are activated stimulating neurosomatic learning. The use of documentation, sketching, nature journals, gathering information and data, and returning to the same site in ongoing investigations can be great tools for outdoor education. Different practices from simple awareness to scientific skill sets can support observation.

Recently, my love for nature has really grown and my sense of connection to place, to the earth the plants, trees, animals, and ecosystems, particularly in my area where I live. I feel like I was given such a gift to have had the experience of Gazebo, but my experience in nature was part of my life outside of school as well. I feel so lucky to have had the opportunity to be in nature as a child, and I am blessed to still live in Big Sur. When I was about one year old, we moved from Esalen, to the land I grew up on in Big Sur in southern Big Sur where my father cultivated the land.

My father is an avid outdoorsman and hunter. He took me and my siblings and friends hiking and backpacking at a young age and showed us tracking and naturalist skills. He knows many native plants and flowers including the Latin names. He knows the patterns of the animals, their calls, their marks, their scat. He knows when the swallows return, when it is time to prune, and when it is time to plant, and water, and when to harvest. He knows the weather patterns, the marks of the bucks' antlers on the tree bark, the places mushrooms like to grow. Each morning he feeds and watches the birds—the quales and doves gather around him without fear. He knows the time when the light hits certain parts of the property and when it is best to sit in the sun and work at his bench carving local Jade.

For over forty years, he has lived and breathed the land. I have seen this with other old time Big Sur people in that they sort of become part of the land they live on. Other cultures, particularly tribal cultures, but even people who were displaced by colonialism, slavery, genocide, and imperialism, still have an amazing connection to their places of origin or where they call home. I feel Esalen is this for many people who have found healing there, met their mates there, or even had children there. We as humans are connected to the land. We are part of nature. We are no different, no more or less important, than each and every plant, animal or organism, in terms of our contribution and impact within the whole of our ecosystem, environment, and planet. We are connected!

Growing up in Big Sur, we went hiking or we surfed for fun! When I hear the kids in the local high school saying they went hiking this summer, I know as an educator they did much more than just walk in the forest. When in nature, they are identifying plants and animals, learning weather patterns, gaining physical skills through the use of their senses, adapting bilateral movements that are shown to increase cognitive function, and much more. I feel this is important for inner-city children as well and would like to see more cross-cultural connections in our area—inner-city kids contacting nature, rural kids coming in contact people of other walks of life—sharing knowledge. Rites of passage programs, particularly for at-risk children or youth can promote growth as well. I feel blessed to have this love of the earth to share with young people. Connecting children with natured doesn't have to look one way. Gazebo relied on the agrarian life of farming and gardening. Adventure-based programs, survivalist and naturalist programs are also ways in which children can participate in the outdoor education experience. I hope that educators can foster the nature-child relationship, as it is so important for the future of our planet.

Returning to the Native American concept of, "All my Relations" which views the natural world as related to us and to be respected like a family member. Indigenous wisdom shows the way of being in relationship with the natural world. First Nations peoples viewed this reciprocity as not just for what nature can offer humans, but how humans both impact and are in an energetic exchange with the natural world. In this way we are in relationship not just to plants and animals just for their healing ability and for food, but because we are both alive, and potentially contain life in the form of spirit. There is a marriage between spirituality and science. The earth gives its gifts so generously, and within the reciprocity of relationship, we might ask what can we give in return. The answer is highly personal.

In this way, being alone with nature has also been a traditional path of indigenous peoples. There is so much tranquility and wisdom available when we spend time in nature. The Native American vision quest is a ritual in which a person, often a youth coming of age, come to know themselves in a deeper way by being alone in nature. In today's world, there is a lot fear around being safe in the wilderness alone, and that notion certainly is fair. On the other hand, drawing from the ancient wisdom of First Nations people, educators may see the value of nature connection on a very intimate and personal level.

There is something inherently spiritual and transcending to experience the beauty of nature. One can only hope that each person adapts as they build relationship to nature in their own way. When we as humans are truly connected to nature, even an animal sighting such as a hawk and two crows between rain storms can be a personal sign, bringing hope, insight or can even be a spiritual experience.

Kimmerer says,

> I've heard it said that sometimes, in return for the gifts of the
> earth, gratitude is enough. It is our uniquely human gift to express
> thanks, because we have the awareness and the collective memory
> to remember that the world could well be otherwise, less gener-
> ous than it is. But I think we are called to go beyond cultures of
> gratitude, to once again become cultures of reciprocity.[12]

In this way, the life-giving and healing power of nature is real, but
as humans can we find ways to do more than take, but to give back.
The earth is alive with the elements: the earth, fire, water and air, as
being a source of life to all living things in the cycle of life.

We are connected to this web of life and our actions are part
of its delicate balance. The state of our planet is dire. I fear for my
daughter's generation having to pay for our carelessness with global
warming and climate change. Teaching young children that we have
a strong impact, and to care for the natural world at a young age, may
be the hope for the future of our environment. Ultimately, the earth
is our source of life, our food, our air, our water. It is precious more
than just an environment with resources for us but as a relative, in
relation to us. We must teach our children how sacred, how joyful,
how valuable is our relationship with the earth.

The Power of Play

Play is the work of children.

– Jean Piaget

*If we destroy full bodied PLAYING in early human life
we are left with sorrow. The tragedy of human life
without the comedy.*

– JL

Samantha said it was show time and she and Emily sat down on the little wire bistro set with a coffee cup and lid as percussion instruments and sang native chants. What came out of this six-year-old child wasn't just singing, she was deep in it, and she would lift her hands up and Emily would follow. Later, Samantha told me she knew singing from ceremonies with her mom and grandma. She knew about offering food and singing gifts to the spirits. She knew it made them happy. This child that swings like a dancer twirling legs like a ballerina in midair. She who decided to be a tour guide when a group of youth from inner-city Los Angeles were visiting the school. She who decided instead of throwing away a flower plant that had been cut back, she would make bouquets and hand them out to people at Esalen who happened to walk by the school. Each person reacted, smiled, or said, "No thanks," to which she seemed puzzled as to why not. Some were touched, and one woman even cried. I thought she would charge money or offer some trade but she was doing it because it was making people happy and this made her happy.

I have written a lot so far about what Gazebo doesn't do, how not to intervene. *Allow* is probably the most popular word in this book. Yet there is a space for what does unfold that is hard to describe. The processes, the creativity, the play that arises from children being free in the outdoor elements is ever changing and continuously wondrous. It can be anything, and they come up with the most creative ideas! It might begin with curiosity about termites that turns into a project that goes on for weeks during which the children take dead logs apart with different tools. It might be an ongoing love for a certain activity that grows in challenge and interest. My daughter loved the swings and these were places of play, learning, and comfort for her during her time at Gazebo. She gradually learned new ways of playing with them and still goes to swing when she visits.

Nature provides such an interactive learning landscape that in combination with the children's play, there is all manner of possibilities. My daughter and I spent less than an hour in the Gazebo Park the other day visiting the new Big Sur Park School program and touching base with the land and people. So much happened in such the short time we were there. A hawk swooped in and grabbed something as my daughter and her best friend walked their trikes up the hill. They gasped in amazement as it flew off and landed in a nearby eucalyptus tree. A little boy grabbed a trike and flew down the hill full force with infectious joy and abandon. He marveled at two turkey vultures that came to roost in the trees above the bike track. Two boys played on top of a playhouse and made loud noises and seemed to experience great power from their height and position. Another boy climbed a tree by himself, feeling sad he wasn't playing with the girls on the bike track. He lay down on the tree until I came to check in with him, playing some of the bells hanging on the tree while I asked what was going on and if he needed some support. Emotions at the end of the school day came in waves as parents arrived and children remembered how much they missed them. One boy broke out in tears when his mom arrived, then soon after proudly showed off his block buildings. It was amazing how much went on in such a short time and none of it was inspired by teachers, it was all the kids engaging in play and wonder.

While Gazebo provided the setting for children to learn, play was really the vehicle for the learning. "It is the free play, the interplay, of all the child's powers, thoughts, and physical movement, in embodying, in a satisfying form, his own images and interests," said John Dewey.[1] So many theoretical approaches were born out of play because natural play is what children do so well. Experiential learning is key as each child learns through experience and play is such a valuable vehicle for this learning. So, student-led and play-based curriculum design brings a different experiential value to the learning. Furthermore, unstructured and organic timing make so many things possible that otherwise would not be. So, children can take as long as they need in any given experience. They can fully engage in a play process, and integrate their experience. The ability to have a small teacher-child ratio also supports open play processes. Moreover, calculated risk within a play-based environment is a significant element. Play evokes an emergent curriculum based on children's interests and builds resourcefulness, social-emotional development, physical and neurological development, and it is fun!

How do children learn through play? Why is experience more meaningful than direct instruction? How is play social learning? How do mixed-aged groups support learning? What is somatic education? What is emergent curriculum? How do unstructured play and organic timing support children? How is calculated risk valuable? What made the Gazebo approach different from other play-based methods? "I feel like all of the Gazebo learning was embodied learning, none of it was theoretical," Delevett says. Behind these stories and experiences about Gazebo, there are theories and concepts that developed over time, yet it all came from a deep trust in play. According to the National Alliance for Educating Young Children (NAYCE),

> Play and learning go hand-in-hand. They are not separate activities. They are intertwined. Think about them as a science lecture with a lab. Play is the child's lab.[2]

And, what do children want more than anything? Probably, to have a good time, to have fun, to engage life with joy! They do this naturally. They play, and they learn concurrently. Play is what instills the love of learning.

As children play, social dynamics emerge, personal challenges arise and are often overcome, and physical tasks which require small and large motor skills create challenges and triumphs. The outdoor environment is especially supportive of independence, dramatic play, and imaginary play and games. At Gazebo there were very few projects or toys that had prescriptive uses, but there were many moving parts and open-ended activities available in which a child could create and be imaginative. Play was the vehicle for learning. A person might simply see play as play and isolated from development and learning, yet the teachings behind play are much more profound.

There are many aspects to Gazebo, but one of the most awesome was the freedom that children had to be self-directed. The child was the leader in that they got to choose to follow what interested them, they got to decide how long they want to spend exploring what interested them. It was about inquiry, hands-on learning, dramatic play, imaginary play, unstructured play. The learning culture at Gazebo was not about outcome, or creating a beautiful art piece or something to bring home to parents. The culture was about development, about being present in the moment as each child learns about the world and learns to trust themselves within it.

Miller feels that,

> People like to enter into dramatic play with kids. Vygotsky says, 'Ask the right questions or provide the right prop so that they can take it further.' At Gazebo there are all kinds of props. For example, the skills to take the Hot Wheels, the hard work getting it up the hill and the balance coming down, or the bubbles there all of the time.

So, the environment and the allowance of exploration combined made play at Gazebo even more possible. Says Barnes,

> Gazebo being outdoors makes it stand out. The interactive garden and animals are also unique. Gazebo encourages children to be independent. To problem-solve and work out disputes without much adult intervention. Emphasis on unstructured learning.

The possibilities with play are endless.

Why Play?

Play is everything. Play is life. Play is the dance of life.
We should be playing all our lives.

– Lia Thompson-Clark

Thompson-Clark, former Gazebo director, is one of the people that has implemented Gazebo-esque philosophy out in the world with the two schools she created. As director of the Children's Center at Sonoma State University, she brings in play as a strong element of their philosophy. More and more early childhood centers are seeing the value of play-based approach as a best practice for young children. Thompson-Clark relates to Einstein's comment that play is the highest form of research. She suggests that,

> If you you look at it from a scientific perspective, this is their form of research. They are testing ideas, role-playing, practicing being mommy, daddy, brother, sibling, or they have a dog in the family. Maybe there is a new baby in the family and one of them says to the other, 'You are going to be my baby.' They are practicing all these kinds of roles that they see out in the world and it is research. The main opportunities that we saw, that those of us who fell in love with what Gazebo was about, saw that it offered so many rich opportunities for play and basically nonstop play. Even when children were working and being part of a project, which was very much a part of the daily ongoing life because one of Janet's fabulous tenants was about bringing life into the curriculum. There was no different definition between play and work. Just like there was no difference between what was cognitive development, social emotional physical, what was physical development. Everything in early education in the first five years is very much one rather than separated out. Whereas elementary schools get physical education or direct teaching cognitive thinking education. It is all all embedded in play. Play wraps everything up.

Similarly, author and psychologist David Elkind suggests,

> Adults respond so negatively to play because they define it as simply having fun and, therefore, as a waste of time. But though play can be fun, as one of the three essential drives—love, play, work—it contributes to the best kind of learning. Play operates as more than a creative urge; it also functions as a fundamental mode of learning.[3]

Douce echoes how important play has been in his own work by saying,

> The sense of experimentation and play has rubbed off on my teach-
> ing. So, when I teach I look for when the people start letting out
> joy, and then I step back. I teach many different techniques, but
> I am waiting for people to be silly and have joy. It continues from
> there because it is one of the more essential human qualities. We
> are taught to worry about Iraq and the price of cheese at Safeway
> and maybe it is o.k. to be aware of that, but we can focus on the joy
> and pleasure we have too. In my groups I really do teach to wait
> by the various different techniques and the best one, really, is the
> partner work that I teach which I have adapted from Taoist martial
> arts. With my own exploration, like the back-to-back movement.
> People start to do those, and they start to play, they get silly, they
> get goofy, and that is what I want. I had one group of work scholars
> once ask me, 'We get really loud and we're not listening to what
> you are telling us, and we're just doing whatever we want?' I said,
> 'That is what I am trying to do! I am not upset, that is what I am
> trying to encourage, the sense of not listening to everything you
> are told, that sense of playfulness.

Holloman reflects that,

> The realm of play and fantasy is something that is quite developed
> in young children. In some ways as we deal with the stresses of life,
> that creative capacity seems to shut down in a lot of adults. Whereas
> in younger children, along with their bodies, their physical expres-
> sion, the most creatively able portions of their being. So, much
> of how it is that they are experiencing each other, relationships,
> the universe, the immediate environment that they are in contact
> with, even complex relationships like to their parents, or between
> their parents, ends up playing out their impressions, their feelings
> about them get expressed in play. Really it is a way that they make
> an attempt to understand and organize their world and orient
> within it. Within educational structures like Gazebo, children
> can express themselves and this is hugely important as children
> develop, helping them maintain a connection and openness to
> those capacities as they become older, teenagers, and even adults.

Delevett remembers,

> Getting to dress up as a princess all the time. Believing I was
> a princess, still can slip into princess mode at times (not Marie
> Antoinette-like princess) but more like fairy tale princess, like a
> Cinderella, where there are fairies all around, godmothers (good
> people) to help you live your dreams.

And Reese recalls, "Walter and Sage playing with bubbles and just
screaming, playing off each other, squealing like stellar jays. There
are not too many places where those sounds would feel so right and
natural."

The outdoor setting at Gazebo provided a wide open space for
experimentation. Baldwin also speaks to the importance of play,

> Gazebo is a place they can do all sorts of outrageous things. That
> doesn't mean the world is a place they can go out and run in all
> directions and do crazy things. At Gazebo you can do certain
> things that with granny you are not going to do. The stuff you
> can do at Gazebo, you can't do in other circumstances. There is a
> certain sense of the outrageous the school doesn't want to damper.
> Gazebo wants you to know that is possible. So, it is allowing them
> to be people; especially in free play.

The lessons the children were learning through their experience
and experiment provided a depth for many teachings to emerge.
Douce explains,

> In my Feldenkrais training, we would work during the week,
> and I would go back to Esalen on the weekend to work for free. I
> remember there was this one sequence we were working on and off
> for months, it was very complicated. Then one day, I was walking
> down to the baths, and I saw a group of you kids playing, and you
> were doing the movement that we were working on for months,
> giggling and laughing, and doing it in a circle on the way to the
> baths. So, the movements Feldenkrais was teaching, a lot of them
> were movements we already knew, but we were educated to forget
> them.

Experiential Learning

Experience precedes knowledge.

–JL

When I began teaching at Gazebo, I often felt the urge to rush the children, to pressure them to complete tasks like washing hands and going to the bathroom so we could get onto the next project, painting, gardening etc. It took time for me to realize that the washing hands and diapering and toileting were the curriculum. They were learning what they needed to care for their bodies. Also, learning how to do it themselves, they were learning self-sufficiency and hygiene. I would watch as a child would try to turn the handle of the drinking fountain, splash themselves in the face, or struggle to turn it to get the water to come out. I would fight the urge to step in, to do it for them. It would sometimes take minutes, hours, or even days for mastery of a tool such as this. But, when the child did turn that handle by themselves, when they were able to do it themselves, even with a bit of coaching from an adult, it was a triumph that could not have been possible if I had stepped in and did what they could do themselves even with a bit of a struggle.

This is true for relationships throughout our lives and for our struggles as both adults and children navigate independence rather than codependence. It is easy for humans to instinctually want to rescue others, especially children, from their experiences in which they struggle, but it is exactly that experience that will teach them what they need to know to gain independence. When we rescue others, we take away that experience. Also, the notion of "helping" is sometimes dangerous. We want to support others, but we don't want our counterparts to lean on us so much that they cannot stand on their own. Like Douce's back-to-back movement activity has deeper metaphoric lessons, the relationships have a balance. Imagine two people standing back-to-back leaning on each other. They each need to give enough support for balance, but if they lean too much, it is a burden for one, and may even make them fall. In relationship, if one doesn't carry some of their own weight, if they lean so much they can't stand without the other, that is no longer support but dependence. This relationship balance can manifest in physical or emotional support, but we can use it an example of our own dance with codependence and Independence. In this way when we see a child struggle, it is natural for everything in our being to want to help, our instincts often say we must. But if we hold back, allow, trust, support without changing their experience, the triumph, pride, and subsequent resourcefulness that follows is rewarding for both teacher and student.

In this way, Gazebo gave space for children to fully experience learning. "Experience precedes knowledge," Lederman said. Moreover, Charles clarifies, "First the experience, then the learning." So much of our culture in mainstream education dictates what the child is to know, and transmits that information by means of instruction that is often a one-size-fits-all approach. As we know, children learn differently, have different timing and interests, and are successful in different learning environments and conditions. It is not always possible to have optimal learning environments, or student-teacher ratios. There are limitations based on funding and educational standards, and the model of instruction-based teaching as the mainstream in education.

Yet, the experiential learning approach, in a sense, reverses the order. In this way, first comes the curiosity, then comes the inquiry, then the cognition of that experience and making sense of the learning. So, the making sense happens after play and experimentation, having your own relationship with the object of the learning. Then with experiential learning, it becomes an understanding that is individual and relevant. "Play and interaction should not be underestimated—I have a deep appreciation for learning by experience," says Davey.

Charles acknowledges that, "The schooling I had was about having the right answer, it wasn't about the learning. How do I learn how to learn?" Children learn how to learn by making mistakes, struggling at times, working through challenges, problem-solving, developing critical-thinking and critical-feeling skills, learning independence and also learning to ask for help. Wolfinger emphasizes,

> As a teacher, I have taught for ten years in public schools, you know a lot of these kids are just so afraid of failure. 'If I don't do good then I didn't learn anything.' I try to explain to them if you did good all the time, you didn't learn anything. You need to fail to learn. That is the beauty. That is the good stuff. You got to hurt a little bit, and be okay with that pain of having to figure it out for yourself, and be strong enough to do it."

Learning through experience versus instruction was an important distinction at Gazebo; and other institutions such as NOLS utilizes experiential-based education as well. Harper suggests,

> NOLS is very geared around experiential learning. At what point, as the instructor, do you step in, and what point do you step out? I think it was the same thing at Gazebo as a tree. At what point

do you step in and at what point do you step out? These judgment calls can be learned, but I don't know if they can be taught. I don't think as a teacher you can say, 'Here is how you make judgment calls.' I do think I could give you the opportunities that you could learn. I still I have groups at Esalen where I am watching them in a place where the trail washes out. Most of the group is doing fine and someone is having a little trouble, and I am waiting, and watching. I am putting all of my years of experience of teaching rock-climbing, high-risk sports—mountaineering, white water rafting, hang gliding, you name it, I did it. I am putting all that up and watching. At what point do I intervene? Do I need to intervene at all? How can I do it in a way that is minimally intrusive to their process? That is a question I am constantly asking, and teachers of kids need to be asking. But it is work. It is something you need to train in again and again. It is something that you can't learn in a textbook, or you can't be taught out of a textbook, but it can be learned.

How do we create the environment we need to learn? How do we create the supports that we need to learn? How do we come in contact with experience in this way? Price talks about what it means to have direct contact with experience through a continuum of awareness,

> Questions arise that support this awareness such as, 'What am I aware of now? What am I feeling/experiencing now? What am I thinking/doing? What am I perceiving? How do I feel, and what do I feel? Can I feel what I'm feeling?' Words are the second step.

She suggests bringing a curiosity to the present moment. So, within these reflections, there is a shift in focus from intellect to experience. In turning towards sensations in the body, the learning becomes more embodied. Holloman expresses,

> The basic notion is that we understand that an experience-forward model is the most effective way to help the central nervous system develop. Experience first has a lot to do with the body, not just

touch and movement and breath, but hearing, seeing, smelling, tasting. That is the most effective way to awaken and integrate living systems and organisms in humans in particular.

Brain-Body = Mind-Body

When I lived in Africa and studied dance and music, I would arrange or choreograph a dance, and other dancers would say, "C'ést intelligent." It is intelligent. I was amazed that they culturally equated this physical form to intelligence, whereas I was accustomed to the Western view of dance, movement, even sports, as appreciated forms of movement for the athletes and dancers physical ability, but not necessarily for their intelligence.

Growing up at Esalen, the mind-body principles were in place all around us and we were exposed to many types of healing and movement modalities that were offered there. Through learning Esalen massage®, dance, yoga, tai chi, qi gong and more, I was saturated in mind-body practices throughout my life on a very unconscious level. I would watch Chungliang Al Huang and a group of students practice tai chi on the pool deck as the sun set behind them. I could join in Gabrielle Roth's 5Rhthyms® dance workshops as a very young child with my friends and experience free expression of movement and emotions. I could sit in the tub and watch people give massages or experience massage myself at a young age. I began learning African dance and drumming from Babatunde Olantunji at the age of six. I was very blessed with these opportunities and feel they are woven into who I am as a person, and that they also helped me develop these strong mind-body connections.

It wasn't until I began my work as a teacher that I started to see on a conceptual level how the mind-body principles work with these movement practices. When I was an aid to a first-grade autistic child, I got a glimpse of what is possible when and I saw how embodied this student became when he practiced Aikido. Through this experience, and my work in Feldenkrais based movement and touch practices, I began to see how both movement and touch were tremendously healing and addressed the mind and body in a unified way. I saw in my work in a Waldorf inspired school how the use of Eurythmy rods made of copper, by throwing and catching using bilateral movements, could increase cognitive function. I was exposed to Brain Gym in the public school system, a program that addressed physical movement beyond the physical education that was being offered by "enhanced learning through movement." Accordingly, there is more and more scientific evidence that supports the concept of mind-body integration and its importance in academic and cognitive function. Douce shares,

> I came back from somewhere, and I walked into the lodge and there was a group of kids running around the table—but running sideways. The whole group was running sideways, which I teach in my workshops—to get people to walk sideways. People don't walk sideways, they walk forward and back, turn, but they don't walk sideways. This was a group of children that hadn't gone to school yet. We have sideways walking already in the beginning. It is extinguished with school. A lot of the most useful movements were already there. Real school erases them.

Anat Baneil, founder of the Anat Baneil Method® and Neuro-Movement®, states that,

> The idea that the body and the mind are one has been advocated now for quite some time. Yet most people still think of 'the body,' or 'physical movement' as separate, different, and independent from 'mental' activity such as thinking, emotions, beliefs, feelings, and social behaviors. Many people find it hard to comprehend how physical movement can help form and enhance thinking and vice versa. In actual practice, many interventions, such as different therapies and fitness programs, approach the physical as a separate entity from the mental. It is only after we have learned how to move and to think, and interact socially, that we can forget the intimate

relationship and the oneness of mind and body. You take away movement, there is no thinking; you take away thinking, there is no movement. And if you take away feeling, there is no action. It all works as one highly complex system.[4]

Furthermore, international yoga teacher, Mark Whitwell describes the mind-body connection as,

We tend to think of the mind as the brain alone, but this is only one small aspect of mind. Your brain core is the culmination of the whole nervous system, so your mind doesn't start at your neck, but at your feet. When you engage the whole body as a feeling mechanism, you can 'think' better; you are literally in touch with reality. The brain core is the culmination of the whole nervous system. The spinal column gets bigger and bigger and it is all brain. The brain is the body. The nervous system is brain so it is just one embodiment. The mind is this extraordinary refinement of the nervous system; and perceptions. When you engage the whole body as this feeling mechanism, that is so useful to the mind because the mind can think better.[5]

Peter Levine developed Somatic Experiencing® work which integrates mind-body and brings healing by releasing trauma and patterning that is held in the body on a very physical level. This work recognizes the mind-body connection and turns towards the somatic experience as a means of self-work. Levine and Maggy Kline share,

The mammalian (mid brain) or limbic system is also referred to as the 'emotional brain' because it processes memories and feelings. The reptilian or 'lower' brain is responsible for survival through the myriad functions that accompany the regulatory mechanisms of basic existence, such as a heart rate and respiration. These include the workings of our nervous system that interact with our sensory and motor systems to move us quickly out of danger. These primitive brain parts form the basic body-brain connection.[6]

The mind-body is an integrated system that fully engages the brain, the nervous system, and the full body. Siegel states that,

> It is important to remember that the activity of what we're call-ing the 'brain' is not just in our heads......The neural networks throughout the interior of the body, including those surrounding the hollow organs, such as the intestines and the heart, send complex sensory input to the skull-based brain. This data forms the foundation for visceral maps that help us have a 'gut feeling' or a 'heartfelt' sense. Such input from the body forms a vital source of intuition and powerfully influences our reasoning and the way we create meaning in our lives.[7]

Furthermore, neuroscientist Richard Davidson shares,

> I was listening to a talk not too long ago in which a Stanford biologist made the provocative claim which I think is very very important, 'Do you know what is the most powerful pharmaceutical on the planet?' Food—food is the most powerful pharmaceutical because it will impact our gut which has enormous influence over our brain. To say that the mind is just in the brain ignores our bodies, and then there are much more complicated and much more difficult sorts of challenges.[8]

Douce says,

> The question is, what is education? Feldenkrais judged education not only in mental tasks, but in physical tasks. So that a judgment of intelligence also involves your ability to move. The educational system doesn't measure that at all. Except gives you a football scholarship so you can destroy yourself. Dancers are some of the smartest. It is more just become an exercise, dance. A lot of my friends in Bali, the best ones, move paint around. They move their body and they move paint around. So, they are often wearing part of it. So, it is not all being controlled like this. Life isn't just like this, a small focused control.

In today's education system and cultural climate, the emphasis on technology moves children away from an experience of learning in which the mind-body is engaged. Children are more and more focused on smaller and smaller devices and screens. Rather than moving paint around a large canvas, most children are moving the mouse around a small square inch with one finger. There is something very visceral and physical that is lost in this shift to technology. There is an aesthetic that is lost as well. Essentially, children need the use of their bodies through large and fine motor skills in order to develop in a whole way. Consequently, play processes, which include movement and touch, are vital to children's mind-body development.

Neural Somatics and Play

Play leads to discovery, feeding our brains with information to create new and unexpected possibilities.

– Anat Baniel

Play is a process which engages the brain on many levels. As I've discussed, brain research supports the idea that developing the neurological function is not separate from developing the physiological functions. Thompson-Clark comments that, "The children, being able to play so freely, become deeply connected to the somatic system, their nervous system, their brains." The mind-body connection is important in understanding how our brains and bodies function and process our experiences. From body sensations to emotions, play provides a supporting structure for understanding the developing mind-body. Holloman says,

Usually not all play, but a lot of play, involves utilizing parts of not just our bodies, but our central nervous systems, that in a verbal-cognitive adult world are often underutilized. If you underutilize anything, the way that the brain and the body are constructed, we begin to lose the neural muscular or neuro pathways that are connected to certain areas. For instance the limbic systems, which is the emotional, the midbrain, the part of the nervous system that is dedicated to feeling. Feeling is a big part of how we experience richness, fullness, and the depth of life and living. So, I would include things, not just play, but playing music, that evoke feeling in us and involve an engagement with the physical body. A creative endeavor that awakens parts of our central nervous systems then connect us to parts of our being, parts of our way of experiencing this universe, that add depth, richness and meaning to life and living. At Gazebo, I sometimes witnessed parents who had a stiffness or a rigidity to them and the quality of their interactions with their children to where it felt like there was a certain dryness, a lack of depth. I felt like they were experiencing themselves as caretakers of the child's physical well-being, and it was their job to make sure that they were clothed and fed and educated, and that is about the extent of it. In my experience, there is such a huge palette of emotion that is felt and shared. These connect us to processes of life that add tremendous depth of experience to my experience, to my quality of life. For instance when I get very stressed, I notice I am shutting down, for periods of time, my access to those parts of experience. I notice there is a kind of rigidity, a kind if inflexibility, that affects my overall experience of *how* I experience. So, if all three portions of the central nervous system, not just the cerebral cortex, but the limbic system, as well as the brain stem—body, emotion, mind, verbal cognition, if they are all online, the potential for our lives to be rich and meaningful goes way up.

In this way, through play and all its forms–movement, touch, creativity, imagination–the direct experience has profound implications on how we process life itself. The experience of full-bodied play is the vehicle for children to have these experiences that lead to understanding about the world around them essentially, enriching their lives at the same time. Changaris says,

> While this growth is a biological process, it is also driven by the child's interactions and experiences.... The brain continues developing in the second year of life. Some of this development

involves choosing the 'best' circuits to keep, and is less related to change in size.[9]

Though we know now about neuroplasticity, we also know that the early wiring of the child's brain is of vital importance. Children who are not exposed to social play or don't experience contact through touch have brains that develop differently. Thus, both play and touch are fundamental to a child's neurological development.

Play also employs principles of learning about relationships. Changaris suggests, "Play is a way children engage with their environment. Far from being frivolous, play develops many skills including attention and concentration, problem-solving, and conflict resolution."[10] In this way, play is a vital tool for learning not only about ourselves but how we relate to others. Siegel, who developed the term *interpersonal neurobiology*, states,

> Finally, the mind is a *relational* process. Energy and information flow between and among people, and they are monitored and modified in this shared exchange...Relationships are the way we share energy and information flow, and it is this sharing that shapes, in part, how the flow is regulated. Our minds are created within relationships—including the one we have with ourselves.[11]

Similarly, in creating Gazebo, Lederman saw the many ways in which play supported neurological development. Holloman recalls,

> She was aware that many kids' developmental difficulties in terms of how they dealt with emotions would arise. In terms of teaching them math too early or to read too early, the idea is that stuff will come if all of the other capacities of the more archaic portions of the brain are healthy and working first, then there is a natural develop-ment of the cortex of intellect. It is how we are constructed. We will do that by ourselves with the proper support. The educational system, at the time Janet was starting Gazebo, was very cerebral cortex orientated. Get your kids to read as fast as you can. She was aware that for many kids there were developmental difficulties in

terms in how they dealt with emotions or complex relationships. Relational situations would arise from a lack of attention to these more fundamental parts of our experience that are really in the foreground for young children; because those parts of the brain are more developed.

Social-Emotional Development

Some people say community and relationship aren't important, but that is not true for "mental health" (if you want to use that term). "Who I am with" is as or more important than "where I am" or "what I am doing," to some degree. So, how to create a balance between those?

– Dorothy Charles

At Gazebo, children had opportunities to process emotions through play. Handl suggests, "With modern studies and knowledge now about limbic systems and brain connections, so much of it supports what already had been happening at Gazebo for so long." In this way, play is the central process for children to work through social emotional issues and thus more fully develop the parts of the brain responsible for emotions and relationships. Whether it be dramatic or imaginative play, pure play provides opportunities for children to process whatever is influencing them; especially experiences that children find challenging. Holloman feels that play helps children "metabolize difficult emotions." He implores that,

> Adults go to work every day and they fulfill tasks that support them financially and hopefully also provide meaning in their lives. For kids, one of the big ways they organize their experience is through play and that is both in the creative realm of imagination. Also, in the creative realm emotionally, helping them sort through very complex emotional experiences that they don't yet have the capacity to understand intellectually; because that portion of their minds are not yet sophisticated enough to do that.

Davidson states that,

> Emotions play a really key role. They can be both a facilitating of our behavioral and cognitive ability or they can be disruptors, it can go both ways. It is not one way or the other, but they are an intimate part of what we do.

According to Levine and Kline,

> Without words, young children sometimes show parents the parts of their experience that have overwhelmed them. Toddlers, preschoolers and elementary school children easily express their worst fears and unconscious turmoil through their world of make-believe, play and art.[12]

For example, Holloman recalls,

> I remember the experience that I had, a little girl brought Barbie and Ken dolls to Gazebo. One day the dolls were going back and forth slapping each other in the face. I got curious and said, 'That is an interesting game. 'What is the game?' 'The game is divorce.' Her parents were going through a separation and obviously there was some things about the separation that she was finding or experiencing as violence, whether that was overt violence or whether that was just the breaking of the family bonds. She was expressing this through this kind of dramatic play. It was just really clear to me that it was an important expression of what she was experiencing and attempting to orient toward in some way, shape, or form.

Play is a fundamental way in which children process feelings and emotions. So, how do we support the play process when a child is working through difficult emotions and experiences? In this case, Holloman says,

> I supported her by first recognizing that she was doing something very important. I was not judging what was going on or taking the Barbie and Ken away from her and attempting to engage her in

something that I might think was more valuable, like painting or grooming the pony, in other words distracting her. So, once she gave me the explanation, I was just there. As I recall, the game went on for a few more minutes, then at some point she turned the dolls away from each other and got interested in something else. I was just being there and observing, because I didn't know what was the right intervention. Janet encouraged us to be present and observe, to take an observer role—witnessing and just being in the space with the kids. I was just there with her.

Holloman reflects on the importance of this experience by saying,

It gave me a both a great insight into what was happening with her. I remember talking about that at a meeting later on that week. I remember not wanting to interfere in the development and expression of what she was doing, because it didn't seem to me like it was entering into some kind of a harmful or inappropriate realm. It was more that she was expressing something that she was having a great deal of difficulty metabolizing emotionally. I expressed to the other teachers what I had seen, and probably at some point we also expressed to the parents what it was we were witnessing—just as information for them. The little one was taking on everything in her way. Finding expressions for that were in some way shape or form. Helping move the energy, which was creating some kind of confusion or anxiety, was a cathartic expression of some kind that helped her reset her nervous system. They [children] take in everything, even the stuff we think we are concealing from them. They are highly intuitive and in some sense they are absorbing the ripple effect of everything that we are thinking or feeling or experiencing because they are so connected to us, particularly children to their parents.

Thompson-Clark also says,

I recently got excited by the notion of describing play as what we talk about a lot as living systems and thinking about the act of play.

When you animate play I am seeing lots of buzzing bees. So I am beginning to myself play with the notion of writing about play as a pollination, as bees pollinating. So, if children are picking up ideas of one kind of plant or flower and pollinating at another place. I like to have that particular imaginal approach to what goes on because they enrich each other—whether it is the children or the adults and the children.

Thompson-Clark remembers at Gazebo,

The reason the children were able to play so powerfully is: One, the time element. Two, the role of the teacher, which was to allow. So, that pollinating piece goes on in that the play did not get interfered with. That was such a core principle which I think allowed it to be richer, deeper, broader, and more authentic.

Similarly, Holloman says,

I've noticed that in a lot of the Gazebo kids is that, both of my kids for instance, that there is a great deal of play that they engage in as adults—which is a huge part of what I would call the quality of life that they experience.

Within a play-based setting, social development naturally occurs. Interactions between children provide ample learning opportunities in which social learning occurs. Gazebo was a culture of many different social dynamics. Many of us who went to Gazebo maintained connection with community members into our later years. Murphy remarks,

I am an only child without the sibling dynamics that are so character building. Gazebo has a special place in my heart for it gave me connection to a brotherhood and sisterhood to grow with throughout my life.

Thus, the learning about social contact was foundational for lifelong friendships and a sense of community with others.

Handl states, "I guess I wrestle with the sort of American value of rugged individualism versus a dynamic healthy interdependence that is inevitable in human relationships."

Recent discoveries in neuroscience on the existence of mirror neurons affirms that social-emotional learning such as the concept of empathy is affected by the modeling of those around us. Neuroscientist Marco Iacoboni of the University of California at Los Angeles says,

> We use our body to communicate our intentions and our feelings. The gestures, facial expressions, body postures we make are social signals, ways of communicating with one another. Mirror neurons are the only brain cells we know of that seem specialized to code the actions of other people and also our own actions. They are obviously essential brain cells for social interactions. Without them, we would likely be blind to the actions, intentions and emotions of other people. The way mirror neurons likely let us understand others is by providing some kind of inner imitation of the actions of other people, which in turn leads us to 'simulate' the intentions and emotions associated with those actions.[13]

Therefore, as children interact, they are learning and developing as they absorb information through play activity and through peer relationships that are strengthened through play. In this way, Reese says,

> Everything that Walter is experiencing here at Gazebo, through social interactions, he will be experiencing his whole life. Both his role in a group and separating from group. Walter is a more peaceful child because he has been given the ability to make choices for himself and learn from his mistakes. I can tell he feels safe and empowered at Gazebo and I hope when I take him home that we continue and jump off from this block. He 'makes decisions' and 'choices' for himself at home. Walter has gained the opportunity to feel what a leadership role is as he is a little older than the other kids. He's also gained a sense of self that I see when he interacts

with other neighbor kids. He finds a way to engage by asking the other kids questions. I love watching him start a conversation and join in with other kids when they are playing. Social interaction has been huge for Walter at Gazebo and that's mostly due to the unstructured schedule of Gazebo.

So, while Walter was learning leadership, another child might have been learning observation skills. With the mixed-age groups at Gazebo, children learned so much through interaction between the age groups. Elders learned to care for younger children, while younger children watched and learned skills they were going to need later.

Mixed-Age Groups, Pottyville, Diapers to Potties

Bath-rooming at Gazebo, either in diapers or going on toilets, had a lot less pressure around it than in most schools and was part of the learning and fun. Pottyville was an amazing example of social learning. At Gazebo there was an organic and social process which was somewhat unusual in its more public nature. Rather than having a private stall, the children used what was called, 'Pottyville,' which was basically an outhouse with no walls and two potties. There were sometimes little curtains, and it was deco-

rated beautifully. The children would sit together and do their business, but also talk or read a book. Others could gather around or from a distance see how it was done.

Foreman remembers,

> Babies weren't slaves to diapers. They often went without and
> learned the freedom of their bodies, the joy of the sun and air
> on their skin. If their diaper was changed or just came off, they
> learned the responsibility of discarding it themselves. Exquisite
> moments occurred in Pottyville where many needs were met!
> Conversations and discoveries were made there in quiet moments.
> Toddlers observed the process of their older pals, getting a sense
> of their next step to toilet training.

So, the toileting was a social experience, but also it was another
opportunity for self-initiative and choice. With my daughter, I called
it *toilet learning* as it really was a natural and organic process in
which curiosity and ease were fostered. I like to think of the time
for children as toilet 'learning' rather than training as it is a learning
process. Miller feels, "It's great that potties are physically accessible
to children. Before they are really ready to do it by themselves."
Douce adds,

> The whole concept of the children, to make something that is
> usually shushed up about, something that is openly discussed and
> kids are proud of. So, a child could be using Pottyville and sitting
> next to a friend using Pottyville. It was still private, but it was still
> not hidden. Also, you could be going to Pottyville and sitting next
> to your friend. It makes it way more fun.

Baldwin expounds,

> Potty training at Gazebo was always one of the easiest places to do
> it, because the children teach each other. I remember one parent
> thought it was going to take her months for her son to potty train.
> So she went to Costco and bought like 3,000 diapers. Her son's
> best friend had potty trained. So, he basically potty trained the
> next day, and the parents came to me and asked if we want 3,000
> diapers for Gazebo. 'Yeah I will take them.' We don't have any
> rules. With the very young ones, I will take them [to Pottyville]

if they can't walk, but I don't want the very young ones to potty train. So, that is when I might pick a child up to go to the potty station. Then, it is just to make it as fun as possible.

I remember when I began teaching at Gazebo my mentor, Joanna Classen, told me that changing diapers was a very sweet and intimate moment and to really savor that and connect with the child during that time. This sentiment immediately changed any aversion I had to the experience and allowed me to see it as a special bonding time. The bath-rooming was also social in nature between adults and children in the guidance and support that teachers offered. I also remember how powerful it was to have the children participate. The child would wrap up their diaper and throw it in the trash. We would talk to the child about the feeling of wetness on their body and if dryness felt better. There was an exchange and a mutual responsibility that supported the philosophy. Baldwin recalls, one boy hated the experience,

> He couldn't potty train if he wanted to, and he was going to be wearing diapers for a long time. It could be quite an ordeal because of this, because he is coming from a real place. When we would finish, him finishing it, him wrapping it up with me helping, and him putting it in the bucket and saying goodbye. He loved that. It was like we have just gone through this ordeal. It is not teacher's fault. It is not my fault. It is just the way the world is. As soon as it was over, the boy was like, 'Now I can go run and play.' It is good for any child to finish the job and of course washing hands and all that. That is as much curriculum as anything. Again with Gazebo this is all you've got to do. You have got all the time in the world. There is nothing else right now. So, you just sit. If you got a child who is new, its okay to get the [trash] bucket, and bring it to the child. It's not, 'You walk that diaper to the bucket or you will suffer the consequences.' It is more, this child is learning so I might bring the bucket across so all she'll do is lift the diaper and put it in. But next time, she might walk. There is no time that diaper has to be in that bucket by, it is something that is going to get done.

Eizner expounds,

> The importance of having little babies exposed to older kids—that was potty training at Gazebo. We didn't have to do anything. They just have to watch a two or three-year-old going to the bathroom, and then they would go and sit. That was the learning process. The multi-generational, that's how kids learn the songs. The babies are sitting there listening and at some point, they sing the songs. How are they going to learn if they are not exposed? So, the more exposure to all these experiences with older kids, the more experiences that they can learn and the more processes of developing.

The way the staff organized at Gazebo, they accommodated the mixed-aged model. There were certain teachers that were oriented towards the babies, others with toddlers, and some focused on the older children. There were play areas designed to stimulate the babies senses and offered a tactile environment for them to explore. In the early years, there was a open tipi-like structure with different herbs which the babies could smell and feel or even taste. They could learn roll over and crawl on the earth and explore water play and other sensory activities. When I worked at Gazebo, an intern built a circle made from willow branches that was about a foot tall. The babies could nap inside the circle and also pull themselves up on the low fencing. There were openings for comings and goings and a nearby arbor with roses hanging over they could crawl underneath or rest under in the shade. Babies were closely watched as the natural world stimulated their senses, and challenged their newfound abilities. They often parallel played with their baby peers, and they closely observed the older children providing *scaffolding* for benchmarks to come.

While much of the Gazebo approach is based in early childhood education, there are some applications for older children as well. For example Wyatt says,

> In terms of the application with older children, I love the idea of ongoing investigations. Janet looked at it and what she came up with was mentorship and modeling. For older kids Janet's whole

thing was mentoring. At a certain age: what are you interested in? 'Oh, are your interested in airplanes, lets go to the aviation center. Let's build an airplane, let's do a play about an airplane, let's get out some technical books about airplanes.' That was her idea of how Gazebo would work with older kids.

When Gazebo had a kindergarten, they had a special reading yurt for the kindergarteners. The focus bus was designed for children old enough to focus; often those beyond the toddler years. Sometimes, a director would hire people for the summer and organize camps for the older children in which they would do activities outside of the Park, either on the farmhouse lawn or taking adventures around the property. Harper remembers,

> Janet would wait for things that she wanted people to say yes to, not at the beginning and not at the end. She would time it when people were into saying yes. She was a very skilled observer of people and also group dynamics. I think probably all that preface of her watching me as a work scholar. I taught Martha Clark slack line. We put hemp rope between two trees, and Janet was watching all that. One summer, I think the summer where we had just started the farm 79ish or '80, she approached me. She came up to me and said to start a summer kids' program. So, I started doing things like gymnastics class on the lawn, because I had coached gymnastics in college. Kids had seen me do stuff, so we did that, and I did some juggling with them, and swimming. I had coached swimming, so we did swim classes in the pool. The next summer Lia, who was working at Gazebo, and I put together a kids' program again for these older kids.

In this way, different activities were planned to accommodate the different age groups so that each had age-appropriate ways to engage in learning while sharing the same common space and also learning from each other through interaction, observation, and mentoring.

Unfortunately, mixed-age groups in preschools is highly regulated in the state of California. Now, babies, toddlers and school-aged children are generally separated by law. The mentorship aspect is so useful for learning and we lose some of this when we isolate the age groups. Nelson remarks,

> The bigger ones would teach the younger ones, and in that pecking order. The mentorship within the students was a really wonderful part of the school. There is something now where they can't have anyone more than six and I think that is a loss. I think the one-room school house is a good thing. A seven year old can realize that they can help a three year old learn how to wipe their butt, or to read, or to throw a baseball, or learn how to ride Hot Wheels down the hill. I think that is an important thing and I like seeing the generations come in. They come in and the bigger kids would defend the little ones, and gradually they became the mentors of the new generation coming in.

Mentorship was a powerful teaching tool at Gazebo in so many aspects of the learning, but particularly within the social dynamics of mixed-age groups. On the contrary, Davey recalls,

> The mixed-ages aspect of the Park is one of the best and worst things for me. If an older kid could do something that I could not, I would strive to do it. Therefore I would grow and set my sights on something. But also, some of the older kids would leave me in the dust and I would feel ostracized. It used to hurt my feelings if an older kid would play with me one day, and not play with me on another day if another older kid came to the park.

So, as Davey had experienced mixed-age groups could have their challenges as well. Nevertheless, there were amazing benefits from the children interacting and playing in this rich social context. Reese says,

> Walter is one of the older kids now in Gazebo and I see him leading play time. I know sitting down at lunch has been a difficulty. He prefers that time to play by himself, but his decision made it more difficult for the other kids to sit at lunch. He understood how his decision affected Dodge's decision when we talked about it at home. I hope he is making decisions at Gazebo that are helpful

for other kids at Gazebo as well. That is a special thing to learn that is unique for him at Gazebo. It might be slow learning to be a leader for the good of the group. I saw this possibly happening at other childcare centers, and he would have adapted and survived, but Gazebo doesn't ask the child to survive circumstances. I appreciate that so much.

Classen states that,

Traditional ways of raising children, there is a auntie, uncle, neighbor, approach and I really value that. There aren't neighborhoods like there used to be to play in. So, having a place with mixed-age groups and people who aren't your family around is a pretty spectacular thing. The other thing is unstructured time. I think that imagination comes when we have space for it.

Thus, with unstructured timing, there might be boredom at first, but also the breakthrough when they are free to be imaginative and playful in an environment where there aren't a lot of toys or people entertaining you or telling you what to do or how to play with prescribed toys. Rather there are lots of moving parts and natural changing circumstances that give feedback and information and through play. The space where children get to create something is exactly what imagination needs to grow and flourish.

Unstructured Timing

One of the unique elements of Gazebo was the unstructured timing. There were natural tasks and chores done at various times of the day, but there were no lessons that the children were required to do. There were not specific times the children had to do circle. The lunch and the songs that preceded the meal were some of the few timing touchstones of the day at Gazebo. Clean-up was required after each project that used tools or supplies and often an end of the day clean-up was implemented as well. Nevertheless, the timing was organic, and the activities were done at a child's rate. Naps were taken individually often after lunch, but were done with rhythm rather than rigidity. With the open outdoor space supporting free play, this unstructured timing set a different tone for the young children, and it supported full play without limitations.

Foreman remembers, "Reading books and taking naps were always tender moments and occurred spontaneously." Though this kind of timing may not be possible for all programs, there is deep insight for the children within this open timing in that they begin to learn to trust their own biological clocks and inner rhythms. They rest when they feel tired, they read when they are interested in reading, they play when they are ready to be energetic. Eizner adds,

> Other programs have a lot of agendas. At Gazebo, the agenda is to follow the children's lead. We didn't have nap times. We did have lunchtime, but kids could eat anytime they wanted, because food was available anytime. It was a time for us to gather. The teachers try to take care of the environment, and we took care of ourselves, and we related to the kids in a way that awareness was the word. We were paying attention to what we were doing, and to how we affected the kids and the environment, as we related to the kids and the environment. I think most schools don't pay attention to that. They have a structure, and they have a routine, and they have to follow the structure and routine. They don't pay attention to the changes that take place in the environment. Transitions were not forced, and the chores were not forced. I go back to it's not reading time, it is not circle time. I am going to sit down and read a book to whomever is asking me to read a book. All of a sudden you have ten kids listening to me read a book. Now you have your circle time, unstructured circle time, and it could happen anywhere anytime. It didn't have to happen at 10:00–10:20 in the morning because at 10:20 we have to do the next thing. There was time for everything. There were times when kids invited me to play with them and I would play. There were times when kids were playing on their own, and I did not need to be part of their play. Sometimes, somebody will grab an instrument and start playing. Then the kids would

come gather around that teacher and start playing music with that teacher. I am not saying it was initiated by the adult, but in some cases, the adult was having an activity and the kids would join them. It goes back to forcing the kid or the environment inviting the kid for the lessons.

Handl says,

Gazebo is magic—in the stoppage of time and artificial transitions, a beautiful bubble encases the children in a setting that allows a natural unfolding, and an honoring of a myriad of ways of knowing the world.

Thompson-Clark feels,

I think even in the transitional kindergartens and the kindergartens we see here, there is a lot of worksheets, and the children do not have time to play. I think that up until six–seven, I would go to eight, they need to have periods of unstructured play in order to have ideas. In having ideas, they practice finding out how real they are, or how they get to put on their energy and juice into them, so that they make something out of something. It may not be right or wrong, but it is an idea about how things work. We want to establish through the ability to feel, think, sense, be, that they are right in who they are. That is the core of resilience, and that can only really come from full-bodied play. From then on they are always going to know that it is okay to take risks.

Wyatt thinks backs to a student named Jaden at around eighteen months old:

I related to him, so it must have been something I could have used but maybe didn't get as a child. He spent the whole hour-and-a-half time when they first came to the Park and inspecting this tree. He was right by it, looking at it, and touching it. His first time at Gazebo, he spent the whole day at the water fountain. Pushing the lever, getting the water, letting it dribble down his chin, letting it go down, sometimes spitting it out, the whole sensory experience. Just having that permission to be wherever I am at any given moment and having support of that. That had been transformational in that it was healing because I didn't get that as a child. And loving that we could offer that. It feels so basic and fundamental. It is rare to make the space in the world that we are currently in, to slow down to really see. Why was that more valuable to him compared to 'we are onto the next thing and this is our agenda as teachers?' I think because it honors the wisdom of his being. And his being needed to check out the tree or fountain at that moment. I don't even want to begin to speak to his being, and I am just in the presence of and I honor his being. If we needed to go then we needed to go, and that is the way it is, and I would need to interrupt, and I would do some acknowledging of what I am seeing, rather than if I interrupt at that level, without some respecting of what is going on. 'Wow,' I would say, 'I see what you're doing.' I might even touch the tree with him for a little while. So, obviously sometimes you do have to go. But every time I interrupt without acknowledging what is going on, there is an underlying message that says the wisdom of your being, what you choose, is not important. And that, over time, is debilitating, and over time hacks away at self-esteem and knowing myself and thinking that I could even know myself. Pretty soon you have people saying, 'Tell me who I am,' and asking outside of themselves.

Faria observes,

The child finds their own rhythm throughout the day with no need of strict 'time guidelines.' Sequence of events provides predictability most of the time as well as the flexibility for change and creativity without the need for 'time restrictions.' Time expands and a natural state of bliss and harmony reign. The opportunities for challenge and growth then come from the interaction of each child's imagination and some creative wonderings posed by teachers.

Reese agrees,

> I've seen places where they put their hands on the child to shuttle them here and there because there is a time schedule more structured, and I feel it puts a lot of pressure on the child at an early age. Walter was craving child interaction and freedom. Everything Gazebo offers.

Handl feels that,

> In most other educational settings there is a 'herding' effect, a right or wrong answer, a structure to which the human being must mold, instead of allowing the natural unfolding of our humanity within the confines of the laws of nature.

Anyone who has worked in a traditional classroom, or for most of us who has been educated in that manner, will likely understand that it is not our nature as children to sit and listen all day long. London shares that,

> We were for kids to provide a space for sensory awareness. A kid could play with a flower for four hours. Children had that freedom and space, and all the time in world. It was all about present moment. What can I learn about this flower? They were learning by interacting.

Price-Waldrip feels that,

> For me it is the thing about not forcing. Having so much room and space to be able to do what you need to do and not being expected to act any way. There was a strong sense of community but what I really appreciate is when I was overwhelmed or when I was scared I could go be by myself and no one followed me. No one said I am going to worry about you and I am going to be involved in your space. I could just have as much time and space as I needed. I really appreciated that.

Price-Waldrip shares the experience of having time for retreat. So, much like with a tree, personal reflection and space to integrate has value as well as engagement. So, in this way, the integration of experiences is very important, and Gazebo allowed time for this. Douce says,

> Rather than we are going to teach, we are going to control these children, and we are going to make them, and teach good standards of control by sitting in circles, sitting in squares, sitting in artificial desks. Most of the people in our society have back pain and back trouble, because we were taught to sit wrong from the beginning. All the time in those desks led to back trouble later. We are not meant to sit straight, we are not meant to sit in those desks and we are not meant to not move about. Children want to move about. They want to experiment physically too. That was always allowed in Gazebo. You were never restrained to a weird piece of furniture. When I talk to people about this now, they all agree. They all say, 'Oh yeah, that was my problem too.' That is why now with the electronic world they are getting caught more into staring at a small area. The neck trouble and the spinal problems, it is going to be rampant.

So, in a play-based setting, with very little restrictions on timing, it is a more physical experience and there may even be more possibilities for different kinds of learning and development. In Douce's teaching he often speaks of the counterproductive nature of the education system—the damages of children sitting for long hours at desks and in chairs without much movement. Thompson-Clark remarks,

> This temporal approach isn't anywhere else. There is engagement in the world and with each other and that is the best of play because of the depth of experience that the children were able to reach. I think that a factor in growth of intelligence is being able to have a lot of unstructured time and play. I say unstructured, but it wasn't that we didn't have activities that a child wasn't attracted too. Whether it was cleaning the pony corral, or the goats, or feeding

of the animals, or the digging of the garden, or the planting, all of those become very structured activities. A child is choosing to do that when they want to do that, as opposed to, 'Now is the time that we are going to....' There was less routine practice at Gazebo than I have seen in another program.

Thompson-Clark continues by saying

The term 'openness to experience' instead of, 'You have to go here you have to move here,' and, 'We are cutting off your play because the time is up.' I think that kind of world of education of the young child never was a priority at Gazebo. Rather it held the philosophy of allowing time, so children could be authentic in their approach to situations. There was no bias that they were taught, and because it was so open, that allowed children to be open with their understanding and very truthful.

Barnes remarks,

The time schedule is also unique. It allows children to structure their time according to their own schedule, something which is rare these days. At first I felt a completely unstructured day was not going to be good for Olivia—that I wanted to know she was learning something through structured activities because that is what education is about in grade school and it is what we are taught in general. But as I sit here and watch Oli walk about the Park initiating her own activities, I see the importance of 'unstructured play.'

Baldwin states that,

It is child-led, that it is their curriculum. Janet was much more interested with art-work with the process and not the product. It is not about having great things at the end that they can take home that looks just like this, it is much more kids can just get involved. A child can just start doing something, then go in another direction, and to support that. That is child-led. You're there to make sure the paint stays where it is supposed to be, and that the paint isn't going in every direction. They can create it themselves and everyone can add ideas. The teachers can have a certain curriculum they want to bring in and to be flexible with it. Don't be surprised if it goes somewhere completely different. If it is something they want to participate in and they want to do it later, that is okay, as long as they are being complete with it. In other words, they don't just rush in and rush out again. Participate, and you need to wash your brush, and then go on to the next thing. The teacher is often keeping the boundaries rather than inspiring what is actually being made. To me it is not just paint and paper. The transparent thing [plexiglass], they could paint. They could paint bark or the acorns. Janet did not want any glitter or any stuff. Natural tempera paints. Lots of good paper. T-shirts from the free box, and just let it go. Do what works, and if it ends up disintegrating, then that's the way it was supposed to be. If it ends up being something that you can dry and take home, then that is great too. It is really just to do it, and to do it in different ways. Like to just have two colors, blue and red. What happens then? If you only have blue and red, of course you end up with purple. So, children get to get a sense of creation. There, I am adding creativity. I am saying you only having two colors today.

However, some children felt challenged finding their own direction within this more organic timing. I remember the visiting children, educated primarily in other kinds of programs, would often look to me as a Gazebo teacher looking for direction. They say, "What now?" I would shrug and ask them what they thought. It really made them look into themselves for their creativity and take more initiative. Price-Waldrip remembers,

I liked things to be simple and known and safe. The amount of freedom at Gazebo was sometimes hard for me. My challenge was learning how to take risks and learning how to tolerate conflict and discomfort. What I so appreciated at Gazebo was that I wasn't forced into doing anything or asked to act a certain way. I was left alone until I felt ready and wanted to participate. I still had consistent contact and someone checking in with me, but it was on my terms, and I got to step in and step out of what was going on at my own pace.

Consequently, children learned how to self-direct and listen to inner impulses. Curiosity was validated. Nelson says,

Self-confidence and feeling their personal power are things that they got from Gazebo. My kids are grounded and they are not afraid to put their hands on things they are interested in. Gaelen likes to cook and Tyler likes to play soccer. They were out there playing soccer very often, so that was a great basis for his life.

Wyatt resonates with the Cat Stevens' lyrics from the song *Father and Son*, "From the moment I could talk, I was ordered to listen." She felt that that way of educating is, "Taking away a sense of dignity that children have and deserve." So, she continues,

If we have a lot of power as adults. I might now ask directly, 'Does someone want to go paint?' Talking to another child and it becomes an invitation. Curriculum is always that child hearing an invitation and choosing whether or not to take it. Everything is curriculum, with young children, from the moment we meet. More and more early educators get this. Adults don't always get this. Janet said some children need to surround themselves with familiar objects, and some need to explore.

Calculated Risk

I remember when I was less than three-years-old, there was a big climbing wall at Gazebo. It had ropes looped together that you could climb up to a high platform above. It seemed huge to me. I remember sitting at the bottom of that climbing wall for a long time, looking at my sister and my friends climbing up and thinking how unfair it was. I remember trying and not being able to get up there. I remember when I finally did it how amazing it felt!

The hill where the Hot Wheels track was seemed huge to me. I also remember the winding staircase in the Gazebo structure that was missing the bottom step. It was missing the bottom step so that small children could only climb the stairs if you were large and capable enough to get up onto the higher step. The staff prohibited efforts to pull a chair up and climb with a prop. You were only allowed to climb up by yourself, and you had to get down by yourself at Gazebo. Those were the rules. I remember trying to get down from the pony shed roof and the tree; to get down seemed so scary. I also remember having someone talk me through it. It was a scary thing for me, but I felt a trust in that tree more than in the adult. In fact, I don't even remember the adult, I just remember the tree and how it looked and felt on my feet and arms. Day remembers,

> I felt the obvious causal relationship between my actions and the consequences were, it felt like a sense of justice, but it also terrified me. (I remember Amanacer. I gave her a daisy while she was at Pottyville, and she kissed me on the cheek. Then Jovian pushed me off the hay bale when I was sitting on it because he liked Amanacer.)

Calculated risk and mixed-age groups supported experiential learning. So, risk-taking and gaining physical skills was based on physical capacity of a child; to know their level and trust in that, and at times push themselves. Much like Lev Vygotsky's concept of the *Zone of Proximal Development*, by which higher benchmarks can be achieved with skilled partners or peer groups than individually, through mixed-age groups and calculated risk, children are socially inspired and challenged in developing physically and psychologically.

Thus, with scaffolded support from peers and by learning through observation, greater development is possible. Furthermore, the outcomes of risk-taking, making mistakes, and learning natural consequences become more meaningful and relevant than learning through teacher or parent warnings.

Gazebo seemed to offer a balance between freedom and responsibility, with many opportunities for calculated risk. With a strong emphasis on risks taking and finding a way through challenges independently with onlooking support of an adult. Wolfinger says,

> My ability to calculate risk is really really strong because of Gazebo. I can assess a situation so much better because I am not afraid to fail. I am really good at picking myself up and trying again. So, I will try a different way. Gazebo encouraged me as a child to be creative in my problem-solving whether it be interpersonal or physical or personal. That ability to judge and calculate and be able to make decisions made me okay. Calculating situations out in the world. I have always been a huge explorer. I love to go out in the community whether it be in nature or society, and my instincts are good. When I am walking I know where to go to get to the right decision if I follow my instincts. It is really empowering, and I think that that was Gazebo. So, definitely that empowerment of the child to be able to make their own choices and the freedom of expression.

Kevin Harvey says,

> Somehow, as a parent, I felt responsible to keep Sage safe all the time. I wasn't necessarily afraid he wouldn't be safe at Gazebo, but breaking down the fear of not being there to catch him when he falls was good for both of us. To let him fall so he can learn not to fall as often through practice.

The challenge for the adult is allowing some risk for children. It is a challenge as we are here to keep children out of danger, yet allowing them the ability to develop judgment and skill when it comes to physical risks can be valuable for them as they grow into adults.

Even within the daily chores and responsibilities, there was calculated risk, which required mental focus and physical skill. Yet, the children often aspired to master skills that required this focus. Nelson recalls,

> That was one of the typical curricula is that they took a butter knife and they could cut up an avocado or a banana. It wasn't dangerous and they were helping prepare their food and they got the idea that

this tool cuts food into pieces. They were all different, some took to it and some took to it less. One child would spend all day, most of the day hammering—roofing nails into those pine rounds that were there from trees that were moved. She (Ariel) had a small hammer and she hurt/whacked her fingers somewhat. She learned and developed hand-eye coordination, and learned that hammers can hurt your fingers. I think she benefited from it. She learned how to use a tool and have hand-eye coordination. Though there may have been some mild injury with the risk involved, the benefit outweighed it in that there was a greater learning that occurred.

Risk-taking cultivated response-ability and resourcefulness. From using a knife to cut fruit, to using a hammer and nail, there were clear consequences, and thus a clearer focus from the child. With an adult watching closely, children were empowered to try new things if they had the ability. While the children had choice in activities, there was an emphasis on cleaning up, taking care of the environment, and helping to make lunch and wash dishes, etc. It was framed as a responsibility rather than a mandatory task. In other words, this is your work in relation to the land, the space, and the needs of the group. Kevin Harvey says, "Gazebo is an advocate of each child's individual desires. Believing in the child and helping the child to believe in themselves." Charles reflects that,

> Maybe the cutting edge is how do we change from being such a litigious society to having kids who know and understand their own physical limits and take self-responsibility for the risks that they take, and providing an environment that has enough calculated risks in it. What about that? That would be really cutting edge.

Emergent Curriculum

It's universal education—it is learning about the universe.

–Neil Baldwin

Emergent curriculum is when the child's curiosity is the impulse for the teachings. Often, the impulse for conceptual learning stems from pure play. The curriculum emerges from the choice of activities that a child engages in, and the teacher is there to provide resources. Miller feels that,

> Emergent curriculum is taking it from where the children are, and going with it somewhere. It happens a lot at the Gazebo with physical skills and social skills. Those are the foundations of feeling safe and confident in the world.

For example, Nelson says,

> The idea was that they decided. They picked the curriculum for the day and you try to go with it. Their attention span can be pretty short so you tried it, but if you were lucky you could really keep them going for an hour; certainly reading books you could. I was supposed to incorporate them, allow them to come into the work in the kitchen. I wasn't very good at it. I was much less experienced at that time and I wasn't able to integrate them. It's hard to do that. If you give the kids a nail and hammer, they would love to hammer nails into the pine stumps, but it was hard to do the work your doing and keep an eye on the child.

Lederman hired Nelson to build the kitchen before he became a teacher, so his work was not strictly that of a teacher. More often, while Gazebo teachers had projects on the land and routines to tend to, their primary work was to follow the children's interests, provide resources, and let activities play out to completion. This included clean-up and being responsible for tools etc.

One description of emergent curriculum is when exploration is coupled with resources. Therefore, uninterrupted play can lead into more intellectual explorations, and thus more conceptual understanding of the world. Thus, the teachers follow the cues of the student by offering more learning opportunities based on their interests. Teachers can do this by asking open-ended questions. Teachers offer resources and allow children to learn how to be resourceful and find out more about what interests them. The process of emergent curriculum helps create pathways for learning how to learn. Curiosity extends into research and learning; and may later even become ongoing projects. I truly believe children learn in a deeper way when the learning is personal and relevant. When a student is learning because they want to learn about something, they tend to retain the information because they care about the topic. Cognitive knowledge then stems from *intrinsic motivation*. So, they first explore, then discover areas of interest, then investigate and gain understanding. What steps does one take to find out about something that they are curious about? Emergent curriculum teaches content, but it also teaches resourcefulness and thus creates sustainability for lifelong learning.

Moreover, there was a geometric shaped greenhouse in the Gazebo Park where there were new plant starts, drying herbs, microscopes, Audubon field guides, books relating to the natural world, organic objects on tables, and some additional art and science supplies. If a child became interested in a bug or a worm while turning the compost, a teacher could offer to look under a microscope with them. They might bring them a book, and show a page with an illustration and description of the insect. This could turn into an art project or an ongoing investigation in which the child followed their curiosity to completion. For instance, Holloman remembers a student. Holloman says,

> Rick Tarnas' son, Flash, is really a very smart, brilliant, young man. It was obvious that his interest and curiosity in intellectual things dawned at an early age—much earlier than the other kids. We found ways to support that with him.

Chris Tarnas (Flash) remembers the computer bus at Gazebo, where he got interested in computers in the '80s. He is now a software architect the CTO and cofounder of Biotique Systems. Tarnas said Gazebo was an incredibly supportive place for creativity.

Thompson-Clark says,

> The children are born with an inherent love of the natural world, and Gazebo/play offers an almost unlimited opportunity to do whatever it is that their brain and body and nervous system want to learn from the natural world. We can't analyze what is going on and how this child is gazing up at this beautiful butterfly in the eucalyptus. The opportunity is so much greater in a place like Gazebo. So, protected was the child, to go ahead and feel like the child can initiate where to move when they want to move. I think that's probably true of forest schools and kindergartens, because they take that approach of what is most important is that the child is able to gain the wisdom from the ancient trees, gain the wisdom from feet on the ancient earth. Maybe they are in contact with mycelium running, we don't know. But what we believe as Gazebo people is, there is never going to be a way to analyze that, but we sense that this is valuable. It is so important to whatever millions of neurons are growing at that moment and whatever that analysis is will be there forever, will be permanent forever.

Yet, despite the incredible learning that emerges from explorative play, it seems that as educators, there is a need to defend play. Thompson-Clark addresses the defense of play by saying,

> We can talk about people who empower and control textbooks. It is the very same reason that it's hard to describe how powerful and important play is at this period. It is not a field even considered education. There is not enough research on play. In the world you watch children, you babysit children, you have childcare, you have day care for your child, because it is not important—that whole phase of life. We in early education want to raise our fists and say—this is the most important period in education—because of the development of the being and true play. We are struggling to

articulate why that is so important, as opposed to something that can be measured with standardized testing. It is easy to not pay attention to what is important. It is easy to 'dis' it, and it is over. Then, on to elementary schools because you can measure, because you can test. I want to do a school that is zero–eight, because I would like to see protected play go all the way to third grade as a model, as innovative educational practice. So, we have to defend it for the elementary like crazy. I don't think we have to defend it in early education as much if we have a population of parents that is in agreement that it is important (luckily we tend to have, in our university population). Yet, the majority of the people that are parents, even if they are faculty members, they are interested in making sure that you are teaching the 'academic part' of this program. When are the children learning?

I asked Thompson-Clark how she explains the importance of play to these parents at the Children's School and she replied,

> We take them through the steps of talking about how important it is to develop their social-emotional self, and to become very strong co-creators of their own curriculum, we value that, so we don't get much pushback. But I know there are lots of places where the parents want to see the children sitting down in a structured setting, because they have had the play schooled out of them and don't understand how or why it is important.

So, many people don't value play because it is not academic, nor is it measurable. On the other hand, play is the fundamental groundwork for learning and the foundation of neurological and somatic development. Plus, play is fun and natural for children. Play breaks through boredom. For children, play is imaginative, dramatic, theatrical, even magical. Unstructured timing, calculated risk, and Emergent Curriculum are elements that support play-based learning and scaffold the children in their play. Even through the vehicle of play, at Gazebo, there were guidelines, structures, and touchstones.

Yet, any play-based program can cultivate an immense capacity for learning through the foundation of play. While, neural somatic growth and social emotional development are grounded in play, play is also joyful. Play is experimentation, curiosity, imagination, risk-taking, and loving learning. Play is—akin to Joseph Campbell's wisdom—to "follow your bliss."

The Growing Edge

I remember when I first heard of the phrase the 'growing edge.' I was in my teens and though I didn't know or understand it, I was curious about the concept. What is a growing edge? Well, it seems it is a space, in that cusp of comfort and discomfort, from which growth occurs. Sometimes, perhaps it is unknown. Other times it may be something you are working towards, but not yet touching. The growing edge is where you are are, where your limit and growth meet. It is your personal learning, growth, and even your challenges. For adults and children, each individual's growing edge is different at different times. Within the Gazebo philosophy, many people, adults and children alike have met their growing edge.

I have gathered stories for years about Gazebo, and as I discussed Gazebo with various community members, there was an overwhelming alliance and support of the Gazebo approach. On the other hand, there were aspects that really rubbed people the wrong way, and other areas where people felt there were missing pieces. Though folks were more often in alignment than not, within the philosophy there were areas of tension for many people. I want to touch on some of these issues in this chapter and illuminate the shadows, while focusing on positive ways to promote even more possibility of growth and the evolution of these ideas.

So, how does any educator or program implement the concepts presented in this book? This book is meant be used as a reference for history and philosophy through firsthand experiences. This is not a how-to manual. This work is a reference, but one most optimally experimented with using intuition as a strong reference point. It is important to consider your demographics, your cultural climate, your learning community, and your physical environment. Cultural considerations are important to consider as well. The demographics of the Big Sur area, as well as the cultural climate of Esalen Institute, made things possible that might not be in your circumstances and in your community. On the other hand, your community might offer a different cultural component that would enrich your particular program.

It was Lederman's dream to have this work to be taken out into the world. She wanted the private sector to generate and subsidize early childhood programs such as Gazebo; especially in the corporate world. She wanted empty lots all over the country to turn into outdoor learning spaces. She hoped parents could view their children playing and hear their laughter in the workplace. She wanted mothers to be able to breastfeed on lunch breaks, and for mothers and fathers to be able to have close contact with their children. There are ways to apply these ideas to your setting, and people have already created schools around the world inspired by the model of Gazebo. Thus, we will explore some of the ways in which this community views the transference of these methods to other settings.

Finally, it is important that we always look for ways to expand and grow. So, where are there places that change can happen? What can be added or removed? In other words, where is there room to grow?

Cultural and Social Considerations

It was amazing to witness this child coming from Denmark with very little English yet he interacted the entire week with other children. He got his point across. I gave him a pen and paper and told his mother that he could draw something if he wasn't able to be understood. He drew three things: a boy with something coming out of his mouth, a flag, and a big X. At first I didn't get it until his mom wrote below in quotes, "I don't' speak English." Regardless, he astonished me as I watched him throughout the week learning words and understanding and responding to English. It was quite wonderful to witness his process as he intelligently navigated the language barrier.

At Gazebo there were often visiting children that came as drop-ins on holiday or just for short stints. Whether they were from outside of the United States or lived within the US, there was often an adjustment to the Gazebo setting. The level of freedom was awkward for some students. I remember a Korean family being very uncomfortable with their children getting so dirty. They were there all week and on the last day they came dressed in their airport clothing. The mother instructed the children not to get dirty and what do you imagine was the first thing that they did at Gazebo Park? Yes, they got dirty. When she came to pick them up, she was very upset, which in my view also resulted in them feeling upset and ashamed as well. This was a hard situation. While I felt it was healthy for children to play in the dirt, I sensed there was something culturally unacceptable about it for them. So, for me as a teacher, I had to begin the process of removing my own judgments and opinions of right or wrong, and consider ways to be culturally responsive to the families we served.

Eizner was one of the directors at Gazebo who bridged a cultural gap in many ways. He was fluent in Spanish and had positive rapport with the Latino community in Big Sur. The enrollment during his leadership was very high. I believe this was partially due to his receptivity and cultural responsiveness to the Spanish-speaking community. He continues to work with families as a licensed marriage and family therapist, and reflects on cultural behaviors for immigrants in this country. He says,

> I work with a lot of migrant communities. These people know many things about their culture that might not apply to this culture when it comes to discipline. It's not that they don't know, they know many things, but its cultural-based and often gets them in trouble. It has to do with acculturation issues. Cultural and traditional ways of relating to children don't fly well.

For example, this cultural rub happened during my time teaching at Gazebo as well. Sometimes I would feel it when little boys dressed up in dresses, and some Latino fathers in particular would appear distressed by this. Yet at the same time, there seemed to be an inherent respect for the teacher and professional in their culture, and/or a less direct style of communication. This created a dynamic in which concerns such as this were not often openly discussed between families from other cultures and the teaching staff.

I believe there are ways for the staff to address how to be culturally responsive and it is our responsibility as educators to consider this. Bilingual offerings are important as well sensitivities to these kinds of cultural incompatibilities. Having a person who can speak the language is very helpful and can bridge these kinds of communication gaps. Offering written material in multiple languages

292 The Gazebo Learning Project

is also a best practice to keep communication open when language barriers are a factor. Language and culture are areas that require us as educators to see into another person's experience, and through the lens of their culture and language. This is an important element to consider in any program.

Moreover, there were other aspects that were culturally tricky about Gazebo. For example, the American idea of independence and individuality came up. In particular, working with individuals from Non-Western cultures, there were issues that arose around some of the Gestalt language. For instance, we had an amazingly bright, reflective, and curious intern from Columbia. When I met with him about his progress, we discussed how one aspect of the Gestalt language was challenging for him. This challenge may have been partially cultural and partially personal. However, the use of "I" statements in the Gestalt language was difficult for him. He, among others who came through the school, who came from a more collective culture with more of an emphasis on solidarity, had trouble with this use of language. Rather than connecting with the intention of taking responsibility for one's feelings through the "I" statements, for this young man, "I" was perceived as egocentric. Also, he was more oriented towards the belief of "oneness," and thus the "I" statements did not align with his personal belief system. Though the Gestalt orientation is focused on ownership of feelings and taking responsibility, this pathway of communication may not work for everyone from every culture. Consequently, in the nature of remaining culturally responsive, I feel it is important to bring awareness to the fact that many cultures do not value this kind of direct communication. When working with Gestalt and children and families of different cultural backgrounds, remaining open and conscious about language use is of great consequence.

Moreover, so much of how we behave as children and adults is culturally and socially programmed. Douce remarks that,

> With boys, if you have emotion it shows you're weak. Whereas the Japanese can't show emotion. They can't cry. They would come to Esalen a lot to learn how to cry. The same is true for the Chinese, they can't cry. Face, keeping face. How many Chinese are there?

Douce comments on the Eastern cultural challenges with expressing emotion. This observation is not good or bad, but is certainly a contributing factor when working with a child or family. This is especially true when working in a program which allowed and encouraged the expression of emotions.

At Gazebo, issues of gender came up frequently. Baldwin comments,

> I remember when we had a whole group of kids and Felicity Larmour, John Larmour's daughter, (very together) had the ability to orchestrate and choreograph stuff with everybody wanting to be a part of it. For instance, she would hand one of the Hacker boys as 'mum' and he would be totally there. He would have the dress, the cloak and he would be totally playing it because that was his job to be 'mum.' And other children have got their roles because she has really put them in roles that she feels somehow work. Here is this boy who is a tough boy, but he is really happy to be 'mum' and he is really playing it. He's in the rocking chair and he has got the baby and they are all totally doing it. And that is totally child-orientated, but really they are being adults. They are being humans and they are doing what adults do. It allows them to get into those places, explore them. The number of times we would have some macho dad come in with his son come bouncing down in a tutu with the biggest smile on his face, and you could always see how dad was with that. Some dads were like, "You go boy." And other dads were like, "Whoa!" That didn't have anything to do with the boys sexuality as far as I can see. Whether they wear a

tutu or not doesn't have anything to do with how they are going to be out there in life. But at two or three, a lot of them are anxious to get into their feminine sides, and when they do and are allowed a freedom which absolutely Gazebo supports. Some boys, but not all boys, really get into their feminine side. To me that is what it is about finding the boundaries and seeing where you go.

Thompson-Clark recalls,

I remember being surprised, that very often the girls would be involved in domestic kind of play and the boys would be more often involved in a warrior kind of play. Yet, sometimes they crossed. Esalen didn't have a lot of media, certainly in the '80s folks were pretty much devoid of attachment to media imagery, and without a lot of gender-specific toys, or colors, or things that were traditional in other places. So, it was one of my big hopes that there would not be a distinction between girls' and boys' types of play, but I did find it there, and I find it everywhere to this day.

Nevertheless, I believe as educators it is our obligation to honor all expressions of gender—from gender fluidity to gender choice. There has been so much progress with gender rights in the United States which gives more freedom of gender expression today than in any other time in history. This also makes it complicated to always meet the changing needs. In order for the teacher to remain sensitive to issues of social justice, one needs heightened awareness, and continued professional development on social and cultural issues to ensure inclusion. Through education on equity awareness and social justice, educators can stay current, be inclusive and culturally sensitive, and offer an anti-biased education.

Particularly, in regard to racial justice, individuals and groups who don't experience racism directly can be short sighted on this issue. For those of us who experience white privilege, we can easily slip into perpetuating institutional racism and other forms of bias without even knowing we are participants. Without education on this topic, including open dialogue with people of color about racism, many people believe that they are not part of the problem because they are "color blind" and don't feel racist. However, I believe this stance does more harm than good. Historically, people of color have had less opportunities to succeed, as a result of imperialism, colonialism, slavery, internment, the mission system's goal to eradicate Native language and culture, attempted genocide of Native American, the GI bill, as well as a host of other forms of systemic and institutional racism. These forms of institutional racism built a power dynamic of oppression in this country and created a dominant discourse that favors people of European ancestry, and perpetuates the marginalization of people of color.

There are many programs that leadership and staff can utilize such as *Courageous Conversation about Race,* a program designed for educators that helps open a dialogue for people to share their experiences about race. There are resources for educators such as *Teaching Tolerance, The Southern Poverty Law Center, The Zinn Education Project,* and *Rethinking Schools* which offer curriculum and support for teachers looking to bridge the gaps of social and environmental justice. There are also speakers and facilitators who can assist programs in examining their systems and beliefs. In fact, author and former Gazebo teacher, LaVerne McLeod, presents workshops and presentations called *Bridge Building to Equity,* and she has recently presented this work in a TedX talk.

Similarly, I strongly believe that it is the obligation of any educational institution to provide the entire staff with obligatory participation in equity awareness training and education so these important issues are not ignored. Institution-wide equity awareness training is an essential way to ensure that educational offerings are inclusive of people of color, and to ensure that the programs are non-biased. Offering programs and scholarships for low-income people and people of color is one way to address race and poverty. Looking closely at statistics of demographics can also support diversification to make sure the needs of all people are met; especially ensuring the inclusion of people of color.

Moreover, it is important to consider how to address the learning needs of all children and recognize each learner for their strengths and to honor differences in the learning community. Nick Walker, professor at California Institute of Integral Studies, is autistic and active in the neurodiversity movement; particularly advocating for a shift from the "pathology paradigm" to the "neurodiversity paradigm." This shift, especially within the language, celebrates the diversity and culture within variations in neurocognitive functioning. In this way, language is a powerful tool for constructing social patterning, and by bringing awareness to the use of our language regarding learning differences, we can further support all learners and celebrate the diversity within our learning communities. Walker states that,

1. Neurodiversity – the diversity of brains and minds – is a natural, healthy, and valuable form of human diversity.

2. There is no 'normal' or 'right' style of human brain or human mind, any more than there is one 'normal' or 'right' ethnicity, gender, or culture.

3. The social dynamics that manifest in regard to neurodiversity are similar to the social dynamics that manifest in regard to other forms of human diversity (e.g., diversity of race, culture, gender, or sexual orientation). These dynamics include the dynamics of social power relations – the dynamics of social inequality, privilege, and oppression – as well as the dynamics by which diversity, when embraced, acts as a source of creative potential within a group or society.[1]

Within the Reggio Emilia pedagogy, the term "children with special rights" is utilized as opposed to "children with special needs." This philosophy addresses the rights of all children, and views it as an adult's obligation to defend children's rights. Walker states that,

"Neurodivergent, sometimes abbreviated as ND, means having a brain that functions in ways that diverge significantly from the dominant societal standards of 'normal'." In this way, standard education is not well designed in its one-size-fits-all approach. It is important in an educational institution, public or private, to bring awareness to neurodiversity, to make sure each individual child's learning needs are being considered and addressed, and to create a learning community where differences are celebrated.

Joyce Lyke was the first work-scholar to work at Gazebo in 1977. She was pregnant with her first child, Karina, during that time. One of her fondest memories of working at Gazebo Park School was,

> One of the main elements of the Gazebo curriculum was to learn how to be in your body. During the early Gazebo years the staff had the privilege of working with a five-year-old autistic child. Her name was Mandy. She was a beautiful soul. She was able to walk, but her legs were quite stiff, and her hand movements mimicked those of a small infant, stuck in a repetitive pattern. Again and again, her fingers would clutch the other hand and then come apart, she would make sounds, but it was mostly a closed system. As we attempted to reach her, to make personal contact with her during her extended care at Gazebo, I remember feeling deeply touched by her presence. There were moments of discouragement, as she did not respond in the ways another five-year-old would or carry on a conversation about what she was seeing. She had her own language and we were desperately trying to learn it, to reach her, we were all attempting to make a difference. She opened our hearts, deep compassion arose in many of those moments of her tender care, and watching how the other children in the school would be sensitive to her, respectful of her. She was the teacher, and we were learning from her. She deeply impacted us all. She opened our hearts in a gentle way during that year she was at Gazebo.

Lyke, also a Gazebo parent and workshop leader, is now creating a resource for parents called *Parenting to Awakening* in which she shares how parenting can be a path to spiritual growth and emotional healing. Her current work, as well as her own parenting, was informed by her experiences and the depth of her contact at Gazebo.

Lederman wrote in an article for the Esalen catalog in 1980,

> Five year old Mandy spent three months with us. She came to us under pressure, a mass of labels including, 'autistic,' ... Her primary contact had been with people who themselves feel pressure to 'do something.' Often children such as Mandy are literally tortured by those who focus continually on what a child can NOT do and ignore what a child is ABLE to do.[2]

In conclusion, equity awareness for professional development is the responsible action for any learning community in order to offer anti-biased education—and to bring more understanding to issues of age, gender, race, poverty, sexual orientation, immigration, considerations of indigenous peoples, and neurodiversity—honoring people with varying physical and cognitive differences. As we address issues of social injustice, these issues can be painful and it takes courage to bring them into full view, and so perhaps at the same time we seek social justice, we need to learn to accept discomfort and nonclosure. Solutions are not always clear and available in the moment. Regardless, I feel it is important to find ways to acknowledge these issues, and for all people to be represented, to be seen and heard, for differences to be honored, and diversity celebrated.

Supporting Transitions

While many people found transitions following Gazebo to their next life's chapter seamless, there were social and cultural challenges for others. For example, an anonymous community member shared,

> Research associates class mobility with whether or not a child has attended preschool. However, in a rebuttal to the often repressive parenting style the teachers themselves had received, Gazebo

School kids were encouraged in self-expression. This was not offset by complementary training in social awareness and manners. Lower-class children were at a disadvantage here; lower-class kids often receive different social training at home, due to social rules being different in lower-class, and because there is often less time with guiding adults. So, while all the kids lacked social training at the Gazebo School, the middle and upper-class kids got could get caught up in dominant middle class social narratives at home. Lower-class kids, generally speaking, did not emerge from the Gazebo with greater ability to maneuver in complicated social situations. Therefore, it's possible the Gazebo School had class bias unintentionally built into its value system by virtue of omission of these vital social skills.

The culture of Esalen and Gazebo also had its growing edges in contrast to the outside world. Traditionally, Gazebo did not condemn nudity. Being that the school was on the property of the hot springs where nudity was accepted, this carried over into Gazebo. We had little hot tubs and mini massage tables on the preschool grounds. Many of the children preferred to be naked and play outside in the water and sun. This practice became less and less culturally acceptable as the years went on, and as other considerations such as legalities, licensing, and liability arose. Nevertheless, in the early days of Gazebo, most of us kids ran around naked for a good deal of time. Children learning to use the potty could be without diapers and feel their bodies. Douce mentions,

> You know the Europeans accept nudity. Now, in Germany in Munich in the summer, you are in the city and you look into the park and everyone is nude. So you're in the city, so if those nude people came up on the bridge they would be arrested, but in the park it is natural. They accept natural. So a lot of Europeans are very loose about nudity, while Americans are very uptight about it.

While nudity may have been accepted in the 'hippie' culture of Esalen and Big Sur, it was a stretch for many. Concerns about health and safety are always a priority to address. So, within different social norms, and ideas about what is acceptable, Gazebo pushed those edges.

On the other hand, those of us that grew up in the Gazebo and Esalen culture had a different kind of acculturation to contend with. Sometimes transition to public schools was challenging. For example, Marquis states,

> My friends make fun of me all the time. I live in Brooklyn. What's nice is I finally brought it out in my friends we are closer now because we are more emotionally connected and they are more emotionally vulnerable around me, but it wasn't going to work otherwise. I miss it. It is really hard not being around my emotionally available 'hippy dippy' friends. I miss them. That is why we have known each other for twenty-seven years as it is so valuable. We make fun of it, but my boyfriend has had none of this. He had an incredibly militant childhood. He grew up in Virginia as an army brat, and I am coaching him through it, and leading him to communicate because it is not going to work if he doesn't. So the other day he said, 'that sounds like it is really hard for you,' and he was like, 'I am learning.' He was so proud of himself.

Similarly, Zoë Beck, former Gazebo student, talks about her life and adjustments within her cultural context by saying,

> My Dad, who came from North Dakota youngest of five from a Catholic family, has great conversations with my husband about how 'you have to practice and it is going to feel weird and uncomfortable, but I just had to practice for a couple years.'

Furthermore, in transitions into Gazebo culture, social beliefs around parenting could differ from Gazebo philosophy. Lederman made the clear distinction that the way children and teachers interacted in the school was different from the way parents and children interacted at home. Nevertheless, there have been learning curves for parents that are new to the Gazebo approach and those who adapt it to their life at home. Marquis says,

> It is interesting the difference between parents and teachers, like how my parents didn't necessarily follow the Gazebo rules all the time. Where the difference was: you get stuck up on the roof and my parents would come and they would take me down and take me home. I like that they are sort of separate between those different roles. What I realize is it takes a lot of intentionality to let that happen, our first instinct is to stop and protect and to control. We want to protect and corral and remove all the things that could hurt. So it takes trust. That is the vision of Gazebo: to give an opportunity for things to happen and that is okay, but that is hard, and that is not the first instinct for humans. That is why Janet fought for it so hard, and as a kid I didn't know any of the philosophy.

Whitehand says,

> For me learning almost a new way to parent and passing that onto Charlie [my husband]. I learned a new way to view parenting and my children. How to give them some space to do and be themselves. To feel the power of mastery and stand in their own shoes. To understand them better. To love their strengths and weaknesses and their friends strengths and weaknesses for what they bring and allow my children to learn from their interactions. This impacted our family life tremendously. It has nurtured the parent-child relationship to improve our enjoyment of each other. To give the kids space to be themselves. To be okay with making mistakes and learning from them. It improved communication with us, each other, and with friends. They are confident, happy, caring, inclusive kids, who love life.

Beck reflects on co-parenting by saying,

> Raising a kid, and raising a kid with another person, we did not see it coming at all. My husband was not raised anything like us.

He was raised in a very domineering home. His father was born in Scotland and moved to Canada. He was told he was loved five times in his life, and I was told every day of my life. A lot of stuff has come up with us about how we were raised differently. He has very little experience with children, and he is really careful with our son. I am like, 'its okay, he can climb up on the counter, he can have the scissors.' I am okay with him getting hurt, and I really want him to explore his boundaries. I really trust that he knows his abilities or not and that it still going to be okay. I was given so much freedom, and so much trust, and so much belief in what I could do. My abilities had boundaries on the outside, but so much freedom.

Transitions to public kindergarten and elementary school posed some challenges for children who were raised purely in the Gazebo. Vieregge says,

We were getting tremendous feedback that the children were having difficulties in kindergarten and first grade. That is why Janet encouraged me because the dance had already started between the Gestalt Process and the freedom of the Park.

Vieregge's spiral of education whereby relevance, imagination, and intellectual rigor created the balance for the children. In this way, the discipline and focus on the first-aid curriculum and kindergarten preparation really supported the transitions to come. In using a more cognitive approach and experimenting with a more academic education would help them prepare for their later years in more formal education.

Emotionally, there were other challenges, based partially on the fact that Gazebo was a place where touch and teacher-student bonding were accepted. For example, Marquis remembers,

I actually had to train myself to not bond with my teachers at school. I had to teach myself because I would get into trouble sometimes because I would be too close to my teachers. I would bond so much that I had to learn how to stop doing that. I remember that, and I still struggle with that at times. I want to give to everyone.

The social expectations were different in public elementary school, and this was problematic for transitions. At Gazebo, a certain intimacy is accepted. There was a nurturing connection that children experienced with their teachers. These relationships and bonds were different than those in grade school.

Gazebo kids sometimes found it uncomfortable transitioning to other cultural settings. Delevett also recalls,

> I didn't fit in in Germany. I was a Californian run-around-naked-hippie-child, and I went to Catholic school. There was this jarring difference and I always wanted to fit in and be normal. I never would, but it stood out to me that not being normal is great. Gazebo gave me so much love and a good foundation. My German teachers were very clear that you don't name us by our first name and we are not friends. 'What are you talking about, of course my teachers are my friends?' I was having to learn about hierarchy and space and boundaries.

Marquis remarks, "I would just cry in most of my twenties because I couldn't connect with people. 'Why don't they connect?' Because they don't want to connect."

Day, who would transition back and forth from New York to Gazebo remarks that,

> I feel like I am too available, I too readily give, but this place [Gazebo] allows you to do things that it doesn't explicitly state that you can do. Like seeing people interact in a certain way. This is contagious by proximity.

In this way, sometimes outside of the *container* of Esalen and Gazebo, the depth of human contact is different.

Many people experience culture shock transitioning to and from Esalen. Perhaps Gazebo kids have met similar challenges transitioning to more mainstream society. Encountering the world as it operates without the emotional transparency may have been jarring for children as well. Transitions to more traditional schooling and society may have been hard for some Gazebo kids, yet there is no clear solution aside from providing a balance, and again it is individual. Others have found these transitions seamless. So, it is important to ask how can we be gentle with ourselves, and bring awareness to how we support change.

Change is part of life and cultivating resilience is part of the learning process; especially for children. In my experience with my daughter, finding ways to open a dialogue about change in challenging times is one of the hardest things, but also very important. She and I have been through a lot of change and transition in her short lifetime. Acknowledging transitions with conversations, stories, and creating rituals that honor change, have supported these transitions in our life. Essentially, acknowledgement of the depth of experience and the accompanying emotions is one way to help children build resilience. Handl remarks,

> It takes courage as a teacher to be able to stand in that unknowing. What is going to happen that day when you walk into the Park. Be willing to let the student tell you what they need instead of telling them what you think they need.

Application in Education

Through playing–engaging the whole Human Being... aspects of self can emerge with courage and a healthy self esteem. CHOICES become available as mistakes are celebrated as the experiential textbooks of life.

- JL

How is Gazebo philosophy transferable in other educational settings? From schools to parenting to homeschooling, what are the seeds that can germinate from here? How can these ideas be integrated in other settings? Thompson-Clark ran two Gazebo-modeled programs: Gazebo School Park at Kenyon College in Gambier, Ohio and The Children's School at Sonoma State University. She believes in

> Re-Rooting education in 'physiological, emotional and ecological literacy' all of which develop the dispositions of respect, resourcefulness and responsibility and the creation of future stewards of the world.

Her programs are successful examples of the translation of Gazebo principles.

There are many concepts presented in book through the lens of a community who lived it. How can the philosophy be applied in other educational settings? Different people will have different interpretations and ideas depending on their path. Really, so much depends on your educational setting, the space and environment, the history of the people, the social atmosphere, and the people themselves. So, any application of these ideas will be intuitive and culturally, socially, and environmentally responsive.

However, the following is an overview of some core aspects of the Gazebo philosophy and how these principles might be implemented in other settings.

View of the Child

Adults, teachers and parents alike, can open to children's capacity for responsibility at a young age, and help them by creating opportunities for empowerment in young children. Wolfinger remarks,

> The biggest way that Gazebo helped me was that it was empowering. That resonates with me for teaching as many kids as I have taught, at this point thousands. The fact that, I am here to help them, and value them as individuals. Sometimes in a teacher setting, it is like everyone needs to be treated the same, and that there are all the same rules. You get to go to the bathroom once, or whatever rules, just silly stuff that doesn't take care of the person. So, they don't feel valued. I feel like Gazebo really instills valuing each other, and that makes all the difference. If someone is going to open up to you, and all the trauma that they have been through, knowing that someone actually cares. We [Gazebo alumni] are so good at getting people to open up because people really recognize that we are not trying to get anything from them, but we are really there to try to help. And you guys [other alumni] say that you sometimes have problems with too much empathy; which is not necessarily a bad thing in this world. In giving more than you receive, it just feels so good.

Wyatt says, "Self-responsibility is a big piece in our culture and I think most people could use some information around that." Allowing a child to do for themselves what an adult might otherwise do for them can be beneficial to the child's skill building. Handl also says,

> The reasons why I felt magnetized to Gazebo was that there was an honoring of the child's inner teacher, that they know what their next step is, that whatever it is that they want to do over and over again, or push themselves with, the child's way of knowing is honored, versus cognitive or other models that are out there. That really resonates with me, honoring the individual and still honoring the needs of others and the group, and yet at the same time you are saying, 'I trust.' There is a trust in the child to know what their next step is, to know what they are learning.

Charles views the child through this lens:

> So that could be the first point that we recognize their talents and abilities and intelligence and that we focus on that. We offer them a safe, yet risky enough environment for them to learn in. It is not like we are going to impart this wisdom, these ideas, this knowledge to them, to open the top of their heads and pour it in. So, recognizing what they can already do, and building on that would be an important piece of it. And the other is looking at communication and how they communicate, first before they have a lot of language, and then as they develop language and how to use the Gestalt language with them and support them in using it as well. Like being polite to each other and cooperating, for me modeling that is much for powerful than saying to them, 'Say please, say thank you.'

Role of Teacher

Thompson-Clark reflects that,

> I think it is very difficult for teachers to be trained in the model a
> Gazebo teacher is trained, and to allow for the types of experiences
> that happen there. That is a very uncommon practice as an early
> educator. We all knew there were boundaries, yet most people
> want control.

There is no strict blueprint for this model, yet this written work
shares the practices. Perhaps the ideas presented here can offer support
for teachers, giving them permission to allow for time and space to
be with children in a different way.

Teachers may choose to approach children's learning through an
inquiry-based model. Using emergent curriculum, they may follow
the child's curiosity. Wyatt says that

> Teachers are guiding. The teaching tool is in the land stewardship.
> How many carrots popped up? You are doing numbers. We did
> stuff with older kids like geocaching on 2,000 acres in the White
> Mountains in New Hampshire. There are ways to work in different
> environments. They had this amazing place and they spent most
> of the time inside. They could do so many things. They could do
> what Midland [a private grade school in California] did in that
> every subject was related to their land.

Charles says,

> Adjusting to fit the situation is a very important guideline. There
> is no hard and fast rule, it is like, 'No, no to you and yes to you.'
> It encourages flexibility because they have to be present to adjust
> to fit the situation and then I have to be creative in a certain way.

Most importantly, Charles says is, "First the experience, then the
learning." For example, Charles continues,

Because people would come into my groups and say what is going to happen and what are we going to learn? And I would say it is just like Gazebo, first you are going to have an experience, then I will teach you some theory of the experience that you have had, then it will mean something to you. So much of my education was learning facts. So, I use the example of, 'We don't sit at Gazebo, sit them down it front of us and with the mushroom field guide and say, "Okay we are going to go through the first ten pages this morning, and then the next day we are going through the next ten pages.' No, we walk into the Park it has rained the night before. There are some mushrooms, so we say, 'What is this?' We talk about it, ask them questions and say, 'Hey, there is a book that we can look these up in.' That means so much more! Or not, maybe I come to school and I don't care about mushrooms and I just wanted to hammer some nails because I was doing it yesterday and I was getting good at it.

Environment—Outdoor/Nature Education

Baldwin believes that creating a Gazebo-like environment is the starting point.

First would be the space, flower beds, compost, Pottyville, the structure—park that has flow. The more space you can give them, that would be the very first thing. Room to hide. If you don't give them room to hide, you are not supporting them. Children need that place, not to hide like getting lost, but privacy. Little structures don't cost huge amounts of money, and can be built so children can get into them. It doesn't have to be great big stuff, it doesn't have to be custom built. You can build these fabulous classrooms and they are wonderful, but kids would rather have old cardboard boxes with windows that they can paint a flower on the outside. That is going to occupy a two-year-old far more than some beautiful thing made for children.

Baldwin, among others, stresses the importance of allowing the children to be part of the design process.

> It could be a couple of of old tree stumps that the kids helped bring. For example, the process of the 'magic castle' becoming a play area. It was Gofer's old house. I grew up in England, there is always old stuff and that's what gets us going. I grew up with castles, these were not built for children to play on, but god are they brilliant for play. No one planned it. No one thought it out, it just happened, because the children engage with it as if for the first time. Whereas, if it's built by an adult for children, they cannot engage with it for the first time because someone got there first. It was thought out. It was somebody's idea, and they had all sorts of plans. Not that that was bad, but it doesn't have the originality. Ask children what they remember as children. I can remember the pile of earth that my cousin and I used to play on. Nothing much, just a pile of earth in his back garden, and they were doing some work on it. And we would build a little cave, and have our Matchbox toys. We would have our little soldiers, and that pile of earth kept us going for years. It wasn't anyone's idea, it was just there. It's just natural stuff and that is naturally engaging. There is something about originality, and to be original, you need to be at the beginning. So, the magic castle, it's there, and it's a ruin. It's not an idea, it's not a built thing, it's a ruin. So, it begins every time you go there.

One element of creating environment that supports these methods is including opportunities for calculated risk. Eizner says,

> I think Gazebo philosophy is transferable. I think adults will have to deal with their own fears and personal issues and their needs to be many changes and I think it just needs to be understood. The governments—I don't want to get too political—but it needs to be understood and there needs to be a cultural shift. It might be research, it might be people who are willing to take risks and implement different philosophies. I am sure in other cultures with less liabilities, and they may be able to do more.

The people who have taken the philosophy out in the world have done so largely in part with the environment. Lederman used to say the environment is the greatest teacher, so that is a great starting point. It is possible to create the environment with the children. As Eizner remarks, there is a lot more liability in our education system today, yet allowing children to learn with some calculated risk, they learn their physical boundaries, and build life-long skills based on real-life personal experience. Eizner recommends,

> Follow the kids, let it be a kids place, support kids' experience, don't rush, be patient, reflect, be aware of your own feelings, do not project. I am just giving you all the things that Gazebo is for me. Gazebo is a place for kids to be who they are. When you come with all these agendas, which some of the teachers do now, and they do in many other schools, in my opinion Gazebo stops being what it is, or what it could be, or what it was. There were main guidelines that all of us that spent time at Gazebo accepted and respected, like the not picking up the children, supporting them, not rushing, the environment, how we take care of the environment, how we take care of the kids. Don't rush. Create a safe environment allowing experiences to take place. Those were kind of like unspoken and understood rules.

By providing opportunities for calculated risk-taking, children learn vital skills. For example, Price-Waldrip says that

> For me my growing edge was taking risks and tolerating discomfort, because as a kid I was super scared of one, getting in trouble, and two, getting hurt physically—like falling. When I was really little I hit my head and had to get nine stitches, and I was like, 'I am never doing this again.' So, being at Gazebo where there was so much going on and so many places to go and so many things to get dirty and involved in. I was really timid and cautious because I didn't want to get hurt. Also, I was coming in and out of regular preschool, and I had this fear of getting in trouble. I didn't want to test the boundary and then have to realize I am going to get in trouble for it. That was my learning. One, it is okay to get in

trouble, that the world isn't going to end. And two, 'How can I learn about my body and be involved and play with other kids and not feel like I am going to hurt myself.' That was true throughout my whole life. I remember my parents used to tell me that if I got a time-out they would take me out for a milkshake. That was their way that they wanted to encourage me to be bad and take risks, and it wasn't about being good, it was about, 'Okay you will get rewarded for trying something that is scary but will eventually help you with your growth.'

Similarly, in regards to taking emotional risk, Delevett remembers that

Steve Beck did the same thing with me when I was twenty and working in the garden. He said, 'Ama, you get a week of breaking rules.' It was great it was so awesome. Coming from Gazebo to Catholic school and back to Esalen it was like, 'Oh I can just break rules and mess things up and the world is not going to end, and it is really liberating and really fun.' I am grateful to him forever for that.

Zoë Beck concurs about her dad, Steve Beck, "He would say some-times that he was more worried that I didn't break rules than that I might." So, learning in an individualized manner recognizes that each person has different needs and we are all working with different strengths and challenges.

Gestalt

Though Feldenkrais was known as a movement and somatics teacher, his definition of Gestalt very much sums up the practice.

Gestalt therapy puts the stress not on bringing up the unconscious material, but on making the person aware of the role played in his life both by each of the sensations we have mentioned and by some others. Starting from the present, the person is led back into his own life history and brought to realize how much his actions were motivated by these emotions, to sort them out, and to guard against them in the future.[3]

Does one need to be trained in Gestalt practice in order to apply Gestalt practice principles? The experience is helpful, particularly if teachers are working on themselves individually and in groups. There certainly are specific Gestalt courses and trainings available. Price states that,

> The bottom line goal in Gestalt practice is to become more aware. If you go through anything and you come out of it with more awareness, then you win. Awareness, in of itself, is healing.

Price suggests ways of doing this through expanding both inner and outer realms of awareness. The inner realm through the breath and physical sensations. Also, the emotional states and feeling states connecting back to sensations. Moreover, the outer realm of awareness can be in contact with what is outside of self through the senses. Essentially, as Price suggests, the goal is to, "Deepen contact in this moment of what I am experiencing." So, bridging inner and outer—contact with self, others, and to the earth are important touchstones for building awareness. Kevin Harvey feels,

> I think the most important elements of Gazebo's philosophy have to be first in connection to earth and the environment, and secondly, using that connection, our animal connection to environment to develop the emotional literacy and ability to communicate emotions in an effective and productive way.

When using Gestalt with children, Charles shares key questions to ask yourself "from the angle of what can I learn about myself as a result of exploring." She asks,

> Which kid triggers you and work with that? Which kid is your favorite? Who do you feel resonant with? Which parents do you find the most challenging to deal with? And again, what is the learning for me so that I can relate better, but also to continue to grow in that way?"

Charles also stresses,

> I think it is really helpful to ask, 'What is my motivation for speaking now? Who is it for? Is it because I am having so much anxiety about the fact that they are fighting and there is so much discomfort around that? Are they able to tolerate these feelings that they are having? Could I let it go a little bit farther to the place where they might come up with 'I want to stop now?'

Waldrip-Price suggests,

> One thing that I would want to have implemented more widely is what we call when we teach workshops 'process before program.' So, in schools so much is about lets get through the lesson plan and what gets missed is what is happening for a kid that day or what is happening at home or what they are really with in the moment. And I don't think a lot of learning and education can happen if a child isn't being first given that space to be with what is happening right now.

So, I think that "process before program" is super important instead of trying to race through a lot of different material. There is so much happening for kids and adults and beings in the moment that if that is not put first, so much learning gets missed.

Parenting

What the parents resist the children persist.

– JL

Bringing Gazebo methods into parenting is also a way to connect to this philosophy. Davey speaks to her use of these methods in her life by saying,

> I am not a parent yet, but I have watched many children and nannied. I have employed Gazebo methods with every child I have ever met. I usually kneel down and introduce myself and actively

listen to them. If there are questions, I will answer to the best of my ability, or I will say 'I don't know'.

Accordingly, Eizner reflects on his time as a Gazebo teacher while his children were enrolled. He remembers,

> They said they loved it when I was there. As a father I needed to be very careful to not intervene in a situation where my kids were involved with other kids or my kids were struggling with something, and to just let other adults to deal with that. In some situations, this worked out beautifully. I was very careful—definitely in conflict. I would not facilitate conflict between my kids and other kids. When they wanted and would seek my attention, and it was that fine line. I am the dad, and are they wanting my special attention? Is it my role as a father? I am both, I am father, and teacher and director. It is that fine line, so having someone else deal with it rather than not allowing my kids to have that experience. I think understanding about myself, my children, having kids, relationships, helped me to be a better father, and a good enough husband.

Wyatt feels that while parents can apply these practices in similar ways that teachers did in the Park, at Gazebo you could take your time with an activity, and at home you may have different needs. "Out in the real world we don't have all day to get your boots on, and at Gazebo we do. So there is some moving around agendas and schedules." She encourages parents to work with emotions at home and to allow space for children and adults to have difficult feelings. She says,

> The first thing is being okay with my child being sad, my child not liking what is happening, my child disagreeing and being okay with that. That was my biggest learning, and I didn't learn it for a while. In the ideal world, I am clear and holding a boundary, and I am honoring whatever you feel about that boundary, but it is not going to trigger me.

In this way, she points towards learning to tolerate highly-charged emotions and making space for emotional expression in the home. Marquis suggests,

> I am saying the parents should know what the kids are up to and how to model it at home as well. So it is not just the parents come to school, and they get this really cool experience where the teachers are really open and free. We didn't have rules, but the teachers had a ton of rules and guidelines as teachers for what you are allowed and not allowed to do; which is sort of a funny switch. Do the parents really get it and buy in and understand this is how we are learning to communicate? So, you can use these tools at home as well. That it is a full-circle thing versus just at school or just at home. That is one of the really special things about growing up here. I would go to Zoë's house and her dad would say, 'We don't say shut up here because everybody is allowed to have their feelings.'

Room to Grow

Gazebo is always in the process of organization and development.

–JL

Though Gazebo philosophy has many elements that resonate with people, there were also challenges and contradictions for people socially, culturally, and emotionally. Community members shared the sticking points with me. We explored the questions, "Where is their room to grow within this philosophy?"

Parent education was one area that seemed to be ripe for development. Getting families on board with the philosophy and how to implement these ideas at home in order to align home and school. Parents having access to more information on the pedagogy may be helpful. What I experienced was so rich, so it is hard to offer a simple pamphlet. Yet, as a parent educator, Handl offered a course on understanding the pedagogy and supporting parents in elements might be useful at home. Alternately, ongoing groups or meet-up where families could share ideas could be supportive. In these types of groups, core concepts could be shared so families could better understand the practices and how to support the home and school application of them. Also, teachers and parents can share information that might be helpful for their children's development. I find parents thrive on sharing and these exchanges support parents as their children grow. Marquis says,

> My parents were learning then at the same time which was kind of cute. She [my mother] would say I learned something in class today and we are going to use 'I' statements, and I would say, 'Oh, I did that too, I know what you are talking about.' It was interesting to be sharing, and kind of like growing up with our parents here, at least for me and my parents. My mom had never done personal growth work, so she was kind of like growing up at the same time. If you want Gazebo for your kids, don't you want that for yourself?

Wyatt concurs,

> I feel like there is a lot of opportunity for parent education, both ways, them educating us about their home life and their child, and about who they are, where the child is coming from, and we then

sharing Gazebo and the practices and principles and the reasons behind and what we know about learning, growing children. It is an incredibly rich opportunity. What I found in Canada coming from Gazebo, we created a parent education feedback system for the program. The teaching of the philosophy for parents is important especially for those parents that don't ask a lot of questions. Communication was the biggest piece.

On the contrary, even some Gazebo children were uncomfortable with some of the Gazebo practices. Delevett, who later herself became a Gestalt therapist, expressed her annoyance at having to live these ideals as a child.

> I don't know what teacher, probably every one of them did it at some point during the years, said 'What are you feeling? Where are your feeling it? See if you can use the words, 'I am feeling..., I don't like..., don't do that, don't hit me or what?' I remember it as a feeling and trying to put words to it. I remember that place of energy in my body and them trying to kind of coach me. Then later, sitting in Gestalt groups and going, 'They are doing the same thing. Asking, is it hot or is it cold?' I don't know, it is just a feeling. I had this anger.' Sometimes I felt burdened as a little kid of always have to take responsibility for my feelings and my actions. I remember that sense of being like, 'I just want to be a kid and I don't want to have to be responsible for my feelings.'

Some alumni I spoke with felt strongly that some of practices, such as not picking up children and letting them cry, were damaging and cruel. Some children even felt scarred by not being "helped" when they felt upset or stranded. The more radical practices of Gazebo land differently depending on any individual's personal moral landscape. Not every child who went to Gazebo saw it as a utopia, and each of us had challenges, some perhaps more than others. I had resistance, and I remember sometimes that feeling of unfairness. I felt it was unfair not getting help up or down. Now, when I think about it, it is actually more fair because they were treating me like an equal. In terms of fairness, they were saying, "You have capacity to do it as much as I do, and I will help but I am not going to do it for you." I just had that feeling that this is unjust. I think particularly the not picking children up or helping them down was a very controversial point for many people.

For me, a missing link is peace education. I wonder how to build a global community in a place-based program; particularly one that is as rural as Gazebo. How can we build international relationships that support empathy and compassion, and a global consciousness and awareness around social and environmental justice? How can we educate children as global citizens? I feel that compassion is often innate in children yet needs cultivating and that growing empathy can start at a very young age.

In early childhood, we are working within the stage of development and the way they perceive the world in a egocentric way as they begin to distinguish themselves from their parents and have not yet found their place in the wider context of society. Yet, I did a pen pal project with Gazebo children with orphans from Cambodia that I worked with through the "Buds to Blossoms" program which offers pediatric massage to orphans with HIV and AIDS. I hand delivered the Gazebo students' letters and they in turn sent drawings, photos and letters which we posted inside of the "pony shed" for the children to view. These images and writings stimulated discussion and more global awareness. I feel pen pal programs are a wonderful way for children to learn about other people and how they live.

There are a growing number of offerings for compassion and kindness curriculum. "Creating Compassionate Cultures," a curriculum that was developed out of Tara Redwood School which began on the grounds of Land of Medicine Buddha in Santa Cruz, California, has many tools for internal calming and focus as well as peaceful communication. Similarly, neuroscientist and founder of Center for Healthy Minds, Richard Davidson created the Kindness Curriculum for schools based on his research and beliefs. In their work *Altered Traits: Science Reveals How Meditation Changes Your Mind, Brain and Body*, Davidson and coauthor Daniel Goleman suggest,

> We have shown the evidence that it is possible to cultivate these positive qualities in the depths of our being, and that any of us can begin this inner journey...qualities like equanimity and compassion are learnable skills, one we can teach our children and improve in ourselves.[4]

The growing field of mindfulness in education is expanding and is an area ripe with growth and potential for education. Daniel Rechtschaffen, author of, *The Way of Mindful Education*, offers workshops and resources for teachers on mindfulness. There are many mindfulness trainings specifically for educators. I see the potential for mindfulness to enrich the lives of children by providing emotional regulation and centering skills for life. Though children naturally live in the present more than adults, finding ways to be calm and grounded can support the nervous system and open up possibilities for learning in a profound way.

Furthermore, teaching social and environmental justice are important parts of peace education, and part of our responsibility as teachers. I feel it is never too young to bring these topics into the open if it is done with consideration of the age-appropriate attention span and language faculty of the children. I remember having conversations at Gazebo with two and three-year-olds about their different family configurations; some sharing about having two mommies while others shared about more traditional family structures and challenges within them. These issues often arise without our prompting, and so we can be responsive and inclusive in how we address these real-life issues.

In some ways, Gazebo practices did support peace education and social and environmental justice. I think that the basics of peace education begin with addressing our own inner emotional conflicts and outer conflicts in our relationships to others. I feel that if we can start small in this way with young children, we can begin to look at larger social problems such as political conflict and war. Furthermore, educating children about caring, and for the earth at a young age is also something I feel they can grasp early and in their own environments locally, and hopefully this will lead them one day to act more globally. Even little children can become activists if they feel passionate about world peace.

The "how" of making a program work, and the logistics, gathering finances to keep a program running is one major consideration. For many years, Gazebo was supported and subsidized by Esalen, yet there were many challenges with funding—especially in times of natural disasters such as road closures, landslides, and wildfires. In particular, the Esalen grounds and gardens departments helped Gazebo so much and the entire Esalen community gave so much to Gazebo and the kids. Nevertheless, Handl says,

> Gazebo (at the core optimum model) is also held by a greater community that values the early years of growth and surrounds the staff, Park and children with resources, energy and love. This enables the staff to focus on the here and now with the children, without having energy leakages toward gathering resources, proving validity, or creating external buffers so they can have this intense focus.

Nelson adds,

> My general wish is to have Gazebo rise to the surface again to become available so that this generation has all the benefits that I did from raising children here because I feel very fortunate. Day cares for corporations, employers could have children in open lots or spaces. I think it's fantastic and I imagine it would happen. I would like to see Esalen Institute support families. I want Esalen to support housing for families. The availability of housing and the demographics has changed tremendously. I am so lucky I was able to caretake and do four days a week here when it was a thirty-two hour a week schedule.

Many share Nelson's and Handl's sentiments about the importance of supporting children financially, physically, emotionally. Much like in Maslow's concept of the "Hierarchy of Needs," if the basic physical needs are not taken care of, self-actualization cannot be addressed. From what I have seen from a transition from Gazebo to Big Sur Park School, essentially, the Big Sur community cares a great deal about not just the education of children but about the deep needs of the soul and development of their human potential.

Dvora says,

> Each school has a unique identity—some more unique than others. Gazebo Park is a school that was birthed from the passionate vision of one woman {Janet Lederman} in synchronous partnership with a cultural institution {Esalen} that provided fertile ground for an inspired identity to form. Gazebo is a year-round outdoor school for infants, toddlers and preschoolers—which has been serving the Esalen community and the local community of this somewhat remote coastal community for the past thirty-six years. The school's philosophy provides a deep immersion in eco-education, Gestalt practice {an Esalen-style approach to embodying one's experience and embracing one's emotional life fully} and social-constructivism {a pedagogy of listening to & supporting children as they construct their own understanding of the world through direct experience independently and in relationship with others}. The gestalt of Gazebo's original intent continues, while over the years and decades {since the mid-'70s} successive directors have contributed to the sculpting of a school that continues to take shape.[5]

The Outcome?

Dingman liked to talk about how the Gazebo kids grew up to be successful in life. I suppose this depends on how you define success. I personally value health and well-being as important aspects of success. For myself, learning in nature and practicing Gestalt at a young age, taught me how to be in my experience, in my body, in contact with my heart, and to trust that. I was given a set of tools that would support me in my communication for my life. I am grateful for the experience of being free, running wild with my friends, and being outside. I grew up before TV, internet or computers were widespread. Though the world has changed tremendously during my life, I still value so much these connections I have to other human beings and to the earth itself. In part, I attribute my ability to deeply connect to growing up in the Gazebo ways. Yet, I myself am still a work-in-progress, still making mistakes, learning, and growing.

Ken Dychtwald, after reading this manuscript, asked the critical question of what happened to the Gazebo kids? Where is the proof that this method is effective and positive for children as they grow into adults? My response: there are no longitudinal studies to show results, and if there were it comes down to how we measure success? Is it by the numbers in our bank account, our health and well-being, our relationships, our happiness? Perhaps we could model our measure of success after the country of Bhutan that measures Gross National Happiness (GNH). The nine domains of Bhutan's GNH are: living standards, education, health, environment, community vitality, time-use, psychological well-being, good governance, cultural resilience and promotion.[6] Bhutan's system of measuring happiness looks at a wider, more holistic view of a life—which I think is a more comprehensive way to view success.

In truth, after corresponding with many Gazebo children, not all their stories are fairy tales. Some children had challenges with the way things were done at Gazebo and Esalen, and others found it to be as Delevett described, "a utopia." The experiences were very personal and each individual, depending on their temperament, their experiences in the Park, at Esalen, and at home, and thus each was influenced differently by this philosophy. Former Gazebo student, Wolfinger, says,

> Esalen is supposed to be a center for developing human potential, and you can't really develop people if you don't have kids because they are the future. As adults, we learn so much from children.

When people say I grew up at Esalen, it really was a human experiment. I went out in the world, then I moved back to California to be part of what is so integral to human development. I really would like to see this worldwide, but the truth is what is out there is the world is crazy and the way that children are treated is absolutely different. I feel a duty to make a difference in the world in terms of the children.

Delevett recalls,

I get a lot of feedback from people that they feel I am authentic in a way that they don't find in many people. I think what is true is that we learned to say how we are really feeling, that I don't have to hide or pretend. The other thing that stands out to me being a therapist, and maybe because I have worked with so much trauma, is how very little memories of people have of their childhood years. I feel like I have so many real, alive, memories, and sensations—that are my memories and not just pictures. I think that is another factor of having been here at Gazebo is that we remember our childhood.

Marquis finds,

I sit with people and they are freaking out, and they are so upset that they are upset. I am like, "It is o.k. to be upset." I think that comes from here, from having an ability to communicate and learning how to talk about my feelings. I went to theater school, and my teachers asked if it is stressful to have everyone asking how you are feeling all the time. Sometimes it is kind of annoying to be constantly communicating, so I think that I'm trying to find the balance of that. I know how to take care of myself, and it definitely started here from, 'You take care of yourself, and you are responsible for yourself, and it sucks but you have to learn how to do it.' I learned really early where I found comfort as a kid. Like not picking up children, we were independent, we were challenged to be little people.

Gazebo mother, Sarah Harvey feels,

> The most valuable tool Sage has taken from Gazebo so far is self-confidence. He stands up for himself, and believes in himself, because of the tactics he's been taught here. Unfortunately, I did not have much in the way of 'Gazebo-like' advice before we came here. I was raising Sage more of less on instinct, knowing in my heart, I wanted his life to be pure. The culture I came from is not like Gazebo culture. So, coming here, my eyes were opened to this beautiful, unconventional method of child-rearing that I am endlessly thankful for. I learn, with Sage and my husband, how to be an aware person, how to respect myself. I am so grateful for the Gazebo community to be a model, a pillar of strength to be inspired by.

Another Gazebo mother, Hanna Reese says, "Gazebo doesn't ask a child to survive, it meets the child where they are." So, in the nature of individuality, each being is different, each experience is different. To calculate outcomes of these methods is not part of this project. I do know that the experiences have been meaningful to students, teachers, and families, and I know that the experiences people have shared with me about their time at Gazebo were often profound and even life-changing. I can't say that is the Gazebo way is the best way, or the only way, it is just one way that is worth looking with possibility, curiosity, and openness. This is just a glimpse into one experiment in one space in time.

The Gazebo Learning Project,was experimental by nature, from the application of Gestalt methods with children, to letting children be outdoors in nature with very little times structure, none of which were being implemented elsewhere at that time in history. There was a cross-pollination of Esalen teachings and Gazebo teachings and these teachings evolved over time. There was the counter-culture experimentation outside the mainstream social norms. This counter-culture was a response to the restrained structures of 1950's era and perhaps, for some, it swung too far into liberating people without enough boundaries and safety. This is not a sales pitch with a cut-and-dry formula for what is right and wrong. Rather, this is a story, documentation of an oral history that is meant to shine light on these specific alternative educational methods. The response to these methods, and their future application, is another, very personal story.

Room to grow means that there is an evolution of these ideas. So much depends on current best practices, cultural sensitivities, community needs, and latest research and learning about how human beings learn, grow and prosper. One of Lederman's key tenets was that, "Gazebo is always in the process of organization and development." In this way, we examine the tools that have been given, the history that has been laid before us, and proceed in what we feel is needed in education, on a global level, in each community, and with each child.

Afterword

*I*t has truly been an honor to be the record keeper of these stories, to focus my energy and to craft a written documentation of so many people's life experiences. These stories are from a community, a tribe, who lived in Big Sur and were connected by Esalen and Gazebo. There is a collective wisdom here and I feel I was the vehicle to share them through this book. My process seemed endless at times, and I hit many roadblocks along the way. When Esalen chose to close the Gazebo, it was hard not to lose my way. The wind was taken out of my sails for a time; there was no model to demonstrate these ways. On the other hand, I had hope that this book was still relevant, and that it could be used as a seed to plant more programs like the Gazebo worldwide. The Big Sur community rallied and created the non-profit called Big Sur Park School that practices and promotes many Gazebo methods and is a similar program. They even use the grounds of Gazebo Park presently and Esalen is supporting the project in allowing them use of the land. So, like all life there is change, there is life, death and rebirth.

To complete this book has taken so much dedication and determination. With self-accountability and self-discipline, I persevered in writing knowing it is part of my life's work. This book is a continuation of a legacy I wanted to honor. I wanted to put it into writing, so it would not be lost with oral tradition and the passing of our elders. I did this for me, for my daughter, for all children, for Janet Lederman, for all my elders and teachers. In some sense, honoring the legacy of the children is a way for me to honor Esalen, Gazebo, and the Esselen people. This place made me believe in magic long after I had grown-up. I wrote this, because I believe in the heart of the Esalen community. I believe in Lederman's vision, and the brilliance of her experimental approach. I believe in the children, and in this way of being with children that has changed so many lives including my own. My childhood was magic, yet it should be each child's birthright to experience freedom, to be held in the safety of healthy boundaries, to feel respected as a human, and to be nurtured and loved.

I wrote this book because I believe that others could benefit from this information, and I wanted them to have access to it. I was able to do this because I had the skills as a writer and educator, and I am blessed to have the community's love and trust to share their stories with me. It has been an honor to hold and keep these stories and wisdom in a way that it can be preserved and hopefully will serve others. I am blessed to have the tools to capture a piece of time and history and preserve it. I wrote this book because children matter, babies matter, their experience matters. I know children's personalities are formed when they are young, and that their early world helps create who they will grow to be.

I consider myself lucky because when I was young and learned that conflict could lead to closeness, that communication could lead to intimacy, that connection to the natural world was a way to be in connection with the rhythms of life itself and to my own intuition. I learned that I was worthy of respect and trust, and that I was capable, no matter how hard it was not to receive the aid that I thought adults should have given. I learned that I could do for myself—that I was strong and powerful—even as a child. I learned to love learning. I learned who I was, how I was, what it meant to be me, to stand up for me, to trust myself. And I knew that there would always be an auntie or uncle nearby. There would be laps to fall into and a chest to cry on when I lost hope.

And at times, in writing this book, I lost hope all together. Why are kids killing each other in schools, movie theaters, in subways? Why is there so much hate it the world that a person could walk into a church, synagogue or mosque and murder people because they were Black, Jewish, Christian, or Muslim? Why are children being labeled exponentially with more and more psychosis'? How is this related to a deeper illness in our society where early life is not seen as significant; especially in education? How are education systems closely tied to greed, class divisions, to the pharmaceutical industry, to oppression and the continuation of cycles of poverty, institutional racism, gender inequality, and cultural degradation. With big business and corporate enterprises operating with greed consciousness, their leadership is missing the mark by not seeing the investment and returns when their employees are well fed, educated, have health care, childcare, housing, and are happy.

Yet at times, education also connected me to hope, when school is safer than home, when teachers are the only healthy bonds some kids have with adults, when the love for learning inspires people to be who they really are and to share it. My hope was renewed time and time again by people like my own mom who would babysit to give me a few hours to write, or by some Esalen community member who would send me a small check in the mail encouraging me to keep on. The support I felt from people who did care and did understand really kept me going—people like you who are willing to listen, people who knew that this was important work and reminded me that the heart within and without was still alive and beating.

I have listened deeply, to the children, to the children who have grown-up, to the parents, to the teachers, and to my own heart. As an educated person who traveled far and wide from my beginnings, I saw many heartbreaking realities for children. In west Africa, I saw children who couldn't even afford to go to school selling water on five-lane dirt roads just to pay for their next meal. I saw children in Jamaica who could barely scrape by for their uniforms, papers, and books, but went to school barefoot. In northeast Portland, I saw inner-city children of color struggle to focus at school—the black boys being the most vulnerable to discipline by their teachers—while many of their family members were incarcerated and others were victims of gang shootings—and the stark reality of their own probable future based on statistics for incarceration of black and brown men. I looked in the eyes of an orphan with AIDS in Cambodia who suffered from cerebral palsy—sang nursery rhymes with her—saw her brilliance—and knew while she might have cloths, and food and medicine, no one would educate her. I saw enough to come home and see my childhood as a treasure—a rough gem worthy of polishing and shining to see the light through. I am so blessed, privileged really, to have had the experiences I had, to have been loved, nurtured and supported in the ways that I was, to be respected and given the trust to be myself in the world.

So, I persevered and I wrote this book because I saw my elders either passing on, or being cast away. My teacher, Maria Lucia Bittencourt-Sauer and I, had an interview set for her next visit to the states, and she passed on before we had that meeting. The last time I saw her, we had sat on the grass in the Gazebo Park and she met my daughter for the first and last time. She gave my daughter a gift with rainbows and mirrors that shone in that afternoon light under the apple tree. Gazebo grandmother, Bette Dingman, sat at home without the help she needed, racked with post-polio pain, but filled with stories about Gazebo and how it came to be, filled with love for the children. So much had changed from when I was a child to when I was a teacher. While it was still beautiful, I felt the Gazebo ways were becoming diluted because fewer and fewer people were there to pass down that oral tradition.

When I came to work at the school as a teacher, the director left before a new one was hired. While I didn't get that traditional "tree" time, my mentor trusted I would find my way. And though I did, there were times when there was no training guide, no manual, not even readily available guides. Yet, Vieregge was present through it all, and many community members generously came forward to share their stories with me. When I approached people, they gratefully opened up and offered their stories and experiences as contributions to this project. I invited this as universally as I could, though I know I am missing some voices, I did what I could while raising my daughter and trying to make ends meet to bring this project to fruition.

I saw that my teachers were moving on. Some of the elders, and even one of my dear Gazebo students, passed away. While the little beings called children are my greatest teachers, I began to see that the people I was raised with, and saw simply as my aunties and uncles, were also great teachers. I sometimes didn't recognize this until after they were gone. There were so many pioneers using Gazebo as a germination ground for their own work. Gabrielle Roth danced with us as children. Perry Holloman and Dorothy Charles laid the groundwork for their Gestalt work from their time at Gazebo. Many Gazebo teachers took the wisdom of Gazebo and carried it into their work in the world. Former students and interns were influenced by Gazebo and were inspired to take what they learned out into the world in their work that was inspired from the space of exploration at Gazebo. The teachers and the children are important to me. The heart of the community, I feel in my own heart.

Writing this book, bringing myself and my experiences to this work, sharing this work, is part of why I was am here. I offer it up because I know the ideas are worthy—as flawed as documenting them may be. I worked on this book with my love and service, with my responsibility to my community—to carry the stories and traditions when I worried all would be lost. I wrote this book in hopes to capture the essence of something, to suspend that space and time, so it could somehow be preserved like a time capsule.

Perhaps like a message in a bottle, by publishing this book, I will throw this message out to the sea, hoping that in our shipwrecked times, it will be found. Hoping that it will matter enough for people to listen and learn from it. My work, is the channel of a greater work. Yes, I matter, my experiences and service have been critical in creating this book for the world. But the work doesn't belong to me, it belongs to the children.

Esalen administration lost sight of the value of early education for a time. Yet, Esalen is only a microcosm of the greater social problems. The way education is undervalued can be reflected of the way society addresses illness—putting more emphasis on healing than on prevention. There are ways in which we can approach education much like Eastern medicine approaches the human mind-body. Looking at the whole, the circumstances, the environment, what goes in and out of the body, the mind, the heart. All too often we wait to fix the ailments and neurosis of adults, when we don't pay attention to how much it matters when the children are forming into adults. So instead, we need to treat the source of the ailment rather than treating the symptoms alone. We need to address the consciousness where, at best, we put our resources into healing childhood wounds, and instead re-center around creating healthy childhoods.

Education should be valued. Teachers should be fairly compensated for doing highly-complex and challenging tasks. Their pay should equal that of doctors and lawyers, but instead, most teachers make less than the waitress serving your dinner. Education should not be questioned and schools should not be under threat of shut down if they don't meet financial quotas. Education should not be performance-based and academic assessment alone should not be the only indicator of success. We should not have to convince anyone that childhood is an important time in order for it to be subsidized. Simply put, education, teachers, schools, children should be supported in order to flourish. My sister, Lucia Horan Drummond, remembers

> A few years ago when Ken Dychtwald interviewed Anna Halprin [renowned dance movement therapist] at Esalen's big birthday celebration. He asked her, "What is the most important piece of wisdom that you could give to Esalen now?" Her response, 'Invest in the children.' My life is dedicated to helping people all over the world heal. I work backwards every day to try to fix what could have been taught to people as children. The Gazebo school was the most future-forward learning environment.

Early childhood is the most precious, important, vulnerable, potential-filled time in which our personalities and core issues, attachments, and foundations are formed. Bryan Scott, a long-time Esalen community member and Gazebo father, poignantly shared, "Gazebo is not just day care, it was the shaping of the human soul."

Childhood is a time when each human should have the right to live as a child, and learn as a child, and be supported as they grow. The Dalai Lama expresses,

> The only way out of this drunken stupor is to educate children about the value of compassion and the value of applying our mind. We need a long-term approach rooted in a vision to address our collective global challenges. This would require a fundamental shift in human consciousness, something only education is best suited to achieve. Time never waits. So I think it is very important we start now.[1]

I hope that as readers this work may open you in some way; perhaps inspire you to create a space for children that is as alive with wonder as Gazebo was for me. Children are the seeds of hope for humanity and they need to be cared for tenderly, watered with our love and attention, invested in, and nourished as the fruit-bearing trees that they will become. By planting seeds of love and respect early on, we can nourish the children, as I believe they are the source of healing for our world.

May all children be blessed.

May all children be happy.

May all children be free.

GLOSSARY

Reflect: To share with someone what you see is happening with them, or to make a statement based on what you heard them say. For example, "I see that you are crying," or "What I heard you say is that you are angry because..."

Process: Uncovering of the emotional landscape. Self-work, self-inquiry, growth and change in emotional, mental, spiritual, and somatic ways in which people may become open or vulnerable and heal within a process of self-realization.

Response-ability: The ability to respond—cultivated through modeling and opportunities, even for very young children, to respond appropriately in a given situation.

Trigger(ed): A situation, person, or dynamic that stimulates an emotional response and may initiate a conditioned pattern of thought and feeling from the past. Often emotional triggers cause a projection of these past experiences onto the current situation and interfere with the present moment.

Projection(s): A shadow of past cast on a present experience or situation which imposes feelings and thoughts from the past on the current experience or situation.

Unlearning: Learning new ways that question previous education, training, and social conditioning.

Container/safe container: An energetic awareness whereby a facilitator creates safety emotionally and physically for the people, place, and the process.

Witness: To be present with a situation, an experience, or a Gestalt process without participating directly while still being alert, aware, and part of the process.

Space holding/ holding space: Bringing attending to a person, object, or a particular intention, and keeping it/them in our awareness with presence.

Reactivities: Emotional triggers that are reactive to a current situation or incident which bring up unresolved issues from our past.

Field: The consciousness of the environment whereby a group of two or more people create a group energy or field in any given place; the dynamics and energy within the group.

Initiator/Reflector: Within Gestalt practice the terms *client/therapist* shifted to *initiator/reflector* during Dick Price's era. Initiator being the person initiating the process and reflector being the facilitator.

Toilet Learning: Shifting the frame from "toilet training" to an approach with less pressure which allows children to learn how to bathroom through curiosity, self-awareness and modeling.

Scaffolding: This is the process by which learning is supported through building an academic or cognitive foundation, and building on this with support structures that further the development and understanding of any given concept, which continue to provide opportunities for challenge and advancement.

Intrinsic Motivation: Motivation coming with within. So, a child inclined to learn about something that interests them, because it is relevant to them, and because they are curious about it. This is the opposite of extrinsic motivation in which case there might be direct instruction or a more behavioral reward system in place.

Growing Edge: The space between comfort and discomfort where one is learning and growing. What a person is working on in themselves including challenges and areas of growth.

Zone of Proximal Development: Lev Vygotsyi's concept that there is a space where higher levels of learning are possible with peers and adult support.

Additional Resources

PARENTING

Magda Gerber and RIE Methods

https://www.magdagerber.org/blog/magda-gerbers-rie-philosophy-basic-principles

https://www.rie.org/educaring/ries-basic-principles/

https://www.janetlansbury.com/

Susan Stiffleman

https://susanstiffelman.com/

Aware Parenting

http://awareparenting.com/

Parenting to Awakening

https://www.joycelyke.com/

MINDFULNESS, COMPASSION AND NEUROSCIENCE

Interpersonal Neurobiology

https://www.drdansiegel.com/about/interpersonal_neurobiology/

Well-Being Tools and Kindness Curriculum

https://centerhealthyminds.org/

https://centerhealthyminds.org/join-the-movement/sign-up-to-receive-the-kindness-curriculum

Creating Compassionate Cultures

http://www.creatingcompassionatecultures.org/

Mindful Education

http://www.danielrechtschaffen.com/

SOMATICS AND MOVEMENT PRACTICES

Brain Gym
https://www.braingym.com/about/

NeuroMovement
https://www.anatbanielmethod.com/

Somatic Experiencing
https://traumahealing.org/

5Rhythms®
https://www.5rhythms.com/

http://www.luciahoran.com/

Yoga
https://www.heartofyoga.com/

Feldenkrais
https://feldenkrais.com/

Tai Ji & Qigong
https://www.livingtao.org

https://www.chicenter.com

OUTDOOR EDUCATION AND EARTH-BASED TEACHINGS

Tsolagui M.A. RuizRazo, *Tomorrow's Children – A Cherokee Elder's Guide to Parenting.*

Robin Wall Kimmerer, *Braiding Sweetgrass.*

Richard Louv & Nature Deficit Disorder
http://richardlouv.com/

8shields Mentoring
http://8shields.org/

Bioneers

https://bioneers.org/

Bioneers Indigenous Knowledge Podcast

Steven Harper, Wilderness Educator
http://stevenkharper.com/

National Outdoor Leadership School (NOLS)
https://www.nols.edu/en/

Wilderness Medicine
https://www.backcountrymedicalguides.org/

Banana Slug String Band
https://www.bananaslugstringband.com/

GESTALT AND COMMUNICATION PRACTICES

Gestalt Practice
http://www.tribalground.com/

Relational Gestalt Practice
https://www.dorothycharles.com/about-dorothy-charles

Non-Violent Communication
https://www.cnvc.org/

SOCIAL JUSTICE

Courageous Conversation about Race
https://courageousconversation.com/about/

LaVerne McLeod, Bridge Building to Equity
http://lavernemcleod.com/18/

Teaching Tolerance
https://www.tolerance.org/

The Southern Poverty Law Center
https://www.splcenter.org/

The Zinn Education Project
https://www.zinnedproject.org/

Rethinking Schools
https://www.rethinkingschools.org/

Neurodiversity
http://neurocosmopolitanism.com/

ALTERNATIVE SCHOOL MODELS

Big Sur Park School
www.bigsurparkschool.org

Patagonia, *Family Business: Innovative On-Site Child-Care since 1983*
https://www.patagonia.com/family-business-on-site-child-care.html

The Children's School, Sonoma State University
http://childrens-school.sonoma.edu/

Early Ecology
http://www.earlyecology.com/

Outside Now
https://www.outsidenow.org/home

Santa Lucia School, Holistic Peace-Based Education
http://santaluciaschool.org/

ESALEN INSTITUTE

Workshops and Educational Programs
www.esalen.org
https://www.esalen.org/page/voices-esalen-podcast

Notes

View of the Child

1. Peter Levine and Maggie Klein, *Trauma Proofing Your Kids: A Parent Guide to Instilling Confidence, Joy and Resilience* (CA: North Atlantic Books, 2008), 16.

2. Susan Stiffleman, *Parenting with Presence: Practices for Raising Conscious, Confident and Caring Kids* (CA: New World Library, 2015), 214.

3. Moshé Feldenkrais, *The Potent Self: A Study of Spontaneity and Compulsion* (CA: Frog Books, 2002), 42.

4. Bence Gerber and Lisa Sunbury, "Magda Gerber's RIE Philosophy Basic Principles," *Magda Gerber: Seeing Babies with New Eyes*, 1 May 2012, <https://www.magdagerber.org/blog/magdagerbers-rie-philosophy-basic-principles> (Accessed 5 July, 2019).

5. Fredrick S. Perls, *Gestalt Therapy Verbatim* (CA: Real People Press, 1969), 27-28.

Role of the Teacher

1. Sharon Dvora, "Play Nice in the Sandbox?", *Collaborative Design/ Child-Inspired Learning*, 28 June 2012, <https://sharondvoradotcom. wordpress.com > (Accessed 05 July 2019).

2. Sharon Dvora, "The Rights of Children," *Collaborative Design/ Child-Inspired Learning*, 7 June 2012, <https://sharondvoradotcom. wordpress.com/ > (Accessed 05 July 2019).

First Aiders

1. Gregory Bateson, *Mind and Nature* (New York: E.P. Dutton, 1979), 230.

2. Bateson, 147.

Gestalt Practice

1. Gabrielle Roth, *Maps to Ecstasy: Teachings of an Urban Shaman* (CA: New World Library, 1989), 62-63.

2. Janet Lederman, *Anger in the Rocking Chair* (New York: McGraw-Hill, 1969), 21.

3. Lederman, 19.

4. Lederman, 37.

Outdoor Education/ Nature Education

1. Robin Wall Kimmerer, *Braiding Sweetgrass* (MN: Milkweed Editions, 2014), 275.

2. Sharon Dvora, "Changing Reflection,"*Collaborative Design/Child-Inspired Learning*, 23 June 2012, <https://sharondvoradotcom.wordpress.com/ > (Accessed 5 July, 2019).

3. Sharon Dvora, "Sucking Nectar from a PassionFlower," *Collaborative Design/Child-Inspired Learning*, 31 May 2012, <https://sharondvoradotcom.wordpress.com/ > (Accessed 5 July 2019).

4. Michael Changaris, Psy. D., *Touch: The Neurobiology of Health, Healing, and Human Connection* (CA: Life Rhythm, 2013), 83.

5. Michael Merzenich, Ph.D., *Soft-Wired: How The New Science Of Brain Plasticity Can Change Your Life* (TN: Parnassus Publishing, 2013). Also see: < https://www.goodreads.com/work/quotes/25975967-soft-wired-how-the-new-science-of-brainplasticity-can-change-your-life.> (Accessed August 28 2019).

6. Daniel J. Siegel, M.D, *Mindsight: The New Science of Personal Transformation* (London: Bantam Press, 2009), 43.

7. Changaris, 43.

8. Changaris, 43.

9. Linda Hartley, *Wisdom of the Body Moving: An Introduction to Body-Mind Centering* (CA: North Atlantic Books, 1995), 93.

10. Kimmerer, 183.

11. Tsolagui M.A Ruiz Razo, *Tomorrow's Children: A Cherokee Elder's Guide to Parenting* (New Tazewell: TN, World Edition, 2004), 71.

12. Kimmerer, 189.

The Power of Play

1. John Dewey, The School and Society and The Child and The Curriculum (IL: The University of Chicago Press, 1991), 118-119.

2. Laurel Bongiorno, "10 Things Every Parent Should Know About Play," *National Association for the Education of Young Children*, <https://www.naeyc.org/ourwork/families/10-things-every-parentplay> (Accessed 10 January 2019).

3. David Elkind, "The Power of Play: Learning What Comes Naturally," *The Strong: National Museum of Play/American Journal of Play*, <https://www.journalofplay.org/issues/1/1/article/powerplay-learning-what-comes-naturally >(Accessed 5 July 2019).

4. Anat Baniel, "NeuroMovement Approach of the Anat Baniel Method," *Anat Baneil Method- Neuromovement® Wake Up Your Brain for a Vibrant Life*, <https://www.anatbanielmethod.com/aboutabm/neuromovement-2 > (Accessed 5 July 2019).

5. Mark Whitwell, "Part 1: #10 The Mind's Source: Emmercing Mind in Breath and Body," *Heart of Yoga Teacher Training*, < https://heartofyogatraining.org > (Accessed 1 June 2019).

6. Levine and Klein, 18.

7. Siegel, 43.

8. "Richard Davidson: A Neuroscientist on Love and Learning," *On Being with Krista Tippet*, 14 February 2019, <https://onbeing.org/programs/richard-davidson-a-neuroscientist-on-love-and-learningfeb2019/> (Accessed 5 July 2019).

9. Changaris, 28.

10. Changaris, 42.

11. Siegel, 55.

12. Levine and Klein, 41.

13. Macro Iacoboni, "The Mirror Neuron Revolution: Explaining What Makes Humans Social," *Scientific American*, < https://www.scientificamerican.com/article/the-mirror-neuron-revolut/> (Accessed 5 July 2019).

The Growing Edge

1. Nick Walker, "Throw Away the Master's Tools: Liberating Ourselves from the Pathology Paradigm," NEUROCOSMOPOLITANISM: NICK WALKER'S NOTES ON NEURODIVERSITY, AUTISM, AND COGNITIVE LIBERTY. 16 August 2013, <http://neurocosmopolitanism.com/autism-and-the-pathology-paradigm/ > (Accessed 1 May 2019).

2. Lederman, Janet. "From Gazebo." Esalen Catalog, May-October 1980, 10.

3. Feldenkrais, 48.

4. Daniel Goleman and Richard J. Davidson, *Altered Traits: Science Reveals How Meditation Changes Your Mind, Brain and Body* (New York: Avery, 2017), 292.

5. Sharon Dvora, "Identity & Culture: Gazebo Park School," *Collaborative Design/Child-Inspired Learning*, 09 June 2012, <https://sharondvoradotcom.wordpress.com/ > (Accessed 5 July 2019).

6. GNH Centre Bhutan, "The Nine Domains of GNH," < http://www.gnhcentrebhutan.org/what-isgnh/the-9-domains-of-gnh/ > (Accessed 22 August 2019).

Afterword

1. Desmond Tutu and the Dalai Lama, *The Book of Joy* (London: Penguin, 2016), 273.

Credits

Cover art and graphic design: Brian Hendrix at Estero Bay Graphics

Photo credits:

Title page: Janet Lederman

Dedication page: Lucia Horan Drummond

Page 7: Janet Lederman

Page 33: Unknown

Page 35: Sydelle Foreman

Page 49: Karen Lemon

Page 53: Sydelle Foreman

Page 64: Sydelle Foreman

Page 92: Karen Lemon

Page 104: Sydelle Foreman

Page 120: Sydelle Foreman

Page 128: Karen Lemon

Page 140: Unknown

Page 146: Janet Lederman

Page 171: Janet Lederman

Page 178: Sydelle Foreman

Page 184: Jasmine Horan

Page 197: Left to right: Janet Lederman, Sydelle Foreman, Janet Lederman

Page 232: Sydelle Foreman

Page 241: Karen Lemon

Page 249: Karen Lemon

Page 265: Sydelle Foreman

Page 288: Janet Lederman

Page 304: Janet Lederman

Page 334: Left to right: Janet Lederman, Janet Lederman, Janet Lederman, Karen Lemon, Karen Lemon, Janet Lederman.

Author photo: Karen Lemon

CPSIA information can be obtained
at www.ICGtesting.com
Printed in the USA
FSHW020326011020
74272FS